"Miroslav Volf loves a good conversation. And this book is exactly that, a conversation in his honor which explores a theme that he has so illumined with his own work over recent years: what it means for human beings to flourish in relation to each other and to the God who is Love."

—**GRAHAM TOMLIN**, Bishop of Kensington, London; President, St. Mellitus College

"Volf is one of the greatest theological minds of his generation, combining profound theological depth with adept creativity and willingness to mold his theology to address our many contemporary challenges. In this book you'll not only receive a resource to better understand Volf's work, but you'll be taken deep into a conversation that works the very center or aims of theology itself, directing its focus toward the good life. This book promises rich rewards for the interested reader."

—**ANDREW ROOT**, Luther Seminary;
Author of *Christopraxis: A Practical Theology of the Cross*

"How should people of faith think about a flourishing life and the common good? This book powerfully addresses this question through reflecting on the work of one of the most towering theologians and public intellectuals of the twenty-first century, Miroslav Volf. In a society marked by pluralism and conflicting claims about the place of faith in the public square, this text is a must-read."

—**KERI DAY**, Author of *Religious Resistance to Neoliberalism:*
Womanist and Black Feminist Perspectives

"With the theme of 'human flourishing' as a response to, and fruit of, divine love providing a *cantus firmus* undergirding the volume as a whole, these essays unfold a wonderfully rich set of dialogues between Volf's theological vision and a range of theological and ethical concerns that spans continents and schools of thought. In so doing, the volume does theology a great service by laying out the full scope, vibrancy, and significance of Volf's theological vision."

—**LUKE BRETHERTON**, Professor of Theological Ethics, Duke University

"What is the good life, the genuinely flourishing human life? This volume of essays by distinguished American and European theologians furthers the generative life work of Volf and his conviction that we flourish in joyful communion with God and one another. But how are ordinary forms of creaturely wellbeing related to this ultimate vocation, and how can this vision of the good life come to terms with the full spectrum of human diversity? If ever there was a time when the world needed to come together in serious engagement with these questions, it is now."

—**JENNIFER A. HERDT**, Senior Associate Dean of Academic Affairs, Gilbert L. Stark Professor of Christian Ethics, Yale Divinity School

Envisioning
the Good Life

Envisioning the Good Life

Essays on God, Christ, and Human Flourishing in Honor of Miroslav Volf

edited by
Matthew Croasmun,
Zoran Grozdanov,
and Ryan McAnnally-Linz

CASCADE *Books* · Eugene, Oregon

ENVISIONING THE GOOD LIFE
Essays on God, Christ, and Human Flourishing in Honor of Miroslav Volf

Cascade Books
An Imprint of Wipf and Stock Publishers
199 W. 8th Ave., Suite 3
Eugene, OR 97401

www.wipfandstock.com

PAPERBACK ISBN: 978-1-4982-3523-5
HARDCOVER ISBN: 978-1-4982-3525-9
EBOOK ISBN: 978-1-4982-3524-2

Cataloguing-in-Publication data:

Names: Croasmun, Matthew | Grozdanov, Zoran| McAnnally-Linz, Ryan
Title: Flourishing in Christ : Essays on God, Christ, and human flourishing in honor of Miroslav Volf
Description: Eugene, OR: Cascade Books, 2017 | Includes bibliographical references.
Identifiers: ISBN 978-1-4982-3523-5 (paperback) | ISBN 978-1-4982-3525-9 (hardcover) | ISBN 978-1-4982-3524-2 (ebook)
Subjects: LCSH: Volf, Miroslav. | Life—Religious aspects. | Happiness. | Theology.
Classification: BR50 F4 2017 (print) | BR50 F4 (ebook)

Manufactured in the U.S.A.   APRIL 26, 2017

To Miroslav Volf, for your sixtieth birthday

Contents

Contributors

Nancy Bedford, Georgia Harkness Professor of Applied Theology at Garrett-Evangelical Theological Seminary.

Matthew Croasmun, Associate Research Scholar at the Yale Center for Faith & Culture at Yale Divinity School.

Alon Goshen-Gottstein, Director of the Elijah Interfaith Institute.

David H. Kelsey, Luther Weigle Professor Emeritus of Theology at Yale Divinity School.

Natalia Marandiuc, Assistant Professor of Christian Theology at Perkins School of Theology at Southern Methodist University.

Lidija Matošević, Assistant Professor of Theology at the Center for Protestant Theology at the University of Zagreb, Croatia.

Ryan McAnnally-Linz, Associate Research Scholar at the Yale Center for Faith & Culture at Yale Divinity School.

Jürgen Moltmann, Professor Emeritus of Systematic Theology at the University of Tübingen.

Ivan Šarčević, Guardian of Saint Anthony's Monastery and Professor at Franciscan School of Theology in Sarajevo, Bosnia and Herzegovina.

Christoph Schwöbel, Professor of Systematic Theology and Director of the Institute for Hermeneutics and Cultural Dialogue at the University of Tübingen.

Reza Shah-Kazemi, Managing Editor of *Encyclopaedia Islamica* at The Institute of Ismaili Studies, London.

Marianne Meye Thompson, George Elden Ladd Professor of New Testament in the School of Theology at Fuller Theological Seminary and Extraordinary Professor in the Faculty of Theology at North-West University, South Africa.

Linn Marie Tonstad, Assistant Professor of Systematic Theology at Yale Divinity School.

Michael Welker, Senior Professor of Systematic Theology at the University of Heidelberg and Managing Director of the Research Center for International and Interdisciplinary Theology (FIIT), Heidelberg, Germany.

Nicholas Wolterstorff, Noah Porter Professor Emeritus of Philosophical Theology at Yale Divinity School and Senior Fellow at the Institute for Advanced Studies in Culture at the University of Virginia.

Acknowledgments

Our thanks go first of all to Jessica Dwelle, without whom this volume would never have come about. She fielded Zoran's query about putting together some essays for Miroslav's sixtieth birthday, and put him in touch with Ryan. From there it was a matter of Skip Masback at the Yale Center for Faith & Culture (YCFC) signing off on the project and Jim Tedrick at Wipf and Stock agreeing to take it on. We are of course deeply grateful to the volume's generous contributors, who have invested significant time and energy in crafting its chapters. Thanks also to Chris Spinks, Brian Palmer, and the copy editors at Wipf and Stock, and to Brendan Kolb, who helped out with research and the occasional editorial conundrum.

As its subject and the chapters' frequent attention to joy suggest, *Envisioning the Good Life* advances the YCFC research project on Theology of Joy and the Good Life. This publication was made possible through the support of a grant from the John Templeton Foundation. The opinions expressed in this publication are those of the author(s) and do not necessarily reflect the views of the John Templeton Foundation. The contributions by Jürgen Moltmann and Marianne Meye Thompson were originally written for research consultations at YCFC funded by the MacDonald Agape Foundation as part of YCFC's God and Human Flourishing Project.

Introduction

Miroslav Volf and Theology of the Good Life

Matthew Croasmun and Ryan McAnnally-Linz

TOWARD THE END OF his *Critique of Pure Reason*, Immanuel Kant writes: "All the interests of my reason, speculative as well as practical, combine in the three following questions:

1. What can I know?

2. What ought I to do?

3. What may I hope?"[1]

These questions serve to introduce Kant's discussion of God and immortality as postulates of practical reason and of the ideal of the highest good. Of interest here, at the opening of a collection of essays in honor of Miroslav Volf, is not so much the place of these questions in Kant's philosophical project, but his particular turn of phrase: "the *interests* of my reason." Reason, Kant suggests, is not a detached observer considering whatever puzzles or curiosities happen to come its way. It has interests: aims, purposes, concerns. These interests drive reason to ask certain questions and, to put it

---

1. Kant, *Critique of Pure Reason*, A 804–5 / B 833–34. The pages given are from the standard *Akademie Ausgabe* of Kant's works.

1

roughly, to *care* about the answers, to be *invested* in both the asking and the answering.[2]

For Miroslav—we, like several of the other contributors, use this casual mode of reference because this volume is a contribution to a conversation among friends—human persons as a whole are much like Kant's reason in this respect. We are *interested* beings. We inescapably have investments, cares, and concerns. And these drive us to ask certain questions and to care about the answers with the whole of our selves. The questions are diverse, difficult to summarize as neatly as Kant encapsulates the interests of reason. The most basic of them, however, have to do with God. Who is God? What is God's relation to the world? How is God disposed toward us? What does God ask of us? Such questions are not simply intellectual puzzles. They *matter* for us. On Miroslav's view of things, therefore, a disinterested theology would be no *theo*logy at all, for we are fundamentally, at our very cores, "interested" in God. God is the one who concerns us most deeply. Put differently, any theology worth the name is theology "for a way of life."[3] We ask theological question as those whose lives depend on the God whose character we try to articulate in the answers—and also in the asking. How we ask and answer these questions gives shape to our lives.

Bound up with questions about God are a whole host of other questions.[4] What makes a life worth living? What is life *for*? What is the *good* life? What does it look like from the outside? What does it *feel* like from the inside? What does it require of us? In recent years, Miroslav has taken to summing up this set of questions and our answers to them in terms of "human flourishing," "the good life," or "the life worth living." The formulations are relatively new to Miroslav's work. The questions, however, have undergirded that work and the theological vision it presents for the past three decades or more. Miroslav persistently urges his readers and interlocutors to give serious attention to these question, for, he reminds us, they lie at the heart of our lives.

This introduction will briefly trace the trail of concern for human flourishing in Miroslav's work and then offer an overview of the essays in this volume and how they intersect with the driving questions and commitments of Miroslav's theology.

2. Thanks to Brendan Kolb for talking us through how to talk about Kant.

3. See Volf, "Theology for a Way of Life."

4. Some of the following is adapted from a lecture Matt gave at the University of Fribourg in 2015. See Croasmun, "Christ and Human Flourishing."

THE BASIC SHAPE OF VOLF'S THEOLOGY

Two basic sets of convictions underlie Miroslav's theological vision of human flourishing.[5] The first flows from among the most central claims of Christian theology: God is love. This is not to say merely that God loves, but rather that God *is* love. For Miroslav this basic biblical truth takes a fundamentally Trinitarian form. God is the Holy Trinity and therefore God is love of the other and only *via the other* is it possible to talk about self-love in God. Such love is *who* God is.

This God, the God who is love, *creates*. God creates *out of* love and *for* love. Creation is evidence of God's kind of non-self-seeking love—that is, creation is a *gift*. As the gift of a good giver, creation itself is good. Its goodness is contingent and dependent (since creation is not God), but it is creation's own. Moreover, God's creatures are genuinely good for one another. They are genuinely meant to live with and for one another. Not, of course, to the exclusion of God. But God does not demand to be creatures' sole good.

This same God who is love *redeems*. God in Christ and through the Spirit redeems wayward creatures *out of love*. God "dies" for God's enemies. Christ justifies the ungodly. This is God's love of the unlovely—God's embrace of what is other than God even in the face of enmity.

The God who is love *indwells* the human being. Christ dwells in human beings through the Spirit. This work of the Spirit then means that God's kind of generosity is the hallmark of the Christian life: so, the love of enemy is essential to Christian life. The Christian life is not primarily oriented toward God but is oriented toward the world, by participating in God's love, which is working to suffuse the creation. (Jesus says in John: "As I have loved you, you also should love one another . . ." [13:34 NRSV], *not* the reciprocal "As I have loved you, you also should love me.") We love God when we open ourselves in faith to receive God's love and pass it on.

And the God who is love draws all of creation to *consummation*. The world to come is the world *of love*, specifically the eschatological "love that dances," love as it can be in a world of joy.[6] In this world, both the realities that make up our contexts and the features of our interiority—human perceptions, emotions, values, etc.—are transformed. Gone are the enmity and sorrow caused by sin, replaced by joyful communion. In the present world, not yet so transformed, love—Christ's and ours—often needs to suffer; but, for Miroslav, love's suffering is a *means*, love's dance is the *goal*.

5. We draw these convictions and much of the terminology used to unpack them from Miroslav's own articulations of them in personal communications.

6. Volf, "Trinity is Our Social Program," 413.

Importantly, for Miroslav, that goal is a *world* of love, a community of creatures rightly related to God and one another. This world, and not God alone, is our final end.

Such is the first set of convictions, all of which flow from the central conviction that *God is love*. The second set is, in a sense, a "structural" obverse of the more "personal" lineup just described. These deal with the kinds of identities that the above account of love *de facto*—which is to say not philosophically necessarily—presupposes: First, God's Trinitarian nature is a perichoretic unity. A divine person is a person only in relation of "being-in" others and just that "being-in" others is the One God. Again, God is the Trinitarian God of love.

This has an anthropological analogy. Human beings are created to be indwelled by God—that is, for God to be in them and to work through them—and in a different sense by one another. To be human is to be created for this indwelling. Openness to God is not an optional add-on to human life, the human equivalent to a car's power sunroof. It is simply what it means to be human.

This anthropology sets the stage for Christology and Ecclesiology. God's indwelling of humans is realized in a unique way in Christ, whose identity is a Trinitarian reality (as evidenced in his baptism). Christ *is* the Son, sent by the Father, and indwelled by the Spirit. This means that Christian life is not merely one religious choice among many. Rather, Christian life is a unique fulfillment of what it is to be a human being. Christian life is life in which a person is in Christ, and Christ is in that person by the power of the Spirit.

Given the nature of God's perichoretic unity of love and the fact that human beings are created to be indwelled by this God, relations among humans are also of a perichoretic nature, though in a weaker sense than are relations in God and between God and human beings.[7] This means that the community called "church" is *not* extrinsic but *intrinsic* to salvation. Within the church, our identities are—or at least ought to be—porous, which is to say, bounded and yet permeable. This porousness does not compromise our individuality, but rather expands and enriches it. We are richer precisely *as individuals* the more *others* (all and any created good, in fact) across times and spaces "indwell" us. This is the sort of identity Miroslav has called a "catholic personality,"[8] an identity enriched by otherness—"a microcosm of

---

7. See Volf, "Trinity Is Our Social Program," for Miroslav's careful attempt to delineate the proper limits of anthropological and political inferences from the doctrine of the Trinity.

8. Volf, *Exclusion and Embrace*, 51.

the eschatological new creation."[9] This same catholicity applies to ecclesial communities and to Christian relations to cultural goods: churches are enriched by understanding their own identities as being porous to all other churches across time and space, and Christians are better when enriched by the otherness of cultural goods—including other religions. Therefore, it is in the broadest possible sense that "a truly catholic personality must be an *evangelical* personality—a personality transformed by the Spirit of the new creation and engaged in the transformation of the world."[10]

Note the movement in each of these sequences. The core commitments, the ones that organize and propel the whole, are theological in the strict sense. They are claims about God. They drive persistently, however, toward implications for human life in the world in relation to God and others. One cannot just say, "God is love," and leave it at that. To say, "God is love," is to imply a whole vision of human flourishing, a way of life.

GOD, CHRIST, AND HUMAN FLOURISHING IN VOLF'S WORK

A survey of Miroslav's writings demonstrates the abiding importance of these commitments and their slant toward questions of human flourishing in his thought. What we might call the first movement of Miroslav's work began with his dissertation, which he wrote at Tübingen under Jürgen Moltmann, in which he developed a theological account of work in dialogue with Karl Marx.[11] Already, in the work's focus on the nature and purpose of everyday human work, one can see Miroslav's commitment to seeing faith as a way of life and theology as an articulation of a way of life. So, too, in his later refined, pneumatological account of work in *Work in the Spirit: Toward a Theology of Work* (1991).

A second thread of Miroslav's early work—which ran to some extent in parallel with the first—began in 1985 when he became a member of the Pentecostal delegation of the official Roman Catholic and Pentecostal dialogue on church as communion. The dialogue, especially the fact that he was one of the principal authors of the final statement at the end of the five years of dialogue, led Miroslav to consider carefully the relation between the church as a community and the Trinity (this will be familiar from the second set of convictions discussed previously). This work eventually led to his habilitation, published in English as *After our Likeness: The Church as the Image of the*

9. McDonald, *Re-Imaging Election*, 128.

10. Volf, *Exclusion and Embrace*, 52.

11. Published as Volf, *Zukunft der Arbeit—Arbeit der Zukunft*

Trinity God (1998). The conception of church therein is both *egalitarian* and *communitarian*, populated by persons who both have discrete identities and are "catholic personalities" in the sense described above.

Turning to the work for which Miroslav is perhaps best known, his writings on reconciliation, the same thread appears: profound, careful theological reflection funds engagement with the pressing questions of human life. In *Exclusion and Embrace* the father from Luke's story of the Prodigal Son is a chief exemplar of embrace, in his forgiving the prodigal son and embracing his own new identity as father-of-the-prodigal. But the paradigm case, of course, is Christ, who dies for the ungodly. Christ's arms extended on the cross are a picture of embrace. Of course, this concept of "embrace" is rooted in the Trinitarian understanding of the God who is love. The mutual indwelling of Trinitarian persons is the paradigm case of porous boundaries. Thus, when the world rejects the God who made it out of love, the Trinitarian God who is love responds with the cruciform embrace that both opens the way to and points toward the eschatological embrace of the world of love. This theology then grounds an account of how we ought to live in our current sin-scarred world, marked as it is by conflicts small and large, such as the wars in the former Yugoslavia that drew Miroslav's attention to these questions. Human embrace, which entails acting with generosity toward the perpetrator and maintaining porous boundaries of flexible identities, is participation in God's self-giving love, the fruit of the very indwelling of Christ in the human being for which the human was created.

God's embrace, of course, is a modality of grace. And, indeed, Miroslav's next major work after *Exclusion and Embrace* was *Free of Charge* (2005), an exploration of two primary modes of grace, giving and forgiving, and their implications for human life. It is here that the two basic sets of convictions discussed above are most fully thematized in Miroslav's writings: God's identity as love of other frames creation as a gift; God's perichoretic Trinitarian life makes space for this love to express itself in death on the cross for the ungodly.

The End of Memory (2006), too, can be read as a follow-up to *Exclusion and Embrace*. Here, Miroslav extends his exploration of the implications for human life of the theological vision of that earlier work to the question of remembering wrongs. He argues that such remembering must always aim at *embrace*. Mere "truth-telling" focused exclusively on *justice* feeds the process of trying to sort out perpetrators from victims too simplistically, which feeds the very cycles of violence that remembering *rightly* aims to undo. Miroslav proposes that the sacred memory of Christ's passion in terms of enmity and reconciliation (as opposed to merely suffering and deliverance) should guide Christians' remembrance of wrongs suffered. Controversially,

Miroslav proposes, following Isa 43:25, rightly remembering wrongs suffered and committed will result, eschatologically, in non-remembrance of the wrongdoing, in the sense that, in the context of reconciled relationships, wrongdoings will simply not come to mind.

The publication of *A Public Faith: How Followers of Christ Should Serve the Common Good* (2011) marked a new trajectory for Miroslav, though certainly continuities with what came before can be seen. *Exclusion and Embrace* and the two books that followed were quite clearly *politically* engaged, deeply concerned with political wrongs perpetrated by people groups and the reconciliation possible in the light of such wrongs. *A Public Faith*, however, turns attention directly toward the particular forms that questions about God and human flourishing take in the context of pluralistic societies. Miroslav argues that central Christian convictions about God can and should engage with pressing public questions across lines of difference for the sake of the common good.

This interest in pluralism, deeply connected to his passion for reconciliation—along with world events—drove Miroslav into sustained dialogue with Muslim theologians after 2001, including authoring the Yale Response to Prince Ghazi bin Muhammad's open letter to Christendom, *A Common Word Between Us and You*.[12] This trajectory of research and interfaith work yielded *Allah: A Christian Response* (2011), which explores Muslim and Christian doctrines of God. Miroslav finds Muslim so-called "anti-Trinitarianism" to be a helpful corrective to insufficiently Christian forms of Trinitarian theology that ultimately are—on *both* Muslim *and* Christian accounts—forms of tri-theism. The significant (but far from total!) theological agreement Miroslav finds in questions of God's identity and God's commands to love God and neighbor provide resources for significant collaboration in addressing urgent problems of public life in a globalizing, pluralistic world.

Miroslav's interfaith writing is summarized in *Flourishing: Why We Need Religion in a Globalized World*, in which he demonstrates in practice what he described in *A Public Faith*, inviting, on the basis of his personal Christian convictions, an interfaith conversation about globalization and the great world religions' accounts of material life and its significance. Ultimately, he suggests that the key resource the world's religions offer to our globalizing world is their robust accounts of human flourishing. They offer visions of a flourishing life that is more than bread alone, visions that connect the ordinary to the transcendent.

---

12. See Volf, bin Muhammad, and Yarrington, *A Common Word*.

This last finding of *Flourishing* signals a pivot-point into the next season of Miroslav's work, currently underway and continuing to take shape in the work of the Yale Center for Faith & Culture. This current work is focused directly on the question of human flourishing. Yet, as the discussion so far suggests, this pivot should not be understood as something entirely *new* in Miroslav's work, nor, indeed, as another movement simply in sequence with the others. Rather, this new phase is in some sense a *summation* of what has come before—or, perhaps better, a hermeneutical key to the whole. Work, reconciliation, memory, giving and forgiving, working for the common good alongside people of other religious traditions (and the nonreligious)—each is a locus, or at any rate a way of slicing "ordinary life," as it were, and Miroslav has consistently endeavored to show their intimate connection with the God who is love.

But in this new season of Volf's work, the question-behind-the-questions is now thematized and takes the central place. Work and identity in the perichoretic life of the Trinity now finds its place in the context of the whole of life—what it is for, what its abundance, promised in Christ, looks like. Reconciliation now appears quite plainly as a means to an end: namely, right relationship, the sort of maintenance of the self and yet also openness to one another and to God that is a hallmark of flourishing human life and is a necessary condition of the rich peace that characterizes the world to come. The key question of the public theology—the question of the common good—is now put in perspective: To seek the *common* good, we must have a compelling vision of the *good*, of flourishing human life, the ideal to which we aspire. This is the project we share across various lines of difference. This is the shared *human* question: What is the good life? What is a flourishing human life?

Of course, while this is the human question, it is not always the question human societies ask. But it *is* the question that theology ought to ask—and the question theology ought to help society as a whole learn to wrestle with anew. After all, increasingly, we have lost the ability to ask this question in our culture. What is the good life? If somehow the question comes to us, like an overwhelmed student taking an exam, we stare blankly, mouth agape . . . and go on to the next question. Having skipped the question of *ends*, we find that the next questions are all about *means*. These, it seems to us, are simpler—and they are. But with the prior question still blank, the answers we give to the latter are meaningless. Nevertheless, this is how we live. Experts in means, we remain amateurs in ends.[13] We know *how* to get where want to go—we just have no idea where that is.

13. See Volf, "Life Worth Living."

If the business of theology is the articulation of a way of life—if its goal is to describe the flourishing life for which humans were created, a life uniquely possible through the spiritual indwelling of the One who came that we might have life and have it abundantly—then now, when globalized culture falls deeper and deeper into a crisis of meaning, now may be theology's finest hour. If only we can find our nerve, muster our courage and help the Church—and, indeed, the *world*—learn once again to ask the most important questions of our lives.

ENVISIONING HUMAN FLOURISHING: THE ESSAYS OF THIS VOLUME

The call that Miroslav's current work makes—a call to which it also seeks to be responsible—is thus for a theology of the good life, of flourishing human life, the kind of life that Miroslav summarizes as marked by *love*, *peace*, and *joy*.[14] Each in their own way, the essays of this volume answer this call.

Working as a New Testament scholar, *Marianne Meye Thompson* outlines a vision of human flourishing grounded in two sets of Christian convictions about Christ found in the scriptural witness: (1) Christ is *alpha and omega*, the one through whom all things were made and to whom all things are ordered, and (2) that same one lived among us as the particular human being Jesus of Nazareth in the particular time and place of first-century Galilee and Judea. The core of this vision is that flourishing human life is life centered in God and oriented toward others in love, compassion, and mercy. This follows from who God is and how God relates to the world in creating, giving the Torah, sending Jesus, and bringing all things into the new creation.

Building on the framework established in his *Eccentric Existence, David Kelsey* seeks to open space between the theological concept of human *flourishing* and anthropologically-focused ideas of human *wellbeing*. The former considers human beings as "the glory of God" in various senses, based on criteria that follow from the ways God relates to humans and humans in turn respond to God's relating. The latter considers human beings as finite systems of various energies and assesses them on the anthropocentric criterion of the health of those systems (i.e., how well they are supporting human life over the short or the long term). Kelsey's scrupulous elaboration of this distinction and the distinctions between various senses in which humans can be said theologically to flourish allows him to make sense of some forms of flourishing that appear quite counter-intuitive from

14. See Volf and McAnnally-Linz, *Public Faith in Action*, 13–16.

the perspective of wellbeing. He closes with a profound reflection on the ambiguity of human flourishing under the conditions of sin and evil and the challenge of developing capacities for discerning the good gift from God that is each creature in its creatureliness through the camouflage of sin's and evil's distortions of that gift.

Michael Welker tackles a question often asked by Volf: "How should followers of Christ intend to serve the common good?" Welker begins by shining a spotlight on the roles that social groups have in moral communication in contemporary pluralistic societies, arguing that we must take seriously the way that group-level moral logics fundamentally shape what we mean when we speak of "the common good." Among these groups are those shaped by Abrahamic religions, who, on Welker's account, use "God talk" (theology) more and less effectively to make appeal to transcendent values of justice, mercy, and truth that temper a "natural" moral state typified by "robbery." This allows these groups to hold to a normative moral theological orientation (transcendent values) while also maintaining realism about the world as it actually is (the basic creaturely situation as "robbing, finite, and death-bound"). Enacting such transcendent values in the context of this broken world ultimately takes the shape of "creative self-withdrawal in favor of the other," which Welker takes to be central for any account of flourishing in a world "red in tooth and claw" (Tennyson).

Through a reading of Martin Luther's *Disputatio de homine* ("Disputation on the Human Being"), *Christoph Schwöbel* offers the outline of a Christian account of humanity and human flourishing in service of contemporary pluralistic societies and the challenges of hospitality and justice that arise within and between them. What it means for humans to flourish depends on what and who humans are. Schwöbel proposes that the world religions' accounts of humanity share the general feature of understanding human being in terms of relationship. Any further specification of the relationship(s) in question, however, is a matter of the particularities of a given tradition. On Schwöbel's reading of Luther, human beings can only be rightly understood in terms of their relatedness first of all to God and then secondarily to other creatures. Flourishing, therefore, is not a matter of the development of innate human capacities or the self-actualization of atomistic subjects, but a dynamic process worked out in relationship with God and other (human and non-human) creatures.

Alon Goshen-Gottstein translates and comments on portions of a recently-discovered text from highly influential nineteenth- and twentieth -century rabbi Rav Abraham Isaac Kook that were previously unavailable in English. Kook, he argues, presents a theory of human flourishing built around the harmonious interrelation of five "general forces" of human life. Goshen-Gottstein takes Kook to be proposing a pantheistic vision in which both the full development of these forces (*ceteris paribus* more of them is better than less) and the harmonization of them follow from and are necessary prerequisites for the recognition of the fact that the forces are manifestations of the divine life. Following this thread of Kook's text eventually leads Goshen-Gottstein's to argue that Kook implies a call to radical tolerance and deep interreligious dialogue.

Reza Shah-Kazemi takes up Miroslav's invitation in *Flourishing* to elaborate visions of the unity of meaning and pleasure, accounts of a relationship between the transcendent and the mundane that neither portray humans as living "by bread alone," nor denigrate the mundane. Drawing from the metaphysics and aesthetics of the Sufi tradition within Islam, as well as finding resources in the thought of the fourteenth-century German Dominican Meister Eckhart, Shah-Kazemi argues that human flourishing is grounded in prayer and virtue as human modes of connection to the beauty of God. God is the truly real and as real the eminently attractive beautiful. The created world gains meaning insofar as it reveals the divine beauty, becoming transparent to the divine reality that grounds it. And this world is a foretaste of the beatitude of paradise in the hereafter. We truly flourish here and now when we understand ourselves to be ordered to that beatitude and our world to be only a symbol—but *really* a symbol—of the heavenly paradise that is its archetype and its goal. Prayer and virtue draw us into the divine vision that gives this understanding.

Miroslav's *Doktorvater, Jürgen Moltmann*, offers a haunting meditation on the theme of expectation. Each of us, he says, begins as one who is expected. But we do not cease to be the objects of expectation when we are born. Things are expected *for* us—most fundamentally a good life—but things are also expected *from* us. God expects our correspondence to God's goodness and reflection of God's mercy, and we are responsible to that divine expectation. We are not, however, only the objects of expectation. We are also its subjects. If we live well, we live in expectation, ultimately in expectation of the kingdom of God that has drawn near. Such expectation is determinate hope. It is directed, and it directs us. We live in light of what we expect. This light casts its glow even on our deaths, and thus Christian expectation carries with it an *ars moriendi* that forms us as those who do not merely await death but expect it with a determinate hope.

Natalia Marandiuc, one of Miroslav's former students, examines the place of loving and being loved in generating the experience of joy. Using her reading of Søren Kierkegaard's analysis of the double love command in *Works of Love* as her guide, she sketches an account of human persons as both desiring beings who are meant to love and needy beings who are meant to be loved and must receive love in order to flourish. For that love to function properly and actually promote the flourishing life marked by joy, she argues, it must be indwelled by the Holy Spirit. Humans need and yearn for not merely interhuman love relationships but to participate in a complex love story involving God, themselves, and others. God both mediates our love of neighbor (to love God is the *first* commandment) and forwards our love of God to our neighbors. God's permeation of the dynamics of love protects against the sort of despair that arises when we exclude God from our loves and invest a merely creaturely relationship with absolute significance.

Nancy Bedford identifies a serious obstacle to the successful elaboration of theological projects oriented around joy and human flourishing of the sort that Miroslav calls for: theological discourse often functions as a "white space," a discursive space in which whiteness is presumed normative and engagement with "non-white" questions and concerns appears merely optional. Working with Slavoj Žižek's categories of "subjective" and "objective" violence—respectively, violence perpetrated by an identifiable agent and the background of systemic and symbolic violence that fosters it and renders it intelligible—Bedford notes the complicity of Christianity and Christian theologians in racialized violence. She calls theologians coded as white to frank self-examination and a theological *askesis* that refuses the routine acceptance and perpetuation of white privilege. The incisive question at the heart of her chapter ought to stand as a critical proviso over theological articulations of human flourishing and the good life, including, to begin with, the chapters of this volume.

Nicholas Wolterstorff focuses on the place of art that enhances the ordinary activities of work and congregational worship in human flourishing. This kind of art is distinct from art, such as atonal orchestral music, that contributes to human flourishing primarily by rewarding the absorbed attention of skilled observers. Art that enhances the ordinary, such as work songs or liturgical singing, contributes to human flourishing by improving the activity to which it is attached—making it more enjoyable and making it go better. But in such art there is also an element of gratuitous excess that is an intrinsic good apart from its beneficial effects on the activity. It gives *joy* and is thus a sign of the *shalom* that Wolterstorff argues is the heart of a Christian understanding of flourishing. This analysis leads Wolterstorff to suggest a general pattern: the better path to promoting human flourishing is not to deny or straightforwardly transcend the ordinary, but to enhance it.

Lidija Matošević opens the third part of the book with an examination of Miroslav's early Croatian-language writings from the period of 1981 to 1991. She explores the stance of these writings toward (1) the minority Evangelical (especially Pentecostal) population of Yugoslavia, (2) the

Marxism that was the official ideology of the Yugoslav state, as well as the particular Yugoslav brand of communism known as "self-management socialism," and (3) the traditional Roman Catholic and Eastern Orthodox churches of Yugoslavia. Matošević sees the young Miroslav as a theologian at once adopting and moving to critique the sectarianism of his home church, championing real, constructive engagement with "outside" perspectives. She concludes that the driving impulse underlying Miroslav's various positions is the conviction that (1) Christians can and must be joyful and hopeful even in a world that is not as it should be and (2) following a God who brings the new creation out of the old (*ex vetere*) rather than destroying the old and beginning again from nothing (*ex nihilo*), all our engagements with a broken world must seek to find and foster what is of value, what is right amidst the often-overwhelming wrong.

Ivan Šarčević focuses on the period of Miroslav's work that extends from *Exclusion and Embrace* to *The End of Memory* and considers the place of the enemy in the theology of reconciliation these books develop. Driving them, he argues, is the insight that the Pauline idea that God loves God's *enemies* (see Rom 5:8–10) and in so loving works to make them friends carries with it a norm for human life. It grounds Jesus's radical interpretation of the love command. But it also locates us among God's enemies, those who crucify Christ and *for whom* Christ is crucified. The recognition of God's loving, reconciling response to universal sinfulness drives toward a view of human flourishing that requires reconciliation among humans.

At the end of this volume, *Linn Tonstad*, another of Miroslav's former students, considers Miroslav's understanding of the Christian vision of the end of all things. She carefully puzzles through some of the implications of Miroslav's understanding of the "eschatological transition," the process by which this world is transformed and brought into the next, the new creation, the world of love. Driven by deep concern for the weight of evil and suffering in human history and commitment to the Christian proclamation of a world of perfect love that is to come, Miroslav argues that once we are reconciled to one another in the world to come, the wrongs we have committed and suffered must no longer come to mind. But what status do the *cross* and the wounded body of the *crucified* Christ has in such a world? And in what sense, if any, does such a world redeem the very real past suffering of history? Contrasting Miroslav's work on eschatology with that of John Thiel, Tonstad draws out the costs of various ways of maintaining the continuity of human beings across the eschatological transition and suggests that perhaps we need not worry about carving out a place for the cross in the world of love, for what matters is the fact that we will then be face to face with the one whose love, to use Miroslav's categories, once suffered but now uninhibit-edly dances for joy.

The essays of this volume by no means form a single vision of the good life, not even a composite, kaleidoscopic vision. What they share is rather the *activity* of envisioning the good life. They differ in the angles from which they look, the narrowness or breadth of their scope, and their understand-ings of the God whom they all view to be the source and heart of human flourishing. But they all enact theology that cares for the questions of flour-ishing life and boldly owns its investment in answering those questions. This is the sort of theology to which Miroslav has always been committed—and toward which we, his students and friends, endeavor together.

BIBLIOGRAPHY

Croasmun, Matthew. "Christ and Human Flourishing: An Introduction to the Thinking of Miroslav Volf." Lecture at the University of Fribourg, Switzerland, May 13, 2015. Online: http://faith.yale.edu/sites/default/files/christ_and_human_flourishing-volf-croasmun.pdf.

Kant, Immanuel. *Critique of Pure Reason*. Revised 2nd edition. Translated by Norman Kemp Smith. New York: Palgrave Macmillan, 2007.

McDonald, Suzanne. *Re-Imaging Election: Divine Election as Representing God to Others and Others to God*. Grand Rapids: Eerdmans, 2010.

Volf, Miroslav. *After Our Likeness: The Church as the Image of the Trinity*. Grand Rapids: Eerdmans, 1998.

———. *Allah: A Christian Response*. San Francisco: HarperOne, 2011.

———. *The End of Memory: Remembering Rightly in a Violent World*. Grand Rapids: Eerdmans, 2006.

———. *Exclusion and Embrace: A Theological Exploration of Identity, Otherness, and Reconciliation*. Nashville: Abingdon, 1996.

———. *Flourishing: Why We Need Religion in a Globalized World*. New Haven: Yale University Press, 2016.

———. *Free of Charge: Giving and Forgiving in a World Stripped of Grace*. Grand Rapids: Zondervan, 2005.

———. "Life Worth Living: Christian Faith and the Crisis of the Universities." *ABC Religion and Ethics*, April 30, 2014. Online: http://www.abc.net.au/religion/articles/2014/04/30/3994889.htm.

———. *A Public Faith: How Followers of Christ Should Serve the Common Good*. Grand Rapids: Brazos, 2011.

———. "Theology for a Way of Life." In *Practicing Theology: Beliefs and Practices in Christian Life*, edited by Miroslav Volf and Dorothy C. Bass, 245–63. Grand Rapids: Eerdmans, 2002.

———. "'The Trinity Is Our Social Program': The Doctrine of the Trinity and the Shape of Social Engagement." *Modern Theology* 14 (1998) 403–23.

———. *Work in the Spirit: Toward a Theology of Work*. Eugene, OR: Wipf & Stock, 2001.

———. *Zukunft der Arbeit, Arbeit der Zukunft : der Arbeitsbegriff bei Karl Marx und seine theologische Wertung*. Munich: Kaiser, 1988.

Volf, Miroslav, Ghazi bin Muhammad, and Melissa Yarrington. *A Common Word: Muslims and Christians on Loving God and Neighbor*. Grand Rapids: Eerdmans, 2010.

Volf, Miroslav, and Ryan McAnnally-Linz. *Public Faith in Action: How to Think Critically, Engage Wisely, and Vote with Integrity*. Grand Rapids: Brazos, 2016.

1

Alpha and Omega—and Everything in Between

Jesus Christ and Human Flourishing

Marianne Meye Thompson

WHAT MIGHT IT MEAN to consider Jesus Christ to be the touchstone of human flourishing? There are a number of ways to frame an answer to this question. On the one hand, the NT articulates Christ's relationship to the world and to humankind in terms of origins and destiny: from beginning to end, Christ is the origin of all that is, including every human being; Christ is also the end, the *telos*, of all that is. Put differently: Christ is Alpha and Omega, the means of creation and new creation. Since all human life comes from and through him, it is understandable that we should speak of human flourishing as somehow also located in or derived from him.

But this "cosmic Christ," the Alpha and Omega, is also the one who is known by the human name, Jesus, who was ultimately crucified on a Roman cross. He not only has a name; he is identified with respect to a place (Jesus *of Nazareth*) that situates him historically in time and space. Even the designation "Christ"—*christos, messiah*—locates him in a particular historical context and narrative, and relates him to a particular historical set of hopes owned by a particular people. And while one might argue about the significance of Jesus for his own people, Israel, it is not immediately apparent that the one who lived, worked, and died among his people should be the touchstone of flourishing for *all* people, and not just for this *one* people.

This chapter is a reflection on the relationship of Jesus Christ to human flourishing, and is divided into two unequal parts treating respectively the "cosmic Christ" and the historically particular Jesus of Nazareth. "Creation" and "new creation" are typically related to the "cosmic Christ," not to Jesus of Nazareth. But I will here present "creation" and "new creation" as two ends of an arc encompassing the ministry of Jesus, and propose a reading of Jesus' ministry as the embodiment of the goods intended for human kind in creation and destined for them in the new creation.

"ALL THINGS WERE CREATED THROUGH HIM": THE COSMIC CHRIST

In talking about the significance of Jesus Christ, various NT formulations elaborate the Scriptural portrayal of God as the creator of all things to speak of the creation of the world as mediated by Christ (or the Word, or the Son).[1] Whereas in the OT God's Word or Wisdom are the means or even blueprint of creation, in the NT that role belongs to Christ. Nothing comes into creation apart from or without Christ: "*All* things were made *through* [the Word] and without him was not anything made that was made" (John 1:3 ESV; cf. 1 Cor 8:6; Col 1:16).[2] This means that God's purposes in Christ are not antithetical to those embedded in creation: the creational intent of God can be known in Christ and, to turn it around, the purposes of God in Christ have been embedded in creation. According to the NT, the "image of God" in which humankind is created (Gen 1:27) is Christ himself (1 Cor 15:49; 2 Cor 4:4; Col 1:15; 3:10). Human flourishing "in Christ" will thus embody what it means for human beings to flourish as created beings, part of God's created order.

The biblical witness to God as sovereign over all creation includes, in the NT, the mediating role of Christ in sustaining the world: Christ is the one "in whom *all things* [*panta*] hold together" (Col 1:17), the one who upholds *all things* (*panta*; Heb 1:3). If Christ is the agent of creation and

1. In the Psalms, God created the world through his word (Ps 33:6); in Proverbs, through wisdom (Prov 8:22–31); and in Sirach 24, through Torah.

2. In Hellenistic Judaism, *all* characterizes the scope of God's powers: "Creator of all things" (2 Macc 1:24; cf Sir 18:1); Philo (*Her.* 206); Creator and Maker (*Spec.* 2.30; *Somn.* 1.76; *Mut.* 29; *Decal.* 61); planter of the world (*Conf.* 196); "cause of all things" (*Somn.* 1.67); and fountain of life (*Fug.* 198); Josephus (*J. W.* 2.131; *Ag. Ap.* 2.190–192).

of upholding the universe, then Christ also mediates the end, both in its telic and chronological senses, of human life: not only were all things created *through* him, but all things were created *for* him (Col 1:16). The world's ends—what it is made for, and where its true destiny lies—can be found in Christ.

These "ends" are regularly described in ways that reflect the twofold work of God in creating (or giving life) and superintending or governing the world. Thus there are a number of ways in which the NT talks about the "ends" of human life that relate those ends to the origins of life: new creation (2 Cor 5:17; Gal 6:15); new birth (John 3:3; 1 Pet 1:3); new life (Rom 7:6); life (John 10:10); eternal life (Mark 10:30; John 17:3); and renewal in the image of the creator (Col 3:10) or of the Son (Rom 8:29; 2 Cor 3:18). All these realities come about through and in Christ. Human flourishing in Christ thus draws into itself and brings to fruition, even while surpassing, the intent for human flourishing in creation. Similarly, the NT envisions the reality in which human beings participate when God brings his rule to fruition: they enter the kingdom of God and both enjoy the benefits of and participate in the everlasting reign of God (Matt 19:28; Rom 5:17, 2 Tim 2:12, Rev 22:5), when death, sin, and evil are finally overcome, and God is "all in all."

In brief, then, God is the (protological) Alpha and (eschatological) Omega (Rev 1:8; 21:6) whose purposes are worked out through and in Christ, so that Jesus Christ, as the means by which those purposes are brought to fruition, is himself Alpha and Omega (Rev 22:13). This means that the past, present, and future of humankind belong to God in Christ. Every human being who walks the face of the earth is created and sustained through Christ quite apart from whether they have any knowledge of him or make any response to him. It is not faith that *first* brings human beings into "relationship" with God, or with Christ: it is creation.

To take our bearings from the beginning, then, from the account of the creation of humankind in Genesis, we may single out the following as aspects of human flourishing. Humankind is created to belong to a world that "is very good" (Gen 1:31) and participates in the care of God's good and fruitful earth, having been given dominion over it (1:26–28). Human beings live in a world in which God is present, walking among them: the world (or garden) is therefore holy ground (3:8). In this garden, not only do human beings belong to God, they belong to each other: "it is not good for Man (Adam) to be alone" (Gen 2:18). From the beginning, human beings were meant to live interdependently; to live in relationships of trust with each other. Human beings were created to enjoy, thrive on, and cultivate the fullness of the world; they were created to be together, not alone; and they were created to live with God present among them or, to turn it around, to live in the presence of God. God's creation is trustworthy in that it can sustain human life: but it is not without dangers that have the potential to undermine and destroy human life, let alone human flourishing. The danger posed by the serpent to Adam and Eve is the invitation to turn away from dependence on God, from living by the words that proceed from the mouth of God (Deut 8:3). Soon the first humans will find themselves living in a world where one of their sons murders the other.

If we were to take our bearings from the end, that is, from the account of the new heavens and earth in the book of Revelation, we would see a new world, a holy city coming down out of heaven from God (Rev 21:1–2, 10–27; 22:1–5). In this good and fruitful world, the river of life that runs through the city nourishes the trees whose leaves are for "the healing of the nations" (22:2). This new creation is entirely trustworthy: nothing threatens to undermine or destroy God's purposes for human flourishing (22:3). For here the tribes of the earth are gathered, together worshiping around the throne of God and the Lamb (22:1, 3). There is no more warfare, slavery, oppression, or idolatry (21:8; 22:15); there are no tears, because there is nothing to weep for (21:4); there is no death, because the one who is the beginning and end of all things has conquered it (21:6). God reigns forever and ever, and the saints participate in that reign, fulfilling the mandate given in creation to "have dominion" over the earth (Gen 1:26–28; Rev 22:5); God's dwelling is (again) with humankind (21:3); God has sanctified time and space, so that there is no need for a temple (21:22, 27). This world is holy ground. It is a city of light (21:23–25; 22:5).

In the present, human life is lived in a world stretched between creation and new creation, receiving from and participating in the fullness of the earth created by God in Christ but awaiting the new creation, when God's purposes for all the earth are finally and fully brought to fruition.[3] At the intersection of the fullness of created life and the surpassing fullness of eternal life lies the abundant life: it participates in the fullness of creation, while anticipating and experiencing, if only partially in the present, that final (eschatological) fullness to come.[4] Accordingly, abundant life is marked

3. For the emphasis on "the fullness" of the world in the OT see Deut 33:13; Ps 24:1, 104:24; the fullness of the world includes fullness of joy (Ps 16:11); the Lord's glory (Isa 6:3; Num 14:21); knowledge of the Lord (Isa 11:9; Hab 2:14); the love of the Lord (Ps 33:5; 119:64); an abundance of food (Isa 25:6; Joel 2:23–26; Ps 104:28; 144:13; Pr 3:10); and the praise of the Lord (Hab 3:3). For "fullness" in Christ see John 1:16; 1 Cor 3:21; Col 1:19; 2:9–10; Eph 1:3; 3:19).

4. In John, from whence the phrase "the abundant life" is taken (John 10:10), "life" and "eternal life" are received in the present, even while anticipating the resurrection to life with God (which is both a forward and upward looking anticipation or hope).

by a fullness of love (Rom 8:35; 1 Cor 13; 2 Cor 2:4; Gal 5:22), peace (John 14:27; 16:33; Rom 8:6; Eph 2:14–17; 4:3), and joy (John 15:11; 16:24; 17:13; Rom 14:17; 15:13; 1 Pet 1:8), because it is lived in faith, hope, and love (1 Cor 13:13; Gal 5:5–6; 1 Thess 1:3; 5:8; Pet 1:21).

That is the big picture. But what if we turn our gaze from the all-powerful cosmic Christ to Jesus of Nazareth, the first century Jewish prophet, teacher, and messianic claimant, who walked the hills and paths of Galilee and Judea, and whose particular human life would be known, above all, for the death he died? According to various NT formulations, it is precisely the agent of all creation who became flesh, took on the life of a servant, emptied himself unto death on the cross, and so brought the life of the new creation to the world (John 1:1–18; Phil 2:5–11; Col 1:15–23). Typically such NT texts attribute that recreating work especially to Jesus' *death and resurrection*: here he overcomes death in life; the old has become new. But I would like to turn our attention to the particularities of Jesus' *life and teaching*, noting three ways in which these are presented as the renewal of God's purposes in creation.

JESUS OF NAZARETH

We will begin, first, with Jesus' announcement of the kingdom of God, God's powerful work to overcome all powers—disease, demons, death, domination—which threaten the wholeness of human beings and their relationships. Second, we will look at how one lives in this kingdom as defined by Jesus' interpretation of the Torah in terms of the twofold command to love God and neighbor, an interpretation of Torah that focuses not on the peculiar obligations to Israel, but on the glue that binds human beings to God and to each other. Third, we will turn briefly to look at Jesus' own life as an example of dependence on and trust in God, manifested concretely in prayer, generosity, forgiveness, gratitude, and giving oneself to others.

The Gift of the Kingdom: Renewing the World

In Jesus' announcement of the in-breaking "kingdom of God," he proclaimed that while God is and has always been "king" over all the world, that rule is now encroaching in a tangible and visible way. The concretization of God's sovereign rule is nothing else than bringing to fruition God's creational intent, because God's kingdom comes with judgment on all that would destroy or degrade the good purposes of God for humankind and all creation. The kingdom brings God's creational intent to fruition by excluding or expelling all threats to human life and its fullness: disease and illnesses of various sorts; demonic forces of darkness; earthly powers or human authorities that oppress, perpetrate injustice, and use human beings and power for their own ends; the isolating effects and power of sin; and the very power of death itself.

Jesus promises that what God works in the world, what God generously gives, and what God will ultimately accomplish is setting to rights all those things that are wrong. This is effected by God's kingdom, or God's rule, God's sovereign dominion. This kingdom is a gift (Luke 12:32), a surpassing treasure, received with thanksgiving and entered into with joy (Matt 13:20, 44; 25:21, 23; Luke 2:10; 15:7, 10; John 16:20–24; 17:13). The God of the Kingdom is a generous father who gives good gifts to those who ask (Matt 7:11) and rain and sun to all alike (5:45).

In turn, those who follow Jesus are to imitate this gracious God: they are generous and giving; they are merciful and forgiving (Luke 6:36–38; Matt 18:23–33; 17:15–18). They are also characterized by gratitude, as was the Samaritan healed from leprosy (Luke 17:15–18). This way of receptivity, gratitude, and generosity is the way of joy. And so the Gospels show Jesus speaking of the joy of completing the work of God, and of Jesus' "rejoicing in the Holy Spirit" when the disciples report the results of their own mission (Luke 10:21). His disciples celebrate like guests at a wedding: they cannot fast, for the bridegroom is among them (Mark 1:19–20 pars.; John 3:28–29). Jesus promises such joy to his disciples in the future, but they also experience it in following him. In following Jesus, in living as he calls them to live, the disciples are recipients of the fullness of all things that God can give: they are given the kingdom; they inherit the earth. They enter into the joy of their master (Matt 13:20, 44; 25:21, 23). That joy is experienced in the present, in the company of Jesus, and anticipated in fullness when the kingdom comes in all its fullness.[5]

One can see this illustrated clearly in the parable of the prodigal: the older son, begrudging the father's generous welcome of his returned miscreant brother, cannot enter into the celebration that welcomes his brother home (Luke 15:11–32). The older brother expresses grim rejection of his father's generosity because he has not gotten what is owed to him (15:29–30), while the younger son received far more than was his due (vv. 22–23). The older brother knows neither gratitude nor mercy: neither gratitude to his father, nor mercy for his brother. He is turned in on himself, consumed by his own wants and desires, jealous for what belongs to him, and so he has no

---

5. Note also the joy that accompanies Jesus birth (Matt 2:10; Luke 1:14, 44; 2:10) and the discovery that he had risen (Matt 28:8; Luke 24:41, 52).

joy when his brother comes home. Similarly, in the parable of the laborers in the vineyard, when everyone is paid the same amount at the end of the day, those who have worked longest and hardest grumble because the landowner was far too generous to those hired at the eleventh hour (Matt 20:1–16). They experience no joy, because they cannot celebrate generosity; they do not know, or have forgotten, what it means to receive, to be thankful. They can only count the hours the others did not work.

The kingdom comes with the power of God's holy (or sanctifying) Spirit. Throughout the Gospels, Jesus is portrayed as someone who experiences the power of the Spirit upon him, a power that drives or constrains him (Mark 1:12; 3:27; Luke 4:17; cf. Luke 12:50). He did not merely talk about the Spirit and the kingdom: the Spirit and the kingdom were the powers that impelled him and that were experienced by those who participated in Jesus' mission, heard his teaching, imitated his example. When Jesus, the "holy one of God," encounters persons who are labeled "unclean," including lepers (Luke 17:12–14) and the demon possessed, or those with "unclean" spirits (Mark 3:18; 5:1–13; Matt 12:28), he removes or expels that which is unclean. Those rendered clean are able to enter into the presence of the holy: into the temple, into the holy community.[6] One could understand this, in light of Genesis, as a realization of the Edenic picture of human beings living in the presence of God. But it is perhaps better to see Jesus' actions in light of embodying, even if only partially, the renewed heavens and earth where all barriers to divine-human fellowship are torn down, and where human life flourishes.

Jesus' disciples were witnesses to and recipients of such cleansing, healing power. He therefore urges them to seek first this kingdom of God (Matt 6:33; Luke 12:31). The demands of the kingdom are ultimate: one must renounce everything (Matt 10:34–38; Luke 14:25–33) because no one can serve two masters (Matt 6:24; Luke 16:13). The rich young ruler is called to sell all that he had (Mark 10:21): it is possible to store up treasure for oneself but not be rich towards God (Matt 6:20; Luke 12:21). This is not an easy way: the gate to life is narrow, and the way is hard, because it is counter-intuitive.

And yet, paradoxically and simultaneously, Jesus promises that those who come to him will find an easy yoke and rest for their souls (Matt 11:29): for here is the end of striving for security in oneself. In seeking God's kingdom, the disciples find that God has already promised them all things: they will inherit the earth (Matt 5:5); be filled (5:6); receive mercy (5:7); see God

6. This is Jesus' "exclusively one-way mission: to push the boundaries of holiness further and further into the realm of the profane, and to eliminate pollution in order to expand the realm of purity." See Bockmuehl, "Keeping it Holy," 104.

or be in God's presence (5:8); and belong to God as children (5:9). When Jesus urges them to seek the kingdom, he does not exhort them to discover that which is hidden or unattainable: the kingdom comes to them as a gift, a pearl of great price, a hidden treasure discovered in a field; it comes as the cleansing power of holiness, the Spirit of restoration and life at work. In finding the kingdom, the disciples discover not so much that their deepest desires are met, but that those very desires are reshaped, redefined. Finding the kingdom is discovering the fullness that God gives; the response to that gift is gratitude and joy.

"You shall love the Lord your God": The Humanizing Torah

It is within the framework of the gift of the kingdom that Jesus calls his disciples to hear and do the word of God (Luke 8:1, 15, 21); Jesus calls those who do the will of God his mother, brothers, and sisters, his kin (Mark 3:35). The will of God as Jesus interprets it comes from two commands in Torah: the commands to love God (Deut 6:5) and love neighbor (Lev 19:18). When Jesus crystallizes the Torah, the blueprint of creation, with the twin commands to love God and neighbor, he re-centers the Torah (Matt 22:34–40). Nothing that Jesus says is new, but in making these two commands the heart of Torah, he offers a way of interpreting Torah that directs his hearers back to God's purposes not only for Israel but ultimately for humankind. "In the beginning" humankind was created to live together with God and with each other in harmony. For Israel to be truly Israel, to love God and neighbor, means that they will fulfill not only the law but God's purposes for humankind as recounted in Genesis.

Thus the Torah humanizes those who keep it by forming them into the pattern of living with God and others as described in Genesis for all humankind. Jesus explicated the commands to love God and neighbor by interpreting the law in keeping with God's original intent in the creation of humankind. Because the Sabbath was made for human beings (Mark 2:23–28), it is appropriate to heal a crippled woman (Luke 13:10–17) or a man's withered hand (Mark 3:1–6) on the Sabbath day. One cannot dishonor the law if one honors the original purposes of creation, that bodies should be whole. The day that is to be kept as holy in the Torah is a day that marks the completion of creation and is a day in which creation is restored and healed. Divorce, even though allowed by Moses in the law, runs counter to the intent found "from the beginning of creation" that man and woman should become "one flesh" (Mark 10:6–9; Gen 2:24). The Torah, read rightly, honors God's purposes for the world and its inhabitants. God desires mercy, those virtues and practices that ought to characterize human life together, even more than sacrifice, the particular acts of worship commanded of God's people (Matt 9:9–13; 12:1–8; Hos 6:6). God wants justice, mercy, and faith more than the tithe of mint and dill and cumin (Matt 23:23).

Keeping the Torah as Jesus interpreted it ultimately means modeling one's conduct on God's own character, the God in whose image all human beings are created. Thus to fulfill or live out the law means to hear and do it as inculcating compassion and mercy, in keeping with God's own character as compassionate and merciful (Luke 10:25–28; Luke 6:32–36 pars.; Matt 5:43–58; 9:9–13; 12:1–8; 18:23–25; 25:31–46). Jesus not only spoke of such compassion and mercy in parables about sharing meals with the lost, taking the last seat at a table, and going out to the highways and byways to find people to feast at a banquet (Luke 14:7–24), he himself also did all these things, gladly eating with sinners (Luke 15:1–3), and journeying into Gentile territory in order to seek out "the lost sheep of the house of Israel" (Matt 15:24). His ministry demonstrated the love of God and neighbor that were the heart of the law.

"He Trusts in God": Human Life before God

Jesus embodied the kingdom of God and interpreted the Torah as a way of ordering human life before God. In doing so, he called people to trust the God whom he trusts. According to Matthew, as Jesus hung on the cross, bystanders taunted him with the words, "He trusts in God! Let God deliver him now!" (Matt 27:43 ESV). This is, ultimately, where Jesus' commitment to the messianic vocation to which God had called him—his trust—led him. But that trust had been demonstrated throughout the Gospels.

Jesus exemplifies what such trust looks like when he refuses to turn stones to bread to satisfy his own hunger, for "one does not live by bread alone" (Matt 4:4); to manipulate God for his own ends, for "you shall not tempt the Lord your God" (Matt 4:5–7); or to seek any glory or honor for himself, for "you shall worship the Lord your God and him only shall you serve" (4:8–10 ESV). In turn, Jesus teaches his disciples to pray, "Give us this day our daily bread," and calls them to trust the God who feeds the birds of the air and clothes the lilies with exquisite beauty, and who generously provides for all people from the fullness of the earth: the rain falls and the sun shines on just and unjust alike (Matt 6:25–34). Later, Jesus tells a parable in which the hungry were fed through the hands and deeds of those who saw Jesus in the poor and needy (Matt 25:31–46). Apparently, this too is part of how God feeds the hungry, clothes the naked, and takes care of the imprisoned and poor, of how the generosity of God is given to his world. Those who have learned to receive from the fullness of God's earth now feed and clothe the poor and hungry. The fullness that they take in is a fullness that they give out.

Prayer expresses trust and, in some way, dependence—even if the prayer be a lament. In urging his disciples to pray, Jesus describes a God who is a generous father who delights to give good gifts to those who ask him and so urges his disciples to come with their petitions to God (Matt 7:7–11; 18:19; 21:22; John 14:14–16; 15:16; 16:23–24). And because Jesus trusted God, he would not turn stones to bread or seek a sign, some tangible, confirmatory evidence of his own identity as "Son of God," or manipulate God for his own ends; neither would he *give* a sign to authenticate his identity or the source of his power (Mark 8:12). There are no signs for unbelief—or for faith either. The one who is "Son of God" calls those who are "children of God [the heavenly father]" to live with the kind of faith by which he lives.[7] But the disciples are people of little faith (Matt 8:26; 14:31); *others* demonstrate the kind of faith that Jesus commends, seeks, and himself models (Matt 8:10; 9:29; 17:20; 21:21). Recognizing that Jesus lives by the kind of faith that he commends to them, the disciples appeal to him "increase our faith!" (Luke 17:5).

Where does this trust in God lead? When Jesus invites his disciples to "deny themselves and take up their cross and follow" him, it is evident that Jesus speaks of a way of living that entails surrender, self-giving, and even loss. This is not first a giving of oneself to others, but a giving of oneself to God. The rich young ruler is not told simply to sell everything in order to give it to others, but to sell everything and follow Jesus; the rich man who builds bigger barns has made himself rich in all but that which truly matters: he is not "rich towards God" (Luke 12:21). The God whom he ignored can demand his life at any time. Jesus' stark calls to follow him to death, or to surrender oneself, are calls to turn to the God who gives and to live out of the fullness that God gives, rather than out of the counterfeit fullness that earthly goods purport to offer. Jesus calls his followers to love God with their "heart, soul, and mind," and to turn away from those things that distract them from the "one thing" that they should seek after (Ps 27:4). Jesus thus both models and calls for the kind of trust that Adam and Eve failed to exhibit, turning away from God's word and presence to other, short-lived goods.

7. In the Synoptic Gospels, the words for Jesus as "son" and for others as "children" of God are both *huios*; even given the differences in role, there is comparability in the ways that all God's "children" depend upon their heavenly Father. In John, Jesus is called *huios* while others are called children (*tekna*).

The kind of trust and dependence for which Jesus calls grow out of love. In the gospel of John, Jesus's call to "follow me" is the first and last command that he gives his disciples. But at the end of the Gospel, the call is preceded by three questions to Simon Peter: "Simon, son of John, do you love me?" When Peter answers three times that he does love Jesus, Jesus tells him to extend his own care and provision to his disciples to the sheep of Jesus' flock (John 21:15–17). Peter's service will be rendered out of love for Jesus. To be sure: Jesus tells his disciples that to love him is to keep his commands; but this can never reduce love to commandment keeping.

The Gospel of John further develops the relationship between Jesus and the Father, between the Father and the disciples, Jesus and the disciples, and the disciples to each other in terms of love (13:34–35; 14:21, 23; 15:9–13; 17:24–26). Love is the bond between each of these pairs. Following Jesus leads to love: for him, and for the other. Jesus also promises his disciples that, in him, they will have peace (14:27; 16:33; 20:19, 21, 26), and the fullness of joy, the very joy that he has (15:11; 16:20–24; 17:13). In following him, in entering into the bonds of love that connect Father and Son, both of these with believers, and believers with each other, Jesus' disciples also enter into joy. In trusting God, following Jesus, living in faith, loving one another, and receiving Jesus' peace and joy, they live the abundant life that he promises (10:10).

A CLOSING REFLECTION

Jesus demonstrates and calls for life centered in God and impelled towards the other in love, compassion, and mercy. Jesus lodges his teaching in the character of a holy and merciful God, God's purposes in creation as these are embodied in the Torah, and the expectation of a new world, the kingdom of God, that remakes the world. This is also what Jesus lived and died for: the coming kingdom of God that brings to fruition God's purposes for the world. This is the story of the kingdom of God that Jesus both implicitly narrates and lives out. It is a narrative that calls for hope, because it is not yet finished, and its end lies in the hands of God. As Jesus said, "No one knows the hour, except the Father" (Mark 13:32). Hence, this narrative also calls for trust in the God who holds all things in his hands. And it calls for love: one cannot trust a God one does not love, above all because that God's very being is characterized as love.

The Gospels do not speak of a general or generic human flourishing, but of what it means to follow Jesus. Strikingly, however, the way in which Jesus interprets the Torah not only points his hearers back to the purposes for human life in creation, but also focuses attention on patterns of human conduct summarized by love, rather than on laws and regulations peculiar to and characteristic of the people of Israel. But Jesus does not play off his command to love against the Torah: he does not pit "love" against "law." Rather, he calls people to love precisely because this is what God has always asked of his creatures. The heart of the law is love. Jesus explicates what it means to love God and to love neighbor in parable and deed, calling for trust, generosity, receptivity, and gratitude: open-handed and open-hearted living.

While God utters his decisive "yes" through Christ (2 Cor 1:20), this ultimate "yes" reaches beyond any individual human life, beyond the story of the world that God created. There is no closure in the Bible to the story of Israel, the nations, or creation: indeed, the biblical account, in its substance and form, remains radically unfinished, anticipating in faith and hope the new creation. Theologically speaking, the biblical narrative leaves the resolution of "all things" to the one who also made all things; even the Son leaves the hour to the Father. Undoubtedly human yearnings for a good life, a better life, and a good and better world are rooted in our longings for a new Eden: but creation and new creation are the prerogatives of God who is Alpha and Omega. In the meantime, whatever it means for human beings to flourish must take into account that this happens in the unfinished, open-ended, narrative in which we live, that finds its beginning, middle, and ending in the good purposes of God in Christ, through whom the world was created, and who lived among us in faithfulness, compassion, mercy, and love.

BIBLIOGRAPHY

Bockmuehl, Markus. "Keeping it Holy: Old Testament Commandment and New Testament Faith." In *"I am the Lord your God": Christian Reflections on the Ten Commandments,* edited by Carl E. Braaten and Christopher R. Seitz, 95–124. Grand Rapids: Eerdmans, 2005.

2

Created for Their Own Sakes

Counter-Intuitive Senses of Human Creatures' Flourishing

David H. Kelsey

SOME SENSES IN WHICH human creatures may be said on theological grounds to "flourish" are counter–intuitive because they can also count as situations of severe "ill-health" or "ill-being." Consequently, I argue here, it would be wise in theological contexts to stipulate a sharp distinction between "flourishing" and "well-being" (or "health," broadly understood).

I say "some" senses of "human flourishing" are counter-intuitive because in Christian theological contexts human beings are said to "flourish" in many senses. There is no univocal "essence" to flourishing, the core "real meaning" of the word. As usual, etymology gets us only a little distance toward the range of senses of a word. According to the Oxford English Dictionary "to flourish" means in general both "to blossom" and "to thrive." "To blossom" can be used metaphorically of many kinds of living plants to refer to the type of beauty of which each is capable in its kind when it blooms. It can also be used metaphorically of living animals and of entire human enterprises. So too, both a human being and an academic institution may be said to "blossom" when they are on the way to providing metaphorical "fruit" and "seed" on which contemporary others' flourishing depend and on which a subsequent generation's life may depend. For its part, according to the Oxford English Dictionary, "to thrive" derives from the Old Norse, *thrifask,* "to have oneself in hand." So "to flourish" may function as a metaphor for "being of value" (either intrinsic value, expressed either aesthetically as "beauty" or morally as "good," or creatures' value for one another in the interactions with fellow creatures that constitute their interdependencies). And "to thrive" may function as a metaphor for some way of being "self-related" ("to have oneself in hand"; to be "in charge of oneself"; to be "reliably self-regulating and self-directing").

However, in theological discourse "to flourish" and "flourishing" function metaphorically in several different doctrinal contexts each of which gives those expressions a different sense. Two such doctrinal contexts are especially important: First, human creatures flourish as the "glory of God" (in two different senses of "glory") in virtue of the ways in which the triune God relates to them and they to God. Second, God relates to human beings in three irreducibly different ways; hence human beings are the "glory of God" in a different sense in virtue of each of those three ways in which God relates to them. Accordingly they may be said to "flourish" in different senses with respect to each way God relates to them and they in response relate to God.

Those two theological contexts in which human beings are said to flourish in various senses call for a stipulated, and therefore admittedly artificial, technical distinction in theology between human "flourishing" and human "well-being," for which a common metaphor is "health" or "healthy." The first relies on theological accounts of ways in which God goes about relating to human beings for the criteria of what counts as being the glory of God and thus what counts as flourishing. The second commonly relies on quite different criteria for well-being. Those criteria consider human beings as dynamic physical, mental, and social energy systems whose criteria for well-being or health are how well the systems that make for specifically human life function to sustain human beings' social, cultural, and biological lives over both short and long haul. Where the criteria of flourishing are theocentric, the criteria of well-being are anthropocentric. As we shall see, the latter have an important place in theological accounts of human flourishing. The distinction between the two is not invidious. Nonetheless, it does serve to relativize the force of anthropocentric criteria of flourishing by locating them within the conceptually more basic context of theocentric criteria of flourishing.

The next two sections will outline each of those doctrinal contexts. Subsequent sections will focus on senses in which human beings are theologically said to flourish as the glory of the triune God specifically in virtue of God's way of relating to them creatively purely for their own sakes, which gives rise to counter-intuitive senses of "flourishing."

FLOURISHING AS THE "GLORY" OF GOD

Human flourishing is in some sense the "glory" of God. "Glory" is ascribed to the triune God in three senses.[1] The primary sense of "the glory of God" is God's intrinsic glory in and of Godself. God's intrinsic glory is God's attractive self-expressive self-relatedness.[2] God's glory is intrinsic to God in that it is not dependent on God relating to other realities self-expressively. Obviously human beings, precisely because they are not God, are not the "glory of God" in that primary sense. Second, God's ways of relating to all else are themselves *expressive* of God's intrinsic glory. By virtue of the self-expressiveness of God's creative relating, creatures as such are God's self-expressions *ad extra* of God's intrinsic glory. Third, human beings in particular are complex enough to be capable of *intentionally* responding to God's ways of relating to them in ways that are appropriate to the concrete ways in which God relates to them. Reflecting God's glory in the very way in which they live, they are the glory of God in a third sense. The latter two are the senses in which human beings may be appropriately characterized as the "glory of God." It is in being the glory of God in the latter two senses of "glory" that human beings' flourishing is understood in the context of God's relating to them.

1. This analysis of the way "glory" is used in canonical Christian scripture is heavily dependent on Donald D. Evans's illuminating philosophical analysis of the performative force of language used in biblical accounts of God's creative relating to all else in *The Logic of Self-Involvement*.

2. As Donald Evans points out in *The Logic of Self-Involvement*, Old Testament Hebrew terms usually translated in English as "glory," especially *kabod* ("splendor"; perhaps "gravitas"), *hadar*, and *hod* ("dazzling brilliance"; "beauty"), are often used with "expressive" force in connection with God relating to create. One of the tasks of a doctrine of the Trinity is to outline the threefold way in which God is eternally and attractively self-expressive in ways that do not require reality other than God as the term of the relation "self-expressed-to-x" because the self-expressing is an eternal ontological threefold *self*-relating. The inexhaustible richness of God's intrinsically attractive self-expressive self-relating has traditionally called for three different sorts of discourse in doctrines of God: an aesthetic discourse (God as beauty), a moral discourse (God as good) and an ontological discourse (God as truth, or as inherently wise and reliable).

HUMAN BEINGS' THREE-STRANDED
ULTIMATE CONTEXT

The ultimate context in which human beings "live and move and have their being" is constituted by three irreducibly different ways in which, as narrated in canonical Christian scripture, God relates to all else: to create them, to draw them to eschatological consummation, and to reconcile them to God when they have been estranged from God.[3] The three are irreducibly different from one another because each has a different "narrative logic," a term of art I use to refer to the pattern of movement typical of canonical scriptural narratives of each way in which God relates to all else.[4]

The triune God relates to create all else in a steady-state *creative blessing* on creatures that is either present or is not present but does not admit of degrees.[5] The Genesis creation narratives highlight features of creatures that define both the contingency of their God-dependency and the contingency of their creaturely inter-dependency. They tell of God bestowing life, growth, and the power of fertility for animal creatures' wellbeing in their kind across the generations.[6] I have argued elsewhere[7] that the texts in canonical Christian Scripture that most exemplify this description of biblical creation narratives are in canonical Wisdom Literature, especially in Proverbs 8 and, regarding human creatures, in Job. In virtue of God's relating to them in creative blessing, human creatures flourish in *one sense* as the "glory of God" simply as expressions *ad extra* of the triune God's intrinsic glory, and flourish in a *second sense* insofar as their actions, their personal identities, and their socially constructed proximate contexts are appropriate responses to the way in which God relates to them in creative blessing (i.e., they "glorify God" in creation-related *praxis*).

A second sort of "narrative logic" moves canonical narratives of God relating to *deliver* creatures from bondage.[8] The movement of such

3. It has, of course, been the structure of the way New Testament texts narrate how God goes about relating to all else to draw it to eschatological consummation and to reconcile it when estranged from God as an interplay among Jesus of Nazareth, the One he calls "Father" and who calls him "Son," and the Holy Spirit that has historically warranted trinitarian accounts of God whose validity is assumed here.

4. What follows it heavily dependent on Claus Westermann's exegetical analysis of the literary structure of the Pentateuch and of Genesis in particular in *Blessing*; *Creation*; and *Genesis 1–11: A Commentary.*

5. Cf. Westermann, *Blessing.*

6. Cf. Westermann, *Creation*, 24, 46.

7. Cf. Kelsey, *Eccentric Existence*, Chs. 4B, 5B, 6 and 7.

8. Cf. Westermann, *Blessing*, 4.

narratives is driven by conflict between God and powers that hold human creatures in a bondage that distorts "what" and "who" they are.[9] In Christian scripture such "narratives of deliverance" include the stories told in various ways in the canonical Christian Gospels that render all that Jesus of Nazareth does and undergoes, as that in turn is variously interpreted in canonical Epistles. That "interpretation" is usually expressed in one or another of a set of metaphors for what God is doing in and through all that Jesus does and undergoes: (in no particular order) ransom; redemption; sacrifice; expiation; forgiveness; reconciliation, etc. One thing the metaphors have in common is the picture that humankind as a whole is in need of deliverance from its bondage to the power of the consequences to human creatures of their self-estrangement from God and that what God does in and through what Jesus does and undergoes is to accomplish just that deliverance. Thus the Gospels' narratives render God's conflict with powers holding humankind in bondage as coming to its decisive climax in the particularities of what Jesus does and undergoes in his ministry, betrayal, trial, suffering, crucifixion, and resurrection, as all of that is understood in the context of the Old Testament's longer narrative of God's deeds of deliverance of the Patriarchs, of the Hebrew people enslaved in Egypt, and later the release of Judeans exiled in Babylon and allowed to return to Judah.[10] In that larger narrative context the Gospel's narratives can be read as accounts of how God keeps the promise to Abraham that through him all peoples will be blessed. In virtue of God's relating to reconcile estranged human creatures to God they flourish as the "glory of God" in a *third sense* of "flourish" in that their status as already justified estranged creatures, *simul justus et peccator,* expresses *ad extra* the triune God's intrinsic glory. And they flourish in *fourth sense* insofar as their actions, personal identities, and community with one another are appropriate responses to the way in which God relates to them to reconcile them to God by way of the cross (i.e., they "glorify God" in soteriologically oriented *praxis*).

A third sort of "narrative logic" moves canonical narratives that give an account of *eschatological blessing* by which God promises, and then draws creation into, an eschatological consummation.[11] The promise is

9. Because "creative blessing" is a constant steady-state relating and not a episodic event, Westermann vigorously rejects Gerhard von Rad's characterization of the Genesis creation stories as the first moment in "salvation history's" account of liberating events. See Westermann, *Blessing,* 10.

10. Westermann develops his contrasting characterization of narratives of God relating in creative blessing in an analysis of chapters 1–11 of the book of Genesis and not merely chapters 1 and 2. Cf. Westermann, *Genesis 1–11: A Commentary.*

11. In *Creation,* 41, Westermann argues that by reference to the seventh day of

coeval with God's creative blessing. Like God relating in creative blessing and unlike God relating in liberating events, God's relating to draw creation to an eschatological consummation is not an episodic event in history. It is a steady-state relating once it begins with the promise. However, unlike God relating in creative blessing and like God relating in liberative events, God's relating in eschatological blessing is not such that either-it-obtains-fully-actualized-or-it-does-not.[12] According to canonical New Testament narratives the beginning of the fulfillment of that promise is inaugurated (but only inaugurated, not yet fully actualized) in a particular event, the resurrection of Jesus Christ. Hence eschatological blessing is now at once actually inaugurated but not yet fully actualized. In the future, by the work of the Spirit drawing creatures into Jesus' resurrected life with God, the promise will be fully actualized in an eschatological consummation of creation. One consequence of this is that one aspect of human creatures' proximate contexts is that they now live in the "meantime" between, on one side, the actual inauguration of God's keeping of the promise of eschatological blessing in the resurrection of Jesus and, on the other side, God's future full actualization of that eschatological promise. In virtue of that tension between the "now" and the "not yet" of eschatological blessing, human creatures flourish as the glory of God in yet two more senses of "flourish." They flourish here and now in a *fifth sense* insofar as their actions, personal identities, and community with one another here and now are celebrations of and engagements in communities whose common life is, however temporarily, marked by just love and reconciliation and is engaged in practices that make, however incompletely, for increased liberation of their host societies from bondage by the oppression of unjust arrangements of social, cultural, political, and economic power that expresses and is a "foretaste," however ad hoc and fleeting, of the quality of community in God's eschatological "new creation." That is, they flourish here and now in eschatologically oriented *praxis*. When God's eschatological promise is finally fully actualized, however, human creatures will flourish in a *sixth sense* in virtue God's relating to them in eschatological blessing in that they will then fully share in creaturely fashion in the communion that is the triune God's own life. Human creatures' flourishing in that sixth sense of the term just is their participation in God's fully actualized eschatological "new creation." The imagery used in New Testament texts to characterize that flourishing has historically

creation as the day of rest the Priestly editors of Genesis have "suggested the coming into existence of our world in successive stages . . . and, with the repose of the seventh day, [they] pointed to the continuation of this process as it moves toward a goal which transcends the works of Creation."

12. Cf. Westermann, *Beginning and End in the Bible*, 3, 4, 27.

stimulated a great deal of imaginative speculation about "life after death" in both popular and "high" culture (see Dante's *Paradiso*!). However, the few passages in which New Testament writers attempt to characterize human life in the context of fully actualized eschatological blessing seem mostly to exhibit how it escapes our conceptual capacities (see, e.g., Rom 8:18–26; 1 Cor 15:35–56!). The way in which canonical texts use the phrase "new creation" strongly suggests that eschatological human life is social, communal, and in some way a radical transformation of creaturely life, rather than being a new act of *creation ex nihilo* discontinuous with the quotidian creatureliness human beings live here and now. That suggests that human life flourishing in fully actualized eschatological blessing is not "wholly other" than the life we have experienced in virtue of God's creative blessing and can to some extent grasp conceptually. On the other hand, the images used in canonical texts to characterize the flourishing of human life in this sixth sense of "flourish" are remarkably abstract and almost entirely negative: it is life marked by joy, but a joy unlike any human creatures have known before, a life in which there is no loss, no pain, no grief, no suffering, no "darkness," and no death. Concerning the lineaments of this sixth sense of human flourishing the most appropriate stance may be a certain pious agnosticism.

The three ways in which God relates to all else are inseparable but asymmetrically related to one another. They are inseparable in that it is one and the same God who relates to all else in each of them. The triune God's relating to all else in creative blessing is ontologically and logically (but not necessarily chronologically) prior to the other two ways of relating. God's relating in creative blessing, however, does not necessarily entail that God also relates to all else either to draw it into eschatological consummation or, if it is estranged from God, to reconcile it to God. God's relating in eschatological blessing is coeval with creative blessing. However, as canonically narrated, the concrete way in which God goes about making and keeping the promise of that blessing is logically independent of creative blessing. It is free grace added above and beyond the gracious gift of creation and not logically entailed by it. So too, as canonically narrated, the way in which God goes about liberating estranged creatures from the consequences to them of their estrangement is itself grace, not simply above and beyond the graciousness of creative blessing to non-resisting creatures, but given freely in spite of creatures' hostility to God.

God's way of relating to bless eschatologically and God's way of relating to reconcile estranged creatures are also, as canonically narrated, asymmetrically related. They are both narratives about the same human creature as God incarnate: Jesus of Nazareth, "God with us." Yet they are asymmetrically related: The way God goes about beginning to keep the promise of eschatological consummation by way of Incarnation focuses on the resurrection of Jesus Christ which inaugurates God's fulfillment of that promise. But it does not necessarily entail that Jesus' death need be by way of the curse of crucifixion. God's self-commitment in that promise does not necessarily presuppose that creatures are estranged from God or in need of reconciliation. Canonical accounts of the inauguration of eschatological blessing would make sense were there no estrangement. Moreover God's promise of eschatological consummation and the way God goes about beginning to keep it by the resurrection of Jesus Christ do not necessarily imply that that promise also commits God to reconcile creatures should they become estranged. The two are logically independent. On the other hand, as canonically narrated, the way God does concretely go about reconciling estranged creatures to God is also by way of Incarnation, focused on the crucifixion of Jesus who is raised from the dead. It does presuppose that creatures are estranged. It also presupposes that the context of their reconciliation to God is Jesus Christ's resurrection as the inauguration of God's fulfillment of the promise of the new creation that constitutes eschatological consummation.[13]

Together those three inter-woven ways in which the triune God relates to all else constitute the ultimate context within which human beings live. They are human beings' "ultimate" context in that each is a way in which God unilaterally takes the initiative to relate to them for their own sakes. In each of them God relates "preveniently" and not in response to any value, moral or aesthetic, that human beings may have apart from God's relating to them, nor to achieve any further end other than that they exist for their own sakes, or are eschatologically consummated for their own sakes,

13. An upshot of their different respective "narrative logics" and the asymmetries of their relations to one another is that accounts of these three ways in which God relates to all else cannot be conflated into some one extended coherent narrative in which each sort of narrative is one "moment" (e.g., a continuous intelligible narrative moving from creation through "fall" to reconciliation and then to eschatological consummation). To be intelligible or "follow-able" the proposed single narrative would need to have its own coherent narrative logic. Any effort at such a synthesis would unavoidably involve construing some two of the three sorts of narrative as instances of the narrative logic of the third sort of narrative in order to make the whole continuously intelligible. But doing so would require distortion of the narrative logic proper to each of those other two sorts of narrative. Insofar as doctrinal accounts of the ways in which God relates to all else, respectively, to create, to draw into eschatological consummation, and to reconcile are rooted in canonical scriptural narratives of how God relates to all else, that would have the consequence of distorting the theological accounts of at least two strands of the economy. And insofar as those theological accounts of the economy are the contexts within which "flourish" and "flourishing" are used of human beings, that would have the further consequence of distorting the senses in which those words are properly used of human beings in theology.

or are reconciled for their own sakes. God's threefold relating consists of three different ways in which God grounds human beings' reality and value for their own sake such that *just as they are* they flourish as expressions of God's intrinsic glory; and when human beings' personal identities, actions, and socially constructed proximate contexts are appropriate responses to the ways in which God relates to them then they are the "glory of God" in that they glorify God.

We turn now to focus more closely only on the triune God's relating to create. We do so for two reasons. First, as we have seen, God's creative blessing has a certain logical and ontological primacy in the asymmetric relations among the three strands of canonical narratives of how God relates to all else. Second, the way in which God's creative blessing grounds creatures' flourishing as expressions of God's intrinsic glory theologically warrants affirmation of the most obviously counter-intuitive senses of "human flourishing."

FLOURISHING AS APPROPRIATE RESPONSE TO GOD'S GLORY IN RELATING CREATIVELY

Traditional theological characterizations of the triune Creator's creative relating as *creatio ex nihilo* entail a correlative concept of creaturehood-as-such or creatureliness-in-general. Perhaps the defining feature of creatureliness is limitedness or finitude. Human beings' creatureliness is exhibited in four respects in which they are finite.

First, God's creative relating to human creatures (like God's creative relating to every kind of creature) is "internal" to them in that it constitutes them in actual existence *as* creatures. This is entailed by the *ex nihilo* character of God's creative relating: Did that active relating not obtain, creatures would simply not exist. Their actual existence is universally and always contingent on God's creative blessing, constituting both their concretely actual reality and their value. Nor is their existence grounded in "stuff" out of which God must make creatures of various kinds. In this regard human creatures' finitude lies in the fact that they cannot "create" or ground either their own or any other creature's actual reality or value. In those respects they are grounded eccentrically, "outside" themselves. They are radically finite existentially.

Second, human creatures are created through being born as actual living bodies. As bodies they are parts of the physical cosmos as we know it. They are very minor parts of innumerable vast networks of various sorts of inter-related and inter-acting energy systems (particle, molecular, cellular, nebular, solar, ecological, etc.) that are inherently interdependent insofar as they draw energy from one another in hugely complex ways. In this respect human creatures are finite in *necessarily* being limited in the scope and power of their agency by myriad other creatures that impinge on them. Hence human creatures are finite in being inherently fragile, vulnerable to violation by other creatures, accident prone, and mortal.

Third, created through being born, each human being is a center of a specific range (namely, the range specific to *homo sapiens*) of various powers (physical, emotional, intellectual, social, self-expressive) and degrees of energy that are complexly inter-related. That "specific range" constitutes human "nature," the "power pack," so to speak, that is specific to being human.[14] By means of them human creatures enact their agency in the particular physical and psycho-socially constructed proximate contexts in which they live and that constitute their "ecological niches." Like other living creatures, having been born, human creatures go through a process of maturation during which various of those powers emerge in various degrees. While one matures into one's powers, one is born "human"; one does not "mature" into being human. The differences in their particular sub-sets of human powers do not imply that different human creatures are different degrees of "human." There is no one absolute standard for the "perfect specimen" of the class "human living bodies."

The variety of powers with which human creatures are born, the variety of levels of energy they have, and the variety of degrees to which particular powers mature in those who have them require some degree of integration of them all by human creatures as they mature in order for them to function as agents in their own rights. To the extent that those differences are rooted in the particular genomes of different human creatures, they give some individuals advantages and others handicaps in their inter-actions with one another and in their grappling with the opportunities and challenges they face in the physical and social environments that constitute their common proximate contexts. At the same time, the sheer complexity of the relations among these things leaves human creatures internally vulnerable to varying degrees of failure to become "integrated" and, for a variety of reasons both internal and external, to their relative "dis-integration" over time. These differences among human creatures are simply given and are not a function of more or less vigorous human self-disciplining. They manifest a third respect

---

14. Perhaps the most apt way to identify which new-born living bodies count as belonging to the *homo sapiens* population would be by genetic testing. Although *homo sapiens* "normally" have 46 chromosomes arranged in 23 pairs, there are many individuals with chromosomal abnormalities that do not fit that pattern. The point here is that the DNA of which such individuals have an unusual set are nonetheless human.

in which human creatures are finite, in this case limited internally in multiple respects rather than merely from without by other creatures.

Fourth, one of the features of *homo sapiens* that appears to set it off from other kinds of living bodies is that its specific powers are so richly complex that they include remarkable powers for various sorts of conscious intentional self-regulation. They empower human creatures not only to direct their behavior in goal-oriented ways and to select the goals they pursue, but also self-consciously to cultivate and discipline powers they find emerging as they mature in order more effectively to enact the projects they devise in order to realize those goals. Powers of self-regulation also allow them to cultivate and discipline capacities for various forms of complex creative self-expression. They allow human creatures to construct complex societies and cultures. Such powers for self-regulation also warrant holding human beings accountable for their regulation of their own actions, i.e. to treat them as morally accountable agents. It is just those powers of self-regulation that make possible for human beings one aspect of "flourishing," viz. thriving, "having oneself in hand."

Such self-regulating and self-disciplining by human creatures can shape their individual personal identities, "who" each of them is. They are born "human"; but that physical "nature" does not determine any particular personal identity for them. Their "nature" only provides a range of powers and diverse types of energy that will be "shaped" or "formed" into some particular personal identity for each one. Their identities will in any case be partly shaped by factors they cannot regulate (e.g., by the particular sub-set of human powers with which they are born into their proximate contexts, and the particularities of the psycho-socially constructed societies and cultures that are aspects of the proximate contexts in which they mature). Such contexts usually project more or less abstract stereotyped identities that are attached to various roles in society onto human creatures who are being "formed" by those contexts. Personal identities will also unavoidably be "shaped" by emotionally powerful events that are unique to each individual's family of origin and early life. Nonetheless, human creatures' powers of self-regulation can to some extent allow them to shape whether they appropriate, modify, or reject identities socially projected onto them and to shape how they respond to and interpret traumatic events they live through. Thus they may to some extent "self-regulate" their own personal identities. Conversely, those same creaturely powers for self-regulation may be not be engaged at all, or may be engaged to shape identities in morally unacceptable ways, or may be engaged in the pursuit of both of two projects that are inherently in conflict with each other, block and frustrate each other, and shape a self-divided and self-contradictory personal identity. Thus a fourth respect in which human creatures are finite is manifest in internal limits both to their powers of self-regulation and to the energy resources with which they exercise those powers.

It is in virtue of those finite powers of self-regulation that human creatures may be said to flourish as the glory of God in one sense of the term. In being created in their having been born human creatures they are given living human bodies for whose personal identities, dispositions, affective states, and intentional actions they are accountable to God. Human creatures have capacities, limited and constrained as they may be, that can be nurtured and disciplined to be capabilities to respond to God's creative blessing appropriately. When human creatures respond appropriately to God's relating to them in creative blessing, they flourish in the sense that they are the "glory of God" in actively glorifying God. The question is, "What are the criteria of 'appropriate' responses to God's way of relating in creative blessing in which human creatures flourish?"

In a theocentric account of human creatures' flourishing those criteria should lie in the concrete way in which God goes about relating to all else in creative blessing as that is narrated in canonical Christian scripture. As was noted above, the approach to a theology of the flourishing of human creatures that is proposed here adopts the traditional Christian claims a) that God creates *ex nihilo* and b) that the God who does so is triune. Each claim has implications concerning how God goes about relating creatively. Together they imply one criterion of "appropriate" human creaturely response to the way in which God goes about relating to them creatively: the formation of a personal identity one of whose basic and defining dispositions is *faith* understood, to paraphrase H. Richard Niebuhr's formulation,[15] as the disposition to live in our proximate contexts trusting God to ground our concrete actuality and value and being loyal to God's own project in those contexts. As a disposition that shapes a human creature's personal identity it engages the entire human creature, all its powers—emotions, passions, feelings, temperament, perceptual capacities, talents for self-expression, as well as intellect, will, and physical energy.

a) "God creates all else *ex nihilo*" is a wholly negative claim: God does not create "out of" anything whatsoever. It says nothing about the causal nexus of God's creative act.[16] God's creative blessing is an unmediated active

---

15. See Niebuhr, *Radical Monotheism*, 16–23.

16. That comports with Claus Westermann's analysis of the strategy of the "Priestly" editing of narratives they incorporated in canonical text of Genesis. According to Westermann the creation narratives in Genesis are structured in a way that excludes all of the explanations of how the world was created that were available in the ancient world. They do not serve to explain the coming-to-be of creation because they bracket out the

relating directly to each creature that is "internal" to its reality because it constitutes it. It is a relating that is unconstrained by anything other than God's own "identity" (i.e., "who" God is, God's own qualities). Hence in creating God is free to be "closer" to each creature than the creature can be to itself since by definition, a *creature* cannot relate to itself so as to be *causa sui,* cause of it own concrete actuality. At the same time, in creating *ex nihilo* God is radically and freely "other" than creatures because God's creative relating is asymmetrical and non-reciprocal: creatures' actuality is constituted by God's creative relating to them, whereas God's actuality is not constituted by creatures' actively relating to God. Yet the ontological "otherness" of Creator to creature is not an ontological separation or "gap," much less a "chasm." The Creator's "closeness" to and "otherness" from creatures are correlative and not inversely related (as though the "closer" God is, the less "other" God would be, or vice versa). Each is the condition of the possibility of the other. For that reason the creative relating in which the Creator eccentrically grounds the reality of creatures cannot be conceptualized in terms that imply that the relation of Creator to creatures is competitive and by definition potentially conflictual.[17]

The Fathers concluded that the most apt analogy for the unconstrained freedom of the way in which God goes about relating in creating *ex nihilo* is the volitional freedom of a rational agent's intentional action in giving a good gift. Correlatively, to be "created" is to *be* a good gift. Here "intentional action" means an action that is ordered to a goal or end for which its agent can be held accountable to give intelligible reasons. Left at that our account of how God goes about relating in creative blessing, while importantly true, would still be too abstract to be adequate to the way it is narrated in canonical Wisdom literature. There it is made clear that God's "intentional action"

question of how it came to be. Instead their function is to highlight creatures' contingency and finitude, both in their God-dependency and their creaturely inter-dependency. They tell of God bestowing life, growth, and the power of fertility for animal creatures' wellbeing in their kind across the generations. Cf. Westermann, *Creation,* 24, 46.

17. Cf. Tanner, *God and Creation in Christian Theology,* esp. 37–48. God's "transcendence" of creatures and God's "immanence" to creatures must be mapped onto the relation between "otherness" and "closeness" in God's concrete way of going about creative blessing and cannot be construed as inversely proportional to each other. Yet another important implication of the concrete way in which God goes about relating in creative blessing, as canonically narrated, is that, given its ontological priority, the theological explication of the other two ways in which God's relates (i.e., in eschatological blessing and to reconcile estranged creatures) must also be ruled by these three features of the way God relates creatively: radically "other," radically "close," and the two understood to be correlative rather than inversely proportional to each other so that those other two ways in which God relates to all else also do not construe the relation as competitive and potentially conflictive.

of creative relating is not only unconstrained, not only free intentional action of gift-giving ordered to the good of creatures for their own sakes, but—given "who" God is—it is necessarily done graciously and gracefully. It is done not only wisely ("through the Word") but with "delight" (Prov 8:30) and with a certain playfulness:

> O Lord, how manifold are your works!
> In wisdom you have made them all, . . .
> Yonder is the sea, great and wide, . . .
> There go the ships,
> and Leviathan that you formed to sport in it.
> (Ps 104:24, 25a, 26 ESV)

Accordingly, human creatures' self-regulating personal identities are "appropriate" responses to the way the triune God relates to them in creative blessing when one of the dispositions that most basically shapes their personal identities is the disposition always to act trusting that the meaning of their lives is grounded in God's sustaining their reality and value and never to trust in their own projects and intentional actions to further those projects as the grounds of the meaningfulness of their lives. That is the "trust" aspect of Niebuhr's definition of faith.

b) "It is the triune God who creates" says something more about how God goes about relating creatively: expressed in a Trinitarian formula, it is "the 'Father' that creates through the 'Son' in the power of the Spirit." In classical Trinitarian formulas such as the Nicene Creed the Spirit is characterized as "the lord and giver of life." God's creative blessing "in the power of the Spirit" privileges life and is ordered to nurturing its well-being. As for the "Son," according to John 1:1–3a and 14 it is the eternally "begotten" Word of the "Father" through whom God creates. The exegetical proposal here is that John's use of "Word" is best interpreted in terms of the figure of Wisdom in Proverbs 8 and more generally in Proverbs.[18] Thus "The 'Father' creates through the 'Son'" stresses that God's creative blessing is not merely a constant "holding" of creatures in reality. It is also the triune God's self-involving self-commitment to providential care of creatures. It is God's self-commitment to a constant creative relating that is *wisely* ordered to the nurture of the well-being of living creatures, including human creatures, in their kinds and concrete particularities for as long as they last. That self-commitment enacts God's valuing creatures as "good" for their own sakes. It is one sense in which God "loves" creatures. It is enacted through other creatures. Where God's sustaining creatures in reality is an unmediated

---

18. See Kelsey, *Eccentric Existence*, 171–73.

relating to each of them, God's providential nurturing of creatures' well-being is mediated through other creatures. In particular it is mediated through human creatures. Proverbs' narrative of God's creative relating describes God as calling to human creatures through Wisdom, as it is manifest in the particularities of human creatures' physical and social proximate contexts, to act wisely for the well-being of fellow creatures that make up their shared proximate contexts.

Accordingly, human creatures' self-regulating personal identities are "appropriate" responses to the way the triune God relates to them in creative blessing when another of the dispositions that shape their personal identities is the disposition always to act in their proximate contexts in ways that are loyal to God's own commitment to the well-being of their fellow living creatures and the well-being of the proximate contexts that they share because they are constituted by their patterns of interaction. That is the "loyalty" aspect of Niebuhr's definition of faith in the Creator.

Here we come back to the claim that human creatures' flourishing in faith entails but is not the same as, their well-being or health. Their flourishing is defined theocentrically as personal identities shaped by faith as trust in God alone to ground their reality and value. However, their faith also involves their active loyalty to God's own self-commitment in creative blessing to nurture the well-being of fellow creatures, and that well-being is not defined theocentrically. As canonical Wisdom constantly instructs us, the criteria of creaturely well-being are found, not in attending to how God goes about relating creatively to creatures, but in closely attending to interactions among the creatures themselves. Such "attending" has taken different forms in different cultural eras. In the modern world it is evident in the arts and historical studies, but is largely disciplined methodologically in various social and life sciences none of which are ordered theocentrically. Human creatures' well-being assessed in such ways is not itself their flourishing; but human creatures' faithful *pursuit* of the well-being of their shared proximate contexts (including themselves!) and therewith the well-being of fellow creatures that make up those contexts, guided by attentive study of their actions and interactions, *is* a way in which they flourish in expressing the glory of God's own self-commitment to the well-being of creatures. Theologically speaking, a human creature's flourishing is not identical with its well-being (i.e., its relative biological, psychological, and social "health"); but its flourishing, in one sense of the word, does in part lie in its imitation, indeed participation in, God's providential care for the well-being of other creatures.

There are at least three additional general ways in which human creatures can flourish by virtue of their powers of self-regulation. All three are integral to human creatures' flourishing as the glory of God when their agency in their proximate contexts is appropriately responsive to God's way of relating creatively. Hence they are inseparable from shaping their personal identities by acquiring and deepening the disposition of faith, which is the basic criterion of the "appropriateness" of responses to God's creative blessing.

One is the entire set of a human creature's concrete intentional actions that enact the disposition of faith. In some cases an intentional action's end may straightforwardly be a contribution to the well-being of fellow creatures or to their shared proximate context. Such an end is highly particular, defined by and relative to the concrete conditions of the fellow creatures or their proximate context as a whole at a particular time and place. That is, such actions may intend both individual creatures' goods and common goods. In that case its enactment is simply an instance of the enactment of faith as the disposition to act in just that general fashion. But the set of intentional actions that enact faith is not limited to such actions. More often, having the same context-specific particularity, they enact the disposition of faith in the *manner* in which they are enacted rather than in the end to which they are ordered. They are enacted graciously in a manner that is appropriate response to God's graciousness in creating (i.e., in ways that have a certain freedom and lightness because they do not bear the weight of presuming to ground the reality and value of their agent). Intentional actions enacting the disposition of faith constitute existential "hows," particular concrete ways in which their agents set themselves into and orient themselves toward their proximate contexts under the conditions of particular places and times. Their concrete contents naturally change across time as the particulars of their proximate contexts change. What they share and does not change is the disposition they enact: faith as trust in and loyalty to the Creator.

A second general way in which human creatures can flourish by virtue of their powers of self-regulation is a certain type of subjectivity of consciousness, a combination of attitude, affect, and perception. It is a reverent and awed doxological gratitude. Human creatures' appropriate response to God's relating to them in creative blessing is gratitude for the hospitable generosity of the Creator's gift of finite existence that is intrinsically valuable, gives us space and time to be our fellow creatures' neighbors and to respond to God, and gives us complex proximate contexts of inexhaustible beauty at every level of their complexity. Such gratitude's appropriate affect is the "fear of the Lord," reverent and awed, but not terror before the "Wholly Other" or "Transcendence." It is "doxological" gratitude in that it glorifies God by referring all things to God as God's creaturely gifts. To "refer" fellow creatures to God is to perceive them in a certain way, viz., *as* gifts, *as* existentially contingent on God, as *fellow* creatures.

Nurturing reverent and awed doxological gratitude and the disposition for faithful actions necessarily involves a third general way in which human creatures can flourish by virtue of their powers of self-regulation. Appropriate human creaturely response to the way in which God relates in creative blessing, whether in the formation of their personal identities, in their concrete actions, or in their subjective states, is always conceptually formed. It has been clear in the foregoing that "faith" is not a disposition to trust-in-general or to loyalty-in-general, but trust in and loyalty to the particular way in which God goes about relating creatively. It has been clear that the intentional actions that enact faith and the subjective state of doxological gratitude are neither morally responsible action in general or gratitude in general. Rather they are all shaped by a set of concepts centering on the concept of creation *ex nihilo* (e.g., concepts of gift, creature, gracious, graceful, at once radically close and radically other, intentional action). Learning those concepts is not merely an "intellectual" act. It is a person-forming, perception-training, identity-shaping activity that engages all of a human creature's powers. It is traditionally characterized as a "spiritual" and "ascetic" discipline. It too is an exercise of human creatures' self-regulative powers in which, glorifying God, they flourish.

FLOURISHING "ABSOLUTELY"
AS CREATURELY EXPRESSIONS OF GOD'S GLORY

In canonical Wisdom literature Job tells two stories of his creation in his having been born an actual living human body.[19] One is a story of his having been *given* a human body at his birth for whose enacted life he is accountable to God. Thus far we have been exploring implications of that story for a theology of human flourishing as the glory of God in responding appropriately to God's creative blessing. The second is a story of his being created in having been born *as* an actual living human body. We turn now to explore the implications of that story for a theology of human flourishing.

This story shifts the sense in which we may say that a human creature is "the glory of God" and flourishes as such. That shift raises important questions about our account of human flourishing because it necessarily implies some strongly counter-intuitive claims. Where the first story implied that human creatures can be the glory of God in the sense that their

---

19. For an extended discussion of the two-narrative account Job gives of his birth as his creation see *Eccentric Existence*, chs. 6 and 7.

self-regulated lives may be appropriate responses to the way in which God goes about relating creatively to them, the second story implies that they are the glory of God simply because precisely as creatures they are, like each kind of creature in its distinctive way, God's self-expression *ad extra* of God's intrinsic glory. It is just *as* finite, fragile, human bodies vulnerable to inter-creature conflict, accident-prone and mortal, that they are the glory of God. That is in itself a sense in which they flourish. Flourishing in that sense is not contingent on their exercising their creaturely powers in any particular fashion, especially their powers of self-regulation. Where flourishing as the glory of God in virtue of responding appropriately to the way God relates creatively to us is a matter of relative degree of "appropriateness," flourishing as the glory of God in virtue of being God's self-expression of God's glory is given by God absolutely and is not a matter of degree.

Theologically important claims are dependent on that absolute sense in which human creatures are the glory of God. One implication is that human creatures who live with so-called "handicaps," or who suffer forms of illness that are the social consequences of such "other-abledness," none-theless flourish. As living human creatures they flourish in the sense of be-ing God's creaturely self-expressions of God's intrinsic glory. They are that absolutely and not relative to some standard of the "perfectly" actualized specimen of *homo sapiens*. That is one instance of a more basic implication: it is in virtue of being the glory of God in that "absolute" sense that all hu-man creatures have a dignity that is deserving of unqualified respect and must always be treated as ends in themselves for their own sakes and never as merely a means to some further end.

Accordingly, living human bodies that are new-born and do not thrive, or are in irreversible coma and do not respond, or in consequence of advanced stages of Alzheimer's disease have profoundly changed personali-ties, recognize no one, are deeply disoriented, and have no self-concept are nonetheless all living human bodies created by God through their having come to be born. They are in some sense God's self-expressions of God's in-trinsic glory, and therefore have a dignity that commands respect as ends in themselves. In that sense they flourish. They may be incapable of "thriving," of "taking charge of themselves." They may be unable to "blossom." Under certain circumstances in which such human creatures are dying, respect for their dignity may take the form of ceasing to attempt to arrest their dying, allowing their dying, and taking palliative measures to ease their way to death. Nonetheless, the absolute character of flourishing for as long as they do live simply in virtue of being the glory of God in that precise sense is the basic bar against theological support for genocide and euthanasia of the "socially unproductive."

It may be not only theologically warranted but theologically necessary to say that fellow human creatures "flourish" under such circumstances but, as we consider ever more extreme cases, it certainly becomes increasingly counter-intuitive to say so. I suggest that, too, is theologically warranted because the intuition in question is correct. It is an intuition that "things ain't the way they ought to be."[20] It is an intuition that not everything about our bodily lives and our common proximate contexts are God's created gifts ordered to the good of creatures. It is the intuition, not so much of the reality of sin enacted by human creatures, but of the reality of evil distortions of God's creation, indeed the reality of evil that is in some sense systemic and cosmic in the scope of its distortions. Such distortions are experienced in suffering horrendous and sustained physical and psychological pain, or in empathic observations of other living creatures' suffering such pain. Such distortions appear to be randomly distributed, none of which is "fair" or justly proportioned either to foolish imprudence or to moral culpability. Such evil is in some deep way a-rational, inexplicable, and in that sense a "mystery." Yet it is undeniably real and demands acknowledgement.

Rather than denying the reality of the evil dynamically distorting creatures, the theological claim that God creates *ex nihilo* requires acknowledgement of it. At the same time it no more offers a causal explanation of "how" evil came to be distortingly present in God's creation than it offers a causal explanation of "how" God creates *ex nihilo*.[21] Instead it entails a theological account of human creatures and their proximate contexts as thoroughly ambiguous distorted creatures, at once truly God's good creatures and deeply distorted. That ambiguity requires a carefully framed theological description; otherwise the description will unavoidably have pastorally problematic implications.

At one extreme, evil's distortions of creatures cannot be adequately described in such a way that "creaturely" and "distorted" are synthesized so that, as when two primary colors are blended, the result is a third something

20. Cf. Plantinga, *Not the Way It's Supposed to Be.*

21. From very early in Christian intellectual history there have been efforts to develop theories of how it came about that evil distorts God's creation. The theories were impressively imaginative, had virtually no grounding in canonical scripture, and count as well-intentioned pious mythology. Perhaps the most impressive was Origen's. See *On First Principles,* esp. Bk. I, chs. 7 and 8; Bk. II, ch. 9; Bk. III, ch. 5. Canonical Christian scriptural narratives of God relating to draw creation into an eschatological consummation and about God relating to reconcile estranged creatures to God warrant theological claims about what God does to transform creatures' distortions by evil and to set creatures free of bondage to the consequences of those distortion. They are God's "practical" solutions to correct creatures' distortions rather than "theoretical" causal explanations of the origin of evil.

in which "creaturely" and "distorted" cannot in principle be distinguished. When that happens it leads to theological remarks to the effect that horrendous suffering is just "part of nature, part of the way God made the world." That is theologically problematic because it implies that the "cause" of evil distortions of creatures is somehow creatureliness itself, as though the ultimate origin of horrendous suffering were the fact of creaturely finitude. It warrants pastoral remarks such as, "Suffering is the God-given way to flourishing; embrace it and you will flourish," even in cases where the suffering is so horrendous as to destroy the sufferer's capacity to "embrace" anything, and, "There's a reason for this suffering; God sent it; it will lead to your flourishing," which are world-denying remarks because they imply that creation is a vale of tears designed by God for soul-building and that horrendous suffering is "built into" creatureliness by the Creator. Such pastoral remarks suggest that the faithfulness to the Creator in which we flourish should be a doxological gratitude for evil's distortions themselves, including the horrendous suffering they can cause. Against that the claim that God creates *ex nihilo* implies that finitude is definitive of creatureliness and God values it as good. Finitude leaves creatures vulnerable to evil's distortions of it. Some kind of finitude is precisely what evil distorts. Finitude is not itself that evil or its distortions.

At the other extreme, evil's distortions of creatures cannot be adequately described in such a way that creatures are the field of a battle between the good, which is given by the Creator, and absolute evil, which is the Creator's clear moral and ontological opposite. When that happens it leads to theological remarks to the effect that evil distortions of creatures are clearly distinguishable from the Creator's intentional actions ordered to the good and one needs only to identify with God's side in the battle. That is theologically problematic as an exposition of the implications of *creation ex nihilo* because it identifies the reality of evil as a non-creaturely "power" coeval with the Creator. It sets aside God's radically free initiative in creating by postulating a fundamental cosmic dualism of ultimate realities, good Creator and evil Distorter. It is pastorally problematic because it implies the validity of pastoral remarks that sharply distinguish the evil suffered by the "godly" from that suffered by the "godless," blaming the former on the "godless" and the evil the "godless" do on the autonomous power of evil whom they serve. It comforts the "godly" by systematically locating the sources of evil in their proximate contexts outside themselves in others who are by definition "godless." It is a Manichaean description of the actual ambiguity of human creatures and their proximate contexts.

The more apt analogy for the ambiguity of human creatures and their proximate contexts may be military camouflage. Camouflaged uniforms, vehicles, and buildings present a variety of different colors but not a blend (like a mix of two primary color). Camouflage obscures the lineaments of what it covers so that it is difficult to distinguish and identify them (so that they are not as clearly distinguishable as two teams opposed in competition). But it is possible to learn to discern what it is they obscure, possible to make at least roughly correct distinctions among them. Human creatures in their proximate contexts are an ambiguous mix of creatureliness and evil's distortions of their creatureliness in their kind. That is the truth of Augustinian so-called "privative" definitions of evil: evil is a creature (not an autonomous power) dynamically distorted, deprived of the proper functioning of the dynamics of its kind, and consequently a creature dynamic in distorted ways that, in turn, distort fellow creatures. As actual living human bodies created in their being born they continue even *in* their ambiguity to be one way in which the triune God expresses its intrinsic glory *ad extra*.

Nonetheless, as *distorted* by evil such human creatures' "absolute" flourishing as the glory of God is ambiguous. Perceiving that flourishing in fellow human creatures requires cultivation of powers of discernment to distinguish their particular individual set of creaturely powers, gifts, talents, and self-regulated competencies from dynamic distortions of them. Such discernment is never certain. However it is not impossible. Disciplining one's own powers of such discernment is one appropriate way in which one's own doxological gratitude for God's gift of each fellow creature is enacted.

Human creatures can sometimes also flourish in the midst of such ambiguity in the "relative" flourishing that comes with their self-regulation of their defining dispositions, attitudes, emotions, passions, feelings, sensibilities, and conceptual competencies so that they are collectively appropriate responses to the way in which God relates in creative blessing. That too requires the nurture of competencies to discern through the camouflage of that ambiguity the lineaments of God's creative gift of someone's (including one's own) particular set of powers and energies and to distinguish them from ways in which they are distorted. Such competencies are especially important in connection with concrete enactments of faith's doxological gratitude to God for a particular person. As trust in and loyalty to God and God's own project, faith does not entail doxological gratitude for any human suffering. It certainly does not entail gratitude for horrendous suffering in consequence of evil distortions of the dynamics of the set of powers with which some human creature is born. Such "gratitude" for them would be blasphemy. Faith's patient, generous, and compassionate attention to another's life can yield a discernment through that life's ambiguity that distinguishes, however roughly, between its distortions which we lament and the good gift of its creatureliness in which it has flourished, for which we ourselves glorify God.

BIBLIOGRAPHY

Evans, Donald. *The Logic of Self-Involvement*. London: SCM, 1963.

Kelsey, David H. *Eccentric Existence: A Theological Anthropology*. Louisville: Westminster John Knox, 2009.

Niebuhr, H. Richard. *Radical Monotheism*. New York: Harper, 1963.

Origen of Alexandria. *On First Principles*. Translated by G. W. Butterworth. Gloucester: Peter Smith, 1973.

Plantinga, Cornelius, Jr. *Not the Way It's Supposed to Be: A Breviary of Sin*. Grand Rapids: Eerdmans, 1995.

Tanner, Kathryn. *God and Creation in Christian Theology: Tyranny or Empowerment?* Oxford: Basil Blackwell, 1988.

Westermann, Claus. *Beginning and End in the Bible*. Translated by Keith Crim. Philadelphia: Fortress, 1972.

———. *Blessing*. Translated by Keith Crim. Philadelphia: Fortress, 1978.

———. *Creation*. Translated by John J. Scullion, SJ. Philadelphia: Fortress, 1974.

———. *Genesis 1–11: A Commentary*. Translated by John J. Scullion, SJ. Minneapolis: Augsburg, 1984.

3

God and the Ascent of Life

Michael Welker

The following contribution picks up a question asked and answered by Miroslav Volf in many of his publications: "How should followers of Christ intend to serve the common good?" It also resonates with vibrant concerns raised in his recent masterpiece on flourishing.[1]

In the search for an answer to this question, I will first try to identify ethical possibilities in today's challenging moral communication. The second part attempts to offer a genuine theological account related to this question. It will be based on key insights of the Abrahamic faith traditions in general and on biblical insights into the ethically orienting powers of God in particular. In the third part, I will sketch five aspects of spiritual life in the service of a multidimensional ethical orientation: 1) a great example of shaping cultural and canonic memory; 2) a paradigmatic existential-ethical experience; 3) an impact on a humane social-political ethos; 4) an impact on justice-seeking communities; 5) an impact on truth-seeking communities.

---

1. See Volf, *A Public Faith*; Volf, *Flourishing*.

1. ETHICAL POSSIBILITIES AND CHALLENGES OF MORAL COMMUNICATION TODAY

Any serious search for ethical orientation has to face the complexity of moral communication in general. In moral communication, human beings influence each other by giving or withdrawing respect.[2] We influence each other's thinking, acting, and behaving by giving or promising respect, by not paying respect, or by threatening to withdraw it. The modes of respect come in a broad spectrum from a sharp, short view on each other to vibrant admiration. The communication of respect starts in early childhood with seemingly simple operations: "If you do this, your mom will be pleased. If you refuse to do that, your grandpa will be sad." From seemingly simple attempts to teach a child up to the most elaborated functionalization of complex global media systems to cultivate general moral moods, from adolescent mindsets to the categorical imperative, moral communication is indispensable for common human life. We have to mutually attune our ways of thinking, acting, and behaving. We foster this attunement by moral communication, by giving or withdrawing respect, by promising to give or threatening to withdraw respect. The indispensability of moral communication for social life is the reason why a naïve perspective automatically links moral communication with a positive ethical orientation. Sadly, this is not necessarily adequate.

Whereas many people still regard the processes of moral communication as occurring primarily in groups of interacting individuals, the contemporary situation challenges us to address a broader spectrum, too. As William Schweiker rightly emphasizes, media-based global dynamics and "global reflexivity, the ways in which communities appear in 'the gaze of the other' [are] of great moral import."[3] In unprecedented ways, moral communication becomes culturally, politically, and religiously loaded and ideologically vulnerable. This observation should intensify worries generated by lessons learned from the past. We not only know of what one could term robber morals and a Mafia ethos. We have also been shocked to hear of, or witnessed, the brutal fact that vast parts of human societies have been corrupted by ideologies of fascism or apartheid or ecological brutalism. Vast parts of human societies have given respect to evil forms of thought and action, and continue to do so. And they have developed and still develop routinized forms of withdrawing respect from those who speak up against the powers of evil. Theologically, we are dealing with the difficult topic of

2. Particularly illuminating: Luhmann, "Soziologie der Moral."
3. Schweiker, "On Religious Ethics," 12.

"the good law under the power of sin" (Rom 7:23ff.; 8:2ff.). We have to face the sobering fact that the indispensable and formally valuable moral communication among human beings can transport a false and even evil ethical orientation.

The other basic problem associated with talk about ethical possibilities in contemporary situations could be termed the complicated normative texture of pluralistic societies. When most people, even scholars, think and speak of pluralistic societies today, they as a rule still imagine a multitude of free and equal individuals and a multitude of groups and associations with very different backgrounds of education and worldviews, with different political, moral, professional, and religious interests and orientations. In this texture of a vague *plurality* of orientations, some people see an enormous potential for colorful development and flourishing human freedom. Other people evaluate this setting as a chaotic radical individualism and relativism, which endangers or even destroys any normative thinking and any potential for moral education.

The perception of pluralism as a vague plurality of individuals and social formations, however, can only grasp one aspect of late modern societies in the West. It appreciates the affirmation of individual freedom, radical equality, and the human right to participate as a respected voice in all sorts of general and specific moral reasoning at any time. However, this understanding does not see that pluralistic societies are also heavily normatively coded. More than thirty years ago, David Tracy opened our eyes to the fact that all theological and moral discourse has to differentiate among academic, ecclesial, and moral-political publics and their different styles of communication and normative orientation. With his great book *The Analogical Imagination*, he took an important step toward a serious analysis of the culture of pluralism.[4]

Many of us began to acknowledge that in late modern pluralistic societies there are different overt or latent value systems, institutionalized rationalities, and normative expectations that guide or even dominate the different so-called *social systems* (i.e., large organizational structures that are indispensable for common life and the common good). They include not only politics, the academy, and religion, the famous Tracy differentiation, but also the legal system, market and media, family and education, even the systems of healthcare and the military and police. All these social systems form a complex pluralistic network of normativity and moral orientation in present-day societies in the West. This network is hard to grasp since healthy pluralistic societies refuse to bring the different value systems under the

4. Tracy, *Analogical Imagination*.

dominance of just one of these large organizations, institutions, and pow-ers.[5] In the 1930s, the Germans destroyed an emerging pluralistic society in their country by permitting the dominance of politics, technology, and the military (the Nazi *Gleichschaltung*, an enforced alignment) over the other systems. Today, many of us fear that the market, the media, and technology are imposing their rationalities and dominant values on the other domains of our societies and doing so in distortive and even destructive ways.

Late modern pluralistic societies, however, are not only shaped by a general affirmation of individualism and by the powers of diverse social systems. They also develop a multitude of publicly operative associations, interest groups, parties, lobbies, social movements, etc. A significant num-ber of these associations are interested in shaping the flux of power between the large social systems in pluralistic societies. Together, these associations form what sociologists have called *civil society*.[6] Civil society stands between social systems and the plurality of individual identities. If we want to identify ethical possibilities in contemporary Western contexts, we have to deal with the complex configuration of individualism, the highly normative bind-ing powers of the social systems, and the creativity of civil societal groups and institutions. We have to identify the different hierarchies of values that govern the different social systems and their moral textures.[7] Thus, for fam-ily, "love" seems to dominate the other values and virtues; for the law, it is "justice"; for the media, "resonance"; for the academy, "truth," etc. But it is not the case that a single value alone dominates and rules the whole system. Neither is it the case that just one set of values rules the whole society. The different hierarchies of values are interwoven and interconnected in various ways, giving a complex social and moral coherence and a deep, though often vague, sense that they serve "the common good."[8]

Any realistic search for ethical tasks and challenges in contemporary contexts has to decode the moral fabric of complex pluralistic societies at least partially. It has to ask how the interplays and the conflicts among

5. Cf. Welker, *Kirche im Pluralismus*; Welker, "Pluralism."

6. An important diagnostic mistake is being made when all associations in a so-ciety—from canary breeding and stamp collecting clubs to the churches—are seen as forming the civil society. This mistake results in difficulties in understanding the flux of power in pluralistic societies. See my critique of Habermas's wishful description of the "democratic process" in Welker, "Habermas and Ratzinger on the Future of Religion." Cf. Habermas and Ratzinger, *Dialectics of Secularization*; Habermas, *Between Facts and Norms*, 329–87.

7. Cf. Luhmann, *Soziale Systeme*; Luhmann, *Die Gesellschaft der Gesellschaft*.

8. Cf. for different levels of reflexivity and praxis, Gaita, *A Common Humanity*; McCann and Miller, *In Search of the Common Good*; Chrislip and O'Malley, *For the Common Good*.

different value systems shape the character of individuals and their moral visions. Where do the social systems show moral boundaries and even display distortive powers that have a negative impact on promoting the common good? What are their intrinsic strengths that should be emphasized in an individual's upbringing, in public education, in the political, legal, and religious shaping of minds and mentalities? The identification of mutually strengthening interconnections of normative radiations between orienting powers in law, religion, the academy, family, media, the market, politics, and education will be crucial. With this complex texture in mind, we have to ask for theological insights and accounts that have or can have an impact on ethical orientation today.

2. THE ORIENTING POWER OF GOD AND THEOLOGICAL ACCOUNTS IN A FINITE WORLD

In the academy in particular, we have become used to speaking of *theology* in generalist and relaxed ways. All sorts of metaphysical and popular philosophical God-thoughts pass as *theological* references to God. Examples are the absolute, the infinite,[9] the first cause,[10] the ground of being,[11] the ultimate point of reference,[12] and the all-determining reality.[13] Many scholars declare this speculative toolbox a theological resource, and they even assure us that real communities of faith can identify in these speculative ideas and thoughts the God in whom they invest their faith and put their trust and whom they worship and adore.

A basic problem with many of these God-thoughts was and still is that the more perfect and powerful the God they presented looked, the more they ran into problems to make sense of the real world that their God-idea was supposed to rule. Think, for example, of Bultmann's and Pannenberg's God "as the all-determining reality" (*die Alles bestimmende Wirklichkeit*)—how does this idea relate to a world in which we witness the death of thousands by a tsunami, children dying of cancer, and what are termed "civilized" societies erecting concentration camps and murdering millions of innocent people?

9. Nicholas of Cusa, *On the Vision of God*; McGinn, *Harvest of Mysticism*, ch. 10.

10. In Dionysius the Areopagite, Thomas Aquinas, and others. Cf. Rorem, *Pseudo-Dionysius*.

11. Tillich, *Systematic Theology*, 1:235–92.

12. Kaufman, *In Face of Mystery*, 301–426; Kaufman, *The Theological Imagination*.

13. Bultmann, *Glauben und Verstehen I*, 26–37; Pannenberg, *Wissenschaftstheorie und Theologie*, 304–5; and others.

Correspondingly, if we do not deny that nature and life are ambivalent, that all natural life is frail and finite, that natural life must live at the expense of other life, and that, on top of this natural condition of causing decay and death, human persons have enormous powers of sin and destruction—then does this admission not destroy any perspective on God and divine goodness as well as any hope of gaining an ethical orientation from theological accounts?

A first answer to this situation is that we have to differentiate between totalitarian metaphysical accounts and theological accounts that have stood the test of time and experience in communities of faith. Second, we have to admit that realism—i.e., the will to test our insights by relating them to experience in natural space-time—is absolutely crucial for any attempt to gain sound theological orientation in ethical affairs. Serious theological narratives and symbol systems are aware of the fact that the created world not only offers an enormous amount of fecundity, beauty, and life-sustaining order and many reasons for joy and gratitude, but that the same world is neither divine nor a paradise. Even if we are vegetarians, we have to destroy an immense amount of life in order to sustain ourselves. Alfred North Whitehead is absolutely right in his statement: "All societies require interplay with the environment and in the case of living societies this interplay takes the form of robbery. The living society may, or may not, be a higher type of organism than the food which it disintegrates. But whether or not it be for the general good, life is robbery."[14]

At the same time, natural earthly life is frail and finite and tends toward decay and death. It not only develops many good and healthy strategies to fight against its own frailty and against the powers of endangerment and death. Intelligent life is also often quite sophisticated in developing strategies to deceive itself and others and to take much more of the life resources than are needed for its sustenance and defense. This is the sober starting point of an encounter with the real world, a starting point that all honest and realistic faith traditions and theologies challenge us to face. When we ask for divine guidance, care, and empowerment, we have to set out from these conditions and have to ask for an *ascent of life* that does not deny the vulnerability and frailty of natural life and the self-endangerment of all cultural life by the powers of sin.

In many faith traditions, the ascent of life is associated with the power of the divine Spirit. This Spirit, however, must not be confused with a merely intellectual power. Aristotelian metaphysics, with its brilliant identification of spirit, self-reflexivity, reason, and the divine, produced lasting distortions

14. Whitehead, *Process and Reality*, 105.

on this frontier.[15] Here the biblical traditions with their bewildering figure of the *outpouring of the Spirit* offer a helpful corrective. This figure confronts us with a formative, indeed with a constellation-forming, power. The divine Spirit constitutes complex forms of community. At the same time, it challenges and transforms established natural and political orders of dominance and control. The great vision of the prophet Joel (Joel 2), which is repeated and affirmed by the Pentecost account (Acts 2), describes a constellation in which males and females, old and young people, even maidservants and menservants are brought into a spiritual community with its religious, communicative, and ethical radiations. And this is said in a patriarchal environment, in gerontocratic contexts, and in a slaveholder society.[16]

The Pentecost account quotes this vision of Joel and adds a breathtaking multinational, multicultural, and multilingual dimension. Other constellations of Spirit-created communities emphasize polyphony and mutual enrichment and allow for different hierarchies of values and virtues and for their interplay in complex processes of communication. According to the prophetic visions of the biblical canon in both the Old and the New Testaments, the constellation-forming work of the divine Spirit is quite subversive, even revolutionary.

At least in what is known as the Abrahamic faith traditions, central values of the spiritual interplay attributed to God and divine creativity and seen as ennobling human communication in the light of divine wisdom, are correlated with the *law of God*. The central interwoven values of the law are the care for justice, the care for mercy, and the search for truth in the solemn encounter with the divine. The Messianic visions in Isaiah 11, 42 and 61 see "the Chosen one of God" on whom the Spirit rests as exercising justice, bringing mercy to the weak and the poor, and communicating the true knowledge of God to Israel and also to the Gentiles.[17]

This cluster of values—in justice, mercy, and truth-seeking communities—runs against the necessity of earthly natural life to sustain itself at the expense of other life. Particularly revealing is the intrinsic correlation of justice and mercy in both witnesses to God's creative guidance and normative ethical expectations. In a counterintuitive way, the power of mercy—that is, the care for the weak—causes people to exercise a *free and creative self-withdrawal in favor of another life*. Embedded in family life and in parental love, this tendency even appears natural to us. But what brings human beings to

15. See Aristotle, *Metaphysics* XII, 1072b, esp. 19–32; cf. Welker, *God the Spirit*, 283–302.

16. Welker, *God the Spirit*, 147–58 and 228–78.

17. Ibid., 108–33.

exercise mercy and loving care beyond their helpless children, their sick family members, and their old and frail parents and grandparents? The *ascent of life* envisioned by the divine law and by the divine spirit *sees a gain of life* for persons who exercise this merciful creative self-withdrawal in favor of others, a gain of life that to common sense thought can appear paradoxical. In mercy and in love with its added dimension of joy in free and creative self-withdrawal in favor of others, there are an ascent and growth of life that work against the powers of decay and death. This ascent of life has many dimensions with strong impacts on ethical orientations.

3. SPIRITUAL LIFE AND MULTIDIMENSIONAL ETHICAL ORIENTATION

The power of the divine Spirit not only constitutes a polyphonic community, centered on interconnected core values and practices such as the search for justice, the care for the weak, and the search for truth. The power of the divine Spirit also opens the individual and communal human spirit and personal identities in shaping most impressive realms of memories and imaginations. The relation to the living God offers individual persons an enormous extension of the horizons of experience. They stretch far beyond the relations of family life and the relations to good neighbors and friends. One's own identity is seen with the eyes of God in broad historical perspectives. And this can bring an enormous sensitivity and capacity for empathy and responsible action in favor of other human beings in need.

The *first* dimension of spiritual life highly relevant to multidimensional ethical orientation can be illustrated with reference to the biblical traditions by what is called the *motive clause* of Old Testament law. It offers a great example of shaping cultural and canonic memory. The *motive clause* says: *"For you yourselves were once foreigners in Egypt,"* and it says in its expanded form, *"you yourselves know how it feels to be foreigners"* (Exod 22:21; 23:9, NIV; cf. 20:2). This clause can (with characteristic variations) be found throughout the Old Testament's legal corpora.[18] But why does this theological orientation not violate theological realism? Why do people who were never in their life in Egypt allow themselves to be addressed as those who were slaves and freed by God's hand? Why do they allow themselves to be embedded into time-spanning networks of experience and in public collectives that transcend any realm of personally attainable experience? Why was this double identity ("You were foreigners, yet now you are free") not abandoned and lost? Why were these legal and moral impositions of the

---

18. Deut 4:34; 5:15; 7:19; 11:7; 26:8; Lev 19:34; 26:13. Cf. also Deut 5:6, 15.

mercy code not rejected with a Nietzschean furor? How did *the law* come to serve as the bearer of paradigmatic cultural and canonic memory?[19]

We have to deal here with a discovery of greatest spiritual and religious relevance and explanatory power.[20] At each discrete point in time and space, people are incredibly unequal. This perspective changes when we try to see ourselves with the eyes of God on an extended timeline and see both young and old, sick and weak people as not only *with and among* us, but also *in* ourselves. We then gain a sensitivity for the fragility of *all* human life, and this in turn can promote a respect, even an admiration for the co-evolution of the religious, legal, and compassionate moral codes that we encounter in the biblical law. With the motive clause, Israel expands a basic and undeniable experience of natural life to an historical dimension and the historical dimension to a religious and normative framework of experience. It elevates the sensibilities of familial solidarity into an historical, sociopolitical dimension. This generates the mutual normative strengthening of the mercy code and the juridical code in the biblical context, but also in many cultures in general.

With the first explanation of shaping an individual and communal religious identity in favor of ethical orientation, we have related to Jewish and Christian faith traditions, to biblical orientations. My main concern in this line of argument, however, was and is a realistic approach that does not overrun and overrule the hard experience of frail and finite life, the intrinsic stigma of natural life that it must live at the expense of other life, and the frightening potentials of self-endangerment and destructive behavior connected with this creaturely condition. I try to strictly avoid getting involved with images and ideas of God that invite us to ignore or even deny these experiences. Given this background, I attempt to focus on a non-illusionary ascent of life in the middle of robbing, finite, and death-bound natural life. The spiritual realms of memory and imagination, however, differ in the diverse communities of religious and moral communication. So for people in other religious and secular traditions, my first point might fail the claim to be a realistic theological approach. It can only serve as an invitation to discover and develop cultural memories that sustain differentiated and empathetic individual and communal identities.[21]

A *second* set of counter-powers against the tendency of natural life to sustain itself at the expense of others can offer a systematic claim: the

19. Cf. Welker, "Kommunikatives, kollektives, kulturelles und kanonisches Gedächtnis."

20. I elaborate the following in detail in "The Power of Mercy in Biblical Law."

21. Cf. Volf, *Flourishing*, 1–26.

interconnection of justice and mercy and the powers of love are experienced as ennobling beyond the circles of family, friends, and tribes—an ascent of life in the middle of the ambivalent flux of natural life. In mercy, that is, the care for the weaker, and in forgiving, both in the relation of God to humans and in interhuman relations, we witness and experience *a creative self-withdrawal in favor of the other—and this is not to be understood as a loss of life but as a somewhat strange gain and growth of life.* These very down-to-earth spiritual experiences come with an existential broadening and deepening of the individual identity involved, which does not depend on broad cultural and canonic memory. It can be strengthened by such memories but it can also be seen as a general paradigmatic existential-ethical experience. In many inconspicuous emergent ways we witness the constitution of an emergent "community of the Spirit" that exercises empathy and compassion and generates moral standards beyond the realms of members of family, friends and, good neighbors.[22] The theological strengthening of the development of this rich personal and social identity can counter reductionist forms of subjectivist faith and existentialist mindsets, forms that George Lindbeck identified as a stale standardizing "experiential-expressive model" of religious self-awareness.[23] Human beings who are able to experience and exercise a free and creative self-withdrawal in favor of others move beyond the pervading perspectives of self-sustenance and self-preservation. They move freely and realistically beyond what biblical traditions call a merely "fleshly existence."

Third, the interconnection of juridical law and mercy law found in all Biblical law-corpora, most clearly elaborated in the Book of the Covenant in Exodus, sustains values of social welfare, freedom, and equality. It has a shaping impact on a humane social-political ethos. Even as a latent pattern, it gains important educational and political functions and enables the juridical law and thought to become a *moral and cultural teacher.*[24] The mercy law not only shapes moral and political moods in formative ways, but it also draws impulses from, and recursively strengthens, the family ethos. In biblical times, this ethos was certainly connected to patriarchal structures. But even perspectives critical of the remaining role of patriarchy in the shaping of normative expectations should appreciate the fact that "the merciful father" replaced the king as the premier executor of mercy and clemency appeals. The sensitivities against patriarchal, gerontocratic, defensive tribal,

22. Cf. Tanner, "Workings of the Spirit," and Polkinghorne, "Hidden Spirit and the Cosmos."

23. Lindbeck, *Nature of Doctrine,* 31–32.

24. This is the argument in: Kaveny, *Law's Virtues*; cf. also Witte, "Introduction."

racist, and classist structures cultivated by the working of the Spirit are badly needed to cultivate and promote this ethos of justice and mercy also in contemporary environments.

Fourth, in a direct impact on the juridical law, the mercy law and human morals with a normative claim to care for the weak have a strong impact on justice-seeking communities in religious and secular contexts. No case of a person in need and distress is imaginable that could fall in principle below the competence of the law. No person, however weak, poor and miserable, will fall below the levels of the outreach of the law. In the other direction, the systematic and systemic orientation of the law toward mercy and compassion demands the continual refinement of the legal culture and its directedness toward institutionalization and universalization. Beyond this drive toward a universal outreach of the law, the mercy code of the law helps us in dealing with a paradox that creates deep problems for all legal and moral evolution. This paradox is that on the one hand we want to improve and develop the juridical law and our ethical standards, and on the other we want to provide legal and moral security of expectations.[25] How can we take on this difficult, yet unavoidable task of transforming and improving important normative potentials without in this process destroying their binding force?[26] Here the mercy code has a balancing function: subtle and sensitive dynamics as well as normative stability are enabled when justice and mercy, law and compassion, are put in a creative tension and in cooperation.

Fifth and lastly, the readiness for joyful, free, and creative self-withdrawal in favor of others is important for an *ethos of truth-seeking communities*—in education, in the academy, and in communities with serious cultural, religious, and moral communication. All too often the search for truth is reduced to the search for personal certainty or communal consensus. These perspectives on truth, however, are not sufficient. Obvious moral distortions teach us how dangerous the reduction of truth to subjective self-righteousness can be, or, particularly in large publics, a consensus that immunizes itself against any critical perspectives on it. The search for individual certainty and for consensus is important for the search for truth, but it has to work on its constant growth and on the constant critical correlation with the search for correctness, coherence, and rationality.

Particularly in academic contexts, however, we find the other side of the problem, the reduction of truth to adequacy to the topic, to coherence

25. Cf. Welker, "Security of Expectations."

26. On this function of religion, see Assmann, Janowski, and Welker, "Richten und Retten."

and rationality. And here again we have to work toward improvement and the growth of coherent and rational insight into the encounter with sensitivities for certainty and consensus in non-academic experiential realms. In order to promote this double process—the growth of certainty and consensus and the growth of correctness, consistency, and coherence—the search for truth requires the willingness for free and creative self-withdrawal in the communication in truth-seeking communities.[27] The openness for the joyful, free, and creative self-withdrawal in favor of another person materializes here as the openness and eagerness for the better, healthier, deeper, more convincing, more subtle, and more illuminating insight. And this ascent of life in the search for truth is also highly relevant for the flourishing of religious and ethical life.

---

27. Cf. Polkinghorne and Welker, *Faith in the Living God*, chapter 9; Welker, *God the Revealed*: 304ff.

BIBLIOGRAPHY

Aristotle. *Metaphysics X–XII.* Edited by Hugh Tredennick. Cambridge: Harvard University Press, 1935.

Assmann, Jan, et al. "Richten und Retten. Zur Aktualität der altorientalischen und biblischen Gerechtigkeitskonzeption." In *Gerechtigkeit. Richten und Retten in der abendländischen Tradition und ihren altorientalischen Ursprüngen,* edited by Jan Assman et al., 9–36. München: Fink, 1998.

Bultmann, Rudolf. *Glauben und Verstehen I.* Tübingen: Mohr Siebeck 1933.

Chrislip, David D., and Ed O'Malley. *For the Common Good: Redefining Civic Leadership.* Wichita: KLC, 2013.

Gaita, Raymond. *A Common Humanity: Thinking About Love and Truth and Justice.* New York: Routledge, 2000.

Habermas, Jürgen. *Between Facts and Norms: Contributions to a Discourse Theory of Law and Democracy.* Cambridge: MIT, 1996.

Habermas, Jürgen, and Joseph Ratzinger. *The Dialectics of Secularization: On Reason and Religion.* Edited by Florian Schuller. San Francisco: Ignatius, 2006.

Kaufman, Gordon. *In Face of Mystery: A Constructive Theology.* Cambridge: Harvard University Press, 1993.

———. *The Theological Imagination: Constructing the Concept of God.* Philadelphia: Westminster, 1981.

Kaveny, Cathleen. *Law's Virtues: Fostering Autonomy and Solidarity in American Society,* Washington, DC: Georgetown University Press, 2012.

Lindbeck, George. *The Nature of Doctrine: Religion and Theology in a Postliberal Age.* Philadelphia: Westminster, 1984.

Luhmann, Niklas. *Die Gesellschaft der Gesellschaft.* Frankfurt: Suhrkamp, 1997.

———. "Soziologie der Moral." In *Theorie-technik und Moral,* edited by Niklas Luhmann and Stephan H. Pfürtner, 8–116. Frankfurt: Suhrkamp, 1978.

———. *Soziale Systeme.* Frankfurt: Suhrkamp, 1984.

McCann, Dennis, and Patrick Miller, eds. *In Search of the Common Good.* New York: T. & T. Clark, 2005.

McGinn, Bernard. *The Harvest of Mysticism in Medieval Germany 1300 to 1500.* Vol. 4 of *The Presence of God.* New York: Crossroad, 2005.

Nicholas of Cusa. *On the Vision of God.* In *Selected Spiritual Writings,* translated by H. Lawrence Bond, 233–90. New York: Paulist, 1997.

Pannenberg, Wolfhart. *Wissenschaftstheorie und Theologie.* Frankfurt: Suhrkamp, 1973.

Polkinghorne, John. "The Hidden Spirit and the Cosmos." In *The Work of the Spirit: Pneumatology and Pentecostalism,* edited by Michael Welker, 169–82. Grand Rapids: Eerdmans, 2006.

Polkinghorne, John, and Michael Welker. *Faith in the Living God: A Dialogue.* SPCK: London 2001

Rorem, Paul. *Pseudo-Dionysius: A Commentary on the Texts and an Introduction to their Influence.* Oxford: Oxford University Press, 1993.

Schweiker, William. "On Religious Ethics." In *The Blackwell Companion to Religious Ethics,* edited by William Schweiker, 1–15. Oxford: Blackwell, 2008.

Tanner, Kathryn. "Workings of the Spirit: Simplicity or Complexity?" In *The Work of the Spirit: Pneumatology and Pentecostalism,* edited by Michael Welker, 87–105. Grand Rapids: Eerdmans, 2006

Tillich, Paul. *Systematic Theology*. Vol. 1. Chicago: The University of Chicago Press, 1951.

Tracy, David. *The Analogical Imagination: Christian Theology and the Culture of Pluralism*. New York: Crossroad, 1981.

Volf, Miroslav. *Flourishing: Why We Need Religion in a Globalized World*. New Haven: Yale University Press, 2016.

———. *A Public Faith: How Followers of Christ Should Serve the Common Good*. Grand Rapids: Brazos, 2011.

Welker, Michael. *God the Revealed: Christology*. Grand Rapids: Eerdmans, 2013.

———. *God the Spirit*. 2nd ed. Eugene, OR: Wipf & Stock, 2013.

———. "Habermas and Ratzinger on the Future of Religion." *Scottish Journal of Theology* 63 (2010) 456–473.

———. *Kirche im Pluralismus*. 2nd ed. Gütersloh: Kaiser, 2000.

———. "Kommunikatives, kollektives, kulturelles und kanonisches Gedächtnis." In *Jahrbuch für Biblische Theologie*, vol. 22, *Die Macht der Erinnerung*, 321–31. Neukirchener: Neukirchen-Vluyn 2008.

———. "Pluralism." In *The Brill Dictionary of Religion*, edited by Kocku von Stuckrad, 3:1460–64. Leiden: Brill, 2006.

———. "The Power of Mercy in Biblical Law." *Journal of Law and Religion* 29 (2014) 225–35.

———. "Security of Expectations: Reformulating the Theology of Law and Gospel." *Journal of Religion* 66 (1986) 237–60.

Whitehead, Alfred North. *Process and Reality: An Essay in Cosmology*. New York: Free Press, 1978.

Witte, John, Jr. "Introduction." In *Christianity and Human Rights: An Introduction*, edited by John Witte and Frank S. Alexander, 8–43. Cambridge: Cambridge University Press, 2010.

4

Like a Tree Planted by the Water

Human Flourishing and the Dynamics of Divine-Human Relationships

Christoph Schwöbel

IN HIS NEW BOOK *Flourishing: Why We Need Religion in a Globalized World*, Miroslav Volf has presented a persuasive argument that the process of "globalization stands in need of the visions of flourishing that world religions offer" and pointed to religions' "internal resources to interact constructively and contribute to each other's betterment."[1] This raises important questions for Christian theology which transcend the way in which we are accustomed to seeing human flourishing, either as defined by the given structure of what things are and therefore can be become or as enabled by the capacities for human self-development. What would it mean to conceive of flourishing neither as the actualization of the intrinsic potentialities of a given substance nor as the self-enactment of a human subject, but as a process of becoming worked out through God's creative relationships with God's creation? In this essay I shall try to support Volf's impressive large-scale description with a few small-scale remarks on the internal resources that the theology of

---

1. Volf, *Flourishing*, 206.

65

Martin Luther offers for developing constructive perspectives on a fruitful interaction between religious traditions and communities.

HUMAN FLOURISHING IN PLURALIST CONTEXTS

The idea of human flourishing and the process of personal formation are inextricably connected. In all its different varieties, from classical views of *eudaimonia* to late modern ideals of popular psychology, human flourishing is never understood as a simple given but rather as a goal to be achieved by a process of personal formation. The dynamics of personal formation are directed by what is conceived as the ideal of human flourishing in all its different dimensions. Both, ideas of human flourishing and theories and practices of personal formation, are bound to a particular context. Just as the idea of *eudaimonia* in Aristotelian ethics is directed at reflecting the good life of a citizen of a Greek *polis*, so the reformulation of the ideals of human flourishing in the philosophy of the Stoics mirrors the dissolution of the Greek city states and the emergence of empires comprising many cultures and many religions. How human flourishing should be envisaged and in which way personal formation had to be understood in such a situation required already in late antiquity a cosmopolitan outlook. This reveals a dialectic between the particular contexts of the concrete reflection on human flourishing and the processes of instruction and initiation constitutive for personal formation and their wider, potentially universal applications.

The early Christian communities are a good example of this dialectic. Although Christian views of human flourishing are rooted in the beliefs and practices of particular local Christian communities and realized in particular processes of formation, their application—if one only considers the commandments of love of God and love of neighbor and its radicalization in love for one's enemy—transcends the bounds of the community. This universal applicability is rooted in very particular beliefs and practices about God as God is disclosed in Christ and the Spirit, but the content of these particular beliefs already contains the drive towards universality.

Today we live in all dimensions of life in a multicultural situation. Our ideals of human flourishing and our views on personal formation are always confronted with a plurality of other views and practices. If we assume that every culture, as a symbolic universe of signs, beliefs, and practices has a center of meaning, which shapes the whole world of meaning, and is based on a *cultus*, as a set of focal activities and beliefs, our situation is a religiously and ideologically pluralist context. Every community is challenged to clarify in which way its views on flourishing and formation are different from others, specific to one community, and how they relate to others, to other communities and to other particular persons. This challenge has a very concrete form if we consider that the survival and the good life of humans on this planet and in every local context depend on developing common aims for our shared future and on strategies of cooperation between communities and individuals. Multicultural and religiously pluralist societies may not be able to identify a common ground of values for the common good, but they are challenged to conduct an ongoing conversation between the different communities about the common aims that should be achieved and the common rules that have to observed in striving for a shared future. The grounds that are offered for the common aims may be very different, and the reasoning supporting the common rules may not conform to supposedly universal standards of public reason. That, however, is not to be regarded as something negative. The more specific the grounds are and the deeper they are rooted in the beliefs and practices of particular communities, the more persuasive power they will have for members of such communities. All communities are, however, confronted with the question how they can give others a place in their particular reflection and their particular forms. They are confronted with the challenge of hospitality, both on a more theoretical plane of reflection and in very practical contexts of shaping their life together.

THE OMNIPRESENCE OF THE QUESTION OF JUSTICE

The depth dimension of the notion of hospitality becomes evident when we consider that most conflicts of today's global society, whether in a global, national, or local context, revolve around issues of justice. If we scratch the surface of any problem confronting our societies, we discover problems of justice, problems of the right relationship between the sexes, races, the generations, the "haves" and the "have nots." The problem of justice has become pervasive and omnipresent, and it appears in the contexts of politics, economics, education, health care provision, and in all dimensions of the life of society and raises the question of just participation in its goods, be they material or non-material. If one analyzes these problems in a little more detail one discovers that many of the problems are not easily fully described, let alone solved, by applying classic conceptions such as distributive justice or commutative justice, the exchange of one kind of good for another, or the idea of justice as fairness. It seems that there is a deeper dimension which concerns the dimension of the *recognition* of persons and communities in social and personal interaction. Even if the distribution of justice appears just, even if the rules of just exchange are observed, even if all criteria of fairness are applied, there remains a feeling on injustice if justice does not entail a fundamental recognition of persons and communities as bearers of an inalienable dignity which defines the basis for all other forms of justice. The challenge of hospitality, required by the pluralistic situation of our societies, must entail this dimension of fundamental recognition if it is to serve as a practicable aim for living together. This also extends to notions of human flourishing and personal formation. They must be based on a fundamental recognition of a particular dignity, the rights it entails and the duties it calls for, if they are to contribute to living the common life of societies as a good and just life.[2]

"HUMAN NATURE" IN THE RELIGIONS

Ideals of human flourishing and of human formation are based on an understanding of what it means to be human, not just in the sense of a definition of "human nature" but rather in terms of a vision of human destiny. In the religions, the understanding of what it means to be human is understood in terms of their relationship to the god of a particular religion in theistic religions; in the mystical religions it is determined by the relationship to what is seen as ultimate, albeit the ultimate "reality" of the void or emptiness, Śūnyatā, as it is understood—with different emphases—in the various sects of Buddhism. What it means to be human can in this way not be defined in terms of intrinsic attributes of a human nature. What "nature" is and what "human" is, are both understood primarily as defined by the relationship to God or the ultimate. Human being is in this sense essentially relational being, both in an ontological and in an epistemological sense.[3] What humans *are* depends in this way on the relationship to God or the ultimate; what they *know* about God, themselves and the world also depends on the relationship to God or the ultimate in that not only *what* they know, but also *how they know* it depends on this relationship. In both respects, what human being is and what humans know about themselves depend on God or the ultimate and on how God (or the ultimate) is disclosed by God or the ultimate. This has an implication, which—albeit in very different ways—the religions

2. The best discussion of the problem of justice is found in Nicholas Woltertorff's works *Justice* and *Justice in Love*. Cf. also Schwöbel, "The Justice of God and Justice in the World."

3. Cf. Schwöbel, "Human Being as Relational Being"; cf. also Schwöbel, "Recovering Human Dignity."

seem to share. They do not understand human flourishing as something humans can somehow achieve by themselves alone, as the exclusive self-actualization of human potential, since they understand the very "self" of humans and the power to actualize its potentialities as grounded in the god or the ultimate, which they see as the foundational term for understanding human being in relation. And in the same way, human formation cannot be understood in the religions as a process of human self-formation but must be understood as a process where the origin and the goal and the power that drives this process is understood as god or the ultimate. The religions would not deny that human activity comes into play in the processes of both human flourishing and human formation. However, if I see it correctly, the religions deny that this activity is somehow foundational. Since it is always dependent on being enabled by God or the ultimate, it rests on a prior passivity or receptiveness to the activity of God or openness to the ultimate. This seems to be one of the fundamental differences between religions and at least some non-religious world-views and ideologies.

At this point, we can no longer proceed in generalities. What humans are in a specific sense depends on *who* and *what* God is in relation to whom they have their being, meaning, and purpose. We therefore have to turn here to a specific religious view of reality, that of Christian faith, and try to build bridges to the understanding in other religions through analogical extension and dialogical exchange. I shall try to explicate the Christian understanding of what it means to be human in relationship to God, to the world, and to ourselves by following Martin Luther's theses in his *Disputatio de homine* of 1536.[4] This short text is not only a decisive (and controversial!) statement of the view of Reformation theology, as it is developed on the basis of Scripture. In our context it is also particularly interesting because Luther's brief thesis that being human is to be justified by God (*Hominem iustificari fide*), which he ascribes to Paul, takes up the concern for justice, which is so central to the debates in our society.

FLOURISHING IN RELATION TO GOD: MARTIN LUTHER ON WHAT IT MEANS TO BE HUMAN

Throughout the disputation Luther establishes a contrast between the way philosophy sees the nature of the human and the way theology conceives

4. I refer to the Latin text in the Weimar edition of Luther's works: WA 39/I, 175–77. An English translation can be found in Luther, *Career of the Reformer IV*, 133–44. An exhaustive commentary is provided by Gerhard Ebeling, *Lutherstudien*, vol. 2. An excellent theological interpretation is provided by William C. Weinrich, "*Homo theologicus*."

of humanity. Luther starts by quoting the way in which philosophy, understood as human wisdom, defines the human being as a rational, sensitive, and corporeal animal.[5] Luther does not want to get into a discussion of whether humans are called animals in a proper or improper sense. Instead, he emphasizes right from the start that this definition concerns mortal human beings of this life, meaning this life on earth. Luther readily concedes that reason is the main thing, the head, of all things, and above all things of this mortal and earthly life, the best and something quasi-divine (*divinum quiddam*). He even goes on to say that reason is the inventor (*inventrix*) and governor (*gubernatrix*) of all the arts, of medicine, and of jurisprudence and of all the things which in this life humans posses in terms of wisdom, power, competence, and glory. In the universities, where the seven liberal arts are studied and where medicine and jurisprudence form the so-called "higher faculties," reason is indeed both in its power to invent and to govern supreme. The fact that Luther does not mention the third of the higher faculties (i.e., theology) points already to the special status it has for him. With respect to this mortal life reason has a key governing position concerning what humans can know, what they have power *over* and what they have power *to do*, and hence with regard to all the glory that is due to them.

This section of the theses, which one could subsume under the heading "In praise of reason" (Theses 1–9), goes on to say that reason therefore marks the essential difference (*differentia essentialis*) by which humans are distinguished from animals and other things. There follows scriptural proof for this view of reason. It confirms the special status of reason if Scripture posits her as the ruling lady over the earth, the birds, the fish, and the animals by saying "have dominion . . . " (Gen 1:28). Luther here engages in a play on words by relating the Latin of the Vulgate text "Have dominion" (*dominamini*) to reason as the ruling lady (*domina*).[6] The praise of reason goes further by saying that reason ought to be a sun and a somewhat divine power (*numen quoddam*), posited in order to administer the things of this life. This majesty, Luther continues, God has not taken away after Fall of Adam but has rather confirmed. The Fall is in this sense not a deprivation of faculties which humans possessed before the Fall.

---

5. Thesis 1: "Philosophia, sapientia humana definit, hominem, esse animal rationale, sensitivum, corporeum." WA 39/1, 175.

6. Thesis 7: "Quam et scriptura sancta constituit talem dominam super terram, volucres, pisces, pecora, dicens: Dominamini." WA 39/I, 175.

THE LIMITS OF REASON:
THE BOUNDS OF THIS LIFE

After this almost hymn-like praise of reason follows the first qualification, almost like a section that could be headed: "Criticizing Reason." Reason, Luther maintains, does not know its own majesty *a priori*, by way of deduction from first principles, but only *a posteriori*, by way of inferences from experience, from its practice and its effects.[7] What would it mean if the self-knowledge of humans were given *a priori*? If we follow Luther's argument here, it would mean giving an account of what it means to be human in terms of the traditional four causes of the Aristotelian scheme of causality.[8] This proceeds on the premise that we can only know something if we know how it is caused, if we are able to give an answer to the question "why?" This, Luther claims, is not possible for philosophy or for reason, and if that is so, then we know almost nothing about human beings. He goes on to list the different causes. We do not know enough about the material cause of human being: we cannot say "out of which" (material) it is made. Furthermore, philosophy does not know the efficient cause of human beings, that which makes them be, and similarly, not their end, what they are there for. As the end of humans, philosophy simply posits the peace of this life. It cannot know the efficient cause, because philosophy does not know that God the creator is the efficient cause of all there is.[9] If one now turns to the formal cause which the philosophers call "soul," there is, according to Luther, no consensus among philosophers. Aristotle's definition in *De anima*[10] that the soul is the first act of a body which has the capacity for life Luther regards as Aristotle's attempt to make fun of his readers or listeners.

We have here a rather radical limitation of the capacities of philosophy or reason, which are used by Luther as equivalents. Humans know what they know *a posteriori* on the basis of experience, by reason's explicating its own practice. This, however, is strictly limited to this life. It is almost a view of instrumental reason that Luther seems to be defending. If philosophy attempts to transcend these boundaries by offering causal explanations, it

---

7. Thesis 10: "Tamen talem sese Maiestatem esse, nec ea ipsa ratio novit a priore, set tantum a posterire." WA 30I/175. Luther employs the distinction in its pre-modern Aristotelian sense according to which something can be known in two ways: from the antecedent reasons (*proteron*) and from the subsequent effects (*hysteron*).

8. Aristotle, *Physics* II.3 and *Metaphysics* V.2.

9. Thesis 13: "Nam Philosophiam [causam] efficientem certe non novit, similiter, nec finalem." Thesis 14: "Quia finalem nullam ponit aliam, quam pacem huius vitae, et efficientem nescit esse creatorem Deum." WA 39/I, 175.

10. Aristotle, *On the Soul* II.1.

fails. If we phrase that in the terminology of relationality, we have to say humans cannot give an explanatory account of themselves in terms of their relationship to themselves or to the world. Offering an explanation not only for specific events and states of affairs in this life, but for what it is to be human in its entirety, would require somehow to be able to conceive of the entirety of the human life. Negatively, this means for Luther that there is no hope that humans can know themselves, especially concerning the most important question of the soul, as long as humans do not see themselves in the fountain of all being and knowledge, in God.[11] The miserable state of such knowledge shows itself in the fact that humans have full and certain power over neither their conscious willing nor their knowing; both seem to be subjected to chance and futility.[12] Conclusion: Knowledge of this life is just like this life itself; considered on its own terms, it remains small, slippery, and highly material, in the sense of being bound to material conditions.

If we apply that briefly to our question with regard to human flourishing and personal formation, we come on the basis of Luther's account to a rather negative result. Since reason cannot provide an account of what causes humans to be what they are, it can neither offer an account of how humans can flourish nor how they are to be formed to flourish. This would presuppose having knowledge of the end, of the form and the efficient cause that shapes the matter humans consist of. But all of those lie outside the reach of reason.

THE WISDOM OF THEOLOGY

With thesis 20 we have the transition to theology. Theology, Luther claims, defines humans from the fullness of its wisdom as the entire and perfect human being. What now comes is a brief summary of the economy of salvation. Humans are God's creatures consisting of flesh and a living soul, created for the image of God without sin, in order to procreate, to rule over things, and in order never to die. This statement of the createdness of humans brackets all further statements, by defining who and what humans are through the relationship to God the creator. The relationship the creator has to humans establishes the framework in which all other statements are to be understood. It follows that humans are beings of flesh and a living soul, that they are from the beginning made for the image of God without

11. Thesis 17: "Nec spes est, hominem in haec praecipua parte ses posse cognoscere quid sit, donec in fonte ipso, qui Deus est, sese viderit." WA 39/I, 175.
12. Thesis 18: "Et quod miserabile est, nec sui consilii, aut cognitionem plenam et certam habet potentiam. Sed in his subiecta est casui et vanitati." WA 39/I, 175.

sin. That they are blessed and called to procreate and to have dominion over other animals indicates that humans are created with an open temporal future that extends into eternity. These brief summary statements establish that God's creative relationship to humans is the basis of a history, which is intended not to end, or rather to find its end in God who alone is eternal. Luther does not say here that humans are created immortal; rather he says that humans are never to die. The history between God and God's human creatures is meant to endure into eternity. This implies that God grants humans eternity, because whatever is created thereby has no control over its being, neither its beginning nor the end. Eternity can therefore only be achieved in communion with the creator who alone is eternal.

The next thesis recounts briefly that humans are subjected to the power of the devil after the Fall of Adam, subject to sin and death, which are both insuperable by human powers and therefore, for humans, unending unless they are overcome by God. The Fall is interpreted in such a way that it involves the subjection of humans to the counter-power of God, namely the devil, whose rule occurs through sin and death. As creatures humans cannot escape from the subjection to the power of sin, death, and the devil; if they could, they would have to be seen as the creative partner in the relationship to God the creator. If God is the creator of human creatures this is the one thing that cannot be. The relationship to God cannot be restored by human powers, and therefore the fallen state endures. This subjection to the rule of God's counter-powers can only be lifted if human creatures are liberated by the Son of God, Christ Jesus, whenever humans believe in him, and then eternity of life is donated to them. The way Luther phrases this makes clear that liberation by the Son of God is the necessary and sufficient condition for humans to regain again eternity of life so that the history established in creation is recreated for all eternity. Being human in the full sense, speaking of the total being of the human, means believing oneself to be saved by Christ.

THE BONDAGE OF REASON

Luther introduces the bondage to the power of the devil as the breaking of the relationship to God from the side of the creatures, which results in falling prey to the rule of God's counter-powers. The immediate implication is that reason as the most beautiful and most excellent thing among all things is nevertheless subjected to the rule of the devil. The relationship either to God or to the counter-powers of God affects all that humans are and have, even their most excellent gifts. There is no substance in humans

and there are no substantial attributes that are not affected by this change
of the dominant relationship. Therefore reason, too, is under the oppression
of the devil. Reason is only an example that this change in the dominant
relationship affects (a) the whole human race, everyone, be they King, Lord,
servant, wise, or just people, and (b) every good of this life, however excellent it may be. Sin is the great equalizer of status and of value. It seems
that Luther wants to assert that all these gifts of the creator which define
the excellence of human creatures are not taken away; there is no *privation*
of the gifts of creation, but there is a *perversion* of all of them. Integrity as
well as perversion are relational attributes. Therefore, Luther maintains, all
those philosophize in an impious manner against theology who claim that
the natural attributes of humans have remained in a state of integrity after
the Fall or that humans might earn God's grace and life by doing what is "in
them" (*quod in se est*). All properties of the human creature are a function of
the creative relationship of God to them so that, where this is denied, they
cannot remain in a state of integrity. That which humans have "in them" is
redefined in terms of the relationship they have to God. Luther therefore
maintains that it is wrong to say with Aristotle, who knows nothing of the
homo theologicus, that reason longs for the best. Whatever humans can do
or cannot do is relative to the relationship in which they are to God. In the
state of estrangement from God under the Fall, it does not make sense to
claim that the light of God's face is in humans—Luther qualifies here his
view of reason as the sun from thesis 8[13]—so that they have a free will to
form the right prescriptions for action and a good will. In the same way, it
appears wrong to say that a human could choose between good and evil or
life and death. This presupposes that humans could stand in a neutral position between good and evil and choose either of them. Not so, runs Luther's
argument. There is no neutral position; either humans are in an unbroken
or restored relationship to God, in which case they are already on the side
of the good and of life, or they are dislocated in the relationship to God and
then they are already bound to what is bad and brings death.

13. In Thesis 8 Luther had stated in interpreting the *dominium terrae*: "Hoc est, ut
sit Sol et Numen quoddam ad has res administrandas in hac vita positum." WA 39/I,
175. Also those philosophize impiously against theology who maintain: "Item, quod in
homine sit lumen vultus Dei super nos signatum, id est liberum arbitrium ad forman-
dum rectum dictamen et bonam voluntatem." (Thesis 29) WA 39/I, 176.

THE DEFINITION OF THE HUMAN: JUSTIFIED BY FAITH

At this point in the disputation comes the turning point in Luther's argument with the famous thesis: "Paul briefly summarizes in Romans 3:28, 'For we hold that a man is justified by faith apart from works of the law' the definition of human being, by saying: A human being is justified by faith."[14] It is not easy to reconstruct exactly how Luther means this brief definition. First, he maintains that when Paul says that humans need to be justified, this presupposes that they are sinners and unjust, guilty before God, but can be saved by grace. And "human being," Luther continues, is here taken in a universal sense, so that it comprises the whole world, whatever is called a human being under sin. It is probably right to read the "universal" and "the whole world" as a gloss on Gal 3:22: "But the scripture consigned all things to sin, that what was promised to faith in Jesus Christ might be given to those who believe." Luther presupposes Paul's argument in Gal 3:22, establishing the universality of sin so that all promises of God are then offered to faith in Jesus Christ in order that they can be accepted by faith in Jesus Christ. One way to make sense of this is to suppose that Luther (and Paul?) understand sin as the broken relationship to God which is newly established in Christ, in a sense that is just as universal as the universality of sin, so that all promises that were given within that relationship are now focused in Christ in order that faith in Christ receives and grasps all of God's promises. If justification is interpreted in this way, it is the creative new establishment of the relationship in which humans regain the future they have been promised from the beginning of creation.

Why should this be called justification? It makes sense, if we interpret justification here as the new establishment of God's justice as the right order of all relationships between God and humanity and the created world. Justice in the sense presupposed here must therefore be seen as creative justice. It does not presuppose as the form of justice, that which defines the shape of what it is to be, that which humans have done since the Fall of Adam under the rule of sin. This justice is neither retributive nor purely corrective. However, it is also not the imposition of an entirely new order, abandoning the old world order. Rather it is the sovereign and free creation of a new being and order of justice out of the material being of the old order. In this sense we can understand Luther's thesis: therefore human being of this life,

---

14. Thesis 32: "Paulus Rom. 3: Arbitramur hominem iustificari fide absque operibus, breviter hominis definitionem colligit, dicens Hominem iustificari fide." WA 39/I, 176. For a more extensive account see Schwöbel, "Promise and Trust."

the life of mortality, under the rule of sin, death, and the devil, is nothing but the pure matter for the future form of their life.[15] The "old order," the history of sin since Adam, is not simply abandoned, but it becomes the stuff with which the new form of justice is established. However, the possibilities of the new justice are not restricted to the inherent potentialities of the old life (which would be the case, if good works could somehow merit God's just judgment). The potentialities are defined by God in God's creative justice. Luther underlines this thought by developing an analogy: just like earth and heaven are to be seen in relation to their completed form after the six days of creation, so human beings in this life are to be seen in relation to their future form when the image of God will have been be re-formed and perfected. In one sense, justification is just like creation *ex nihilo*, in that it is unconditional, having its only necessary and sufficient condition in God's creative will. In another sense, the new creation accepts as its material the old life, so that it posits not a new matter *instead* of the old matter of the life of sinners, but transforms the old life creatively by God's creative will and being. Otherwise, the new creation would contradict God's faithfulness, and anthropologically it would not give sinners now much to hope for because their sinful old self would be replace by a new replica. The promise has the point that the new creation is the old Adam and the old Eve, strictly in the sense in which they are in virtue of God's creative relationship to them. Luther can here apply the scheme of the four causes creatively by identifying this mortal life with the matter on which God acts as the formal, efficient, and final cause. This perspective on the future form of human life qualifies the intermediate time as an interim period in which human beings are day by day either justified or polluted—the existence of believers as justified sinners, *simul iustus et peccator, simul iusta et peccatrix*. The disputation concludes with a disqualification of the kingdoms of reason which by Paul, as Luther quotes from 1 Cor 7:31, are not even called "world" but "scheme of the world," interestingly replacing the more positive word "figura," which could be used in a positive typological sense, with the Greek "schema" and its connotations of shadow and unreality.[16]

With these concluding reflections of the *Disputatio* we have reached the relationship of human flourishing and personal formation. Does Luther's sketch of the understanding of what it means to be human offer some foundations for a constructive Christian account of human flourishing?

---

15. Thesis 35: "Quare homo huius vitae est pura materia Dei ad futurae formae suae vitam." WA 39/I, 176.

16. Thesis 40: "Hinc Paulus ista rationis regna nec Mundum dignatur appellare, sed schema mundi potius vocat." WA 39/I 177.

And how could one develop an understanding of personal formation on the basis of these reflections?

FLOURISHING IN RELATIONSHIPS

What is distinctive about Luther's account of human being is that it is coherently developed in terms of an account of the relationships in which human being exists. If one wanted to develop this view one would have to say that the traditional order of substance and relation is reversed. Relations are no longer seen as connections between already established substances, so that relations are therefore not constitutive for existence and the being of substance. In Luther's view relations seem to be foundational and constitutive for understanding human nature and the nature of everything else. This changes the way in which we see human flourishing. On a traditional account of substance metaphysics, flourishing can only mean the actualization of the end of a particular substance. On this view, human flourishing means actualizing the potential that is already given in human nature. In modern accounts where the notion of the subject takes the place of substance in traditional metaphysics, flourishing becomes the aim of the subject's intentional activity. It is no longer given; it has to be realized. Human subjects become their own projects. This relational view is closely linked to a view of human being, indeed of all created being, as becoming, as existing as a process which goes beyond the given state in which something exists in the present. However, all becoming is bound to and restricted by the self-relationality of human subjectivity.

Luther's formula that the human of this life is God's matter for the future form of human life, a formula which he extends to every creature which is described as God's matter for its future glorious form, brings both aspects together: *relationality* and *becoming*. However, relationality is in Luther neither restricted to the external relations of predefined substances nor to self-relation of the human subject. Furthermore, becoming is not envisaged as based exclusively on the capacities of human self-development, rooted in the reflexive structure of human subjectivity. Both aspects are not developed in the form of a metaphysical system but in an interpretation of the biblical narratives.[17] This does not mean that this view could not be fleshed out in a full-scale metaphysical theory. It does mean, however, that for theology the witness of Scripture comes first, that the narrative and dialogical forms in which Scripture presents both aspects of relationality and

17. For a first attempt in this direction see Schwöbel, "God as Conversation."

becoming have a foundational significance for understanding the view of reality that is presented here.

What, then, as we asked in the introduction, would it mean to conceive of flourishing neither as the actualization of the intrinsic potentialities of a given substance nor as the self-enactment of a human subject, but as a process of becoming worked out through God's creative relationships with God's creation? The relational and narrative structure that Luther presents, is fairly traditional. He starts with the human creature, famously summarized in the words of the Small Catechism: "I believe that God has created me with all other creatures." In Luther's theology this understanding of creation is developed in terms of gift and address. Being created together with all other creatures is God's gift to humans and at the same time the address of the creator to the human creatures. Everything in creation belongs in Luther's understanding to God's vocabulary and it is ordered by the grammar of divine speech.[18] Humans are gifted creatures for which they owe God gratefulness, and as creatures who are addressed by God they are creatures who are called to respond to their creator and are made responsible for creation before God.

The image of God in humans seems to be intrinsically connected to the human capacity to respond to God's address not only in relation to God but also in their responsibility for non-human creatures. All this is given to humans as the beginning of a story, so that creation is from the beginning the unfolding of God's will to be in communion with his creation. The summons to be fruitful and multiply (Gen 1:28), introduced by a blessing, contains the promise that humankind shall have a future, a future that is maintained and reiterated (Gen 9:1) in spite of human contradiction against God (Gen 8:22). Humans are creatures of promise, and this gives a foundation to human flourishing. However, human flourishing is always embedded in relationships. The relationship to God, which is the gift of existence, meaning, and value, obligates humans to respect every other creature: createdness always implies co-createdness. Everything that is, is in virtue of God's relationship to every creature a bearer of meaning and value. What is specific for humans is that they are also addressed as those who are called to respect that value because they are themselves bearers of meaning and value. Respect is the recognition of the relative value of everything because

---

18. In his Lectures on Genesis Luther says: "Sic Sol, Luna, Coelum, terra Petrus, Paulus ego, tu etc. sumus vocabula Dei." WA 42, 17. However, sun, moon, heaven, earth, Peter, Paul, I and you are not only independent words of God but they have and we have meaning as names in the structure of divine grammar: "Quaelibet igitur, avis, piscis quilibet sunt nihil nisi nomina divinae Grammaticae." WA 42, 37. Cf. Wendte, *Die Gabe und das Gestell*, 397–407.

of its relation to God. Denying others meaning and value always implies for humans to negate their own created meaning and value. Questioning one's own meaning and value as God's creature is in this way not only contradiction against the creator but also the denial of the meaning and value of the other creatures of God. This is the structure of justice that is embedded in the created order. It is therefore quite fitting that the tradition identified the state of creation before the Fall as a state of original justice. However, this is, in a sense, only a starting point, because if this were true justice, then the realization of justice would be the return to the garden of Eden. This, however, is not the logic of the biblical narrative, and it contradicts the character of creation as promise. True justice is to be hoped for at the end of God's history with God's creation, in the Kingdom of God, not in a return to Eden.

If we summarize the outcome of these reflections for the understanding of human flourishing, we see that it is always dependent on the creative divine source, like a tree planted by the waters, and that it is always relational with regard to human sociality and with regard to the embeddedness of humans in the non-human creation. According to this view, humans do not need to be egoistic, selfish, destructive of the existence, meaning, and value of others, in order to flourish—indeed, they cannot flourish this way. Its logic is not a logic that achieves flourishing at the expense of others' wilting; its logic is consistently incremental. True human flourishing knows no winners and losers, just winners, but winners who will not ascribe their flourishing as their own achievement to themselves, but will see that at the root of every achievement is the reception of an unmerited gift.

RELATIONSHIPS BROKEN AND RESTORED: THE REALITY OF RECONCILIATION

If we follow the brief account of the divine economy which Luther gives, there follows an almost terse statement that through Adam's Fall humans have been subjected to the power of sin, death and the devil, which cannot be overcome by human powers. Humans can only be liberated from this bondage through the Son of God, Christ Jesus who liberates humans from sin, death, and the devil and gives them eternity of life, a liberation humans grasp by having faith in Christ. While the account of the creative relationship to God revolves around the notions of gift and address, gratefulness and responsibility, this stage of the drama of the divine economy is focused on bondage from which humans cannot liberate themselves and on the liberation achieved by Christ and apprehended by faith. Adam's Fall serves a summary of the whole story, which appears as the revolt of humans against their creaturely status and as trying to usurp the status of God in creation. The gift is abused by listening to another promise than that of the creator, a deceptive promise which sets up God as the envious competitor of humans. The desire to know good and evil as God only knows them, by creatively defining what is good and evil, leads to estrangement from God. The promised knowledge turns into shaming self-knowledge; God, the source of life becomes a threat from which Adam tries to hide. Taken to account for their actions, both Adam and Eve try to evade responsibility for what they have done by blaming the other.

Can this story be read as a story of a misguided attempt at a form of self-directed human flourishing? This would be a form of attempted flourishing that strives to transcend the boundaries of the creaturely, to exchange dependence on the creator for self-dependence and to cut the bond of relationship to God. When Luther describes humans according to philosophical reason, he almost offers a caricature of Eve's reflections when confronted with the fruit of the tree, which focus on her rational ("to be desired to make one wise"), sensitive ("delight to the eyes"), and corporeal ("good for food") nature.[19] The point seems to be that all the faculties and what they perceive are good, if they are seen in relationship to the creator as the gifts of God's creation. When they are desired apart from God, against God's commandment, they turn into the enticements of temptation. Once they are desired and appropriated as objects of desire apart from their character as gift and address of God, they become idols.

The result of the Fall is indeed dramatic because it manifests the depth of human dependence on the creator. Once the revolt against the creator is successful and the human creature is displaced from the network of relationships grounded in God's creative will and being, the negative aspects of createdness make themselves felt. However, neither Luther nor the narrative in Genesis 3 dwells on these aspects. The attempt at self-aggrandizement leads to self-debasement. The one decisive point Luther underlines in his brief reference to Genesis 3 is that the state into which humans bring themselves by dislocating themselves in the relational good order of creation is a state of bondage, of slavery from which there is no escape. The attempt at enhancing one's position leads to a permanent degradation, the impossibility of

---

19. Reconsider Thesis 1 of the disputation *De homine*: "Philosophia, sapientia humana, definit, hominem, esse animal rationale, sensitivum, corporeum." WA 39/I, 175.

returning to the right place in relationship to God. On such a relational view as Luther offers it, cutting oneself loose from the source of life is death, nothingness. There is indeed no alternative to nihilism.[20] The tree that is cut off from the supply of water might as well shout with Nietzsche: "The desert grows, woe to him in whom deserts hide."

That is why the gospel of Christ is such good news. Its content is that the creator not only sustains humans in revolt and takes the effects of that revolt upon himself, but also offers definitive liberation from the powers of sin, death, and the devil in Jesus Christ. The content of the Gospel is the healing of broken relationships, between God and God's estranged creatures, between humans, and between humans and the non-human creation (which seems to be point of the so-called nature miracles of Jesus). The whole story of the message, life, death, and resurrection of Jesus seems to have the one point that God acts decisively to establish a new order of right relationships between God and humanity, by once and for all overcoming the power of sin, by conquering death and defeating the counter-powers of God, personified in the devil. In contrast to this news, the attempts of humans at achieving their own liberation seem utterly futile. The message of the gospel is: freedom has been achieved and we can participate in it by faith in Christ. Where human flourishing appeared before as a law, it now becomes gospel, the promised future of God's liberated human creatures. Humans are relocated in their proper place in the structure of relationships of creation, and the direction of their becoming is no longer directed towards nothingness but towards the glorious freedom of the children of God. However, the detritus of the life in bondage to sin, death, and the devil is not lost. When Luther says that this life is pure matter for the future form of life, two things are said. The past of bondage has lost its determining force for the future, but it nevertheless is to be transformed through God's formation of the future life in us. On this basis, human flourishing does not need to present itself as an unbroken story of progress and success, the cracks in the fabric or our lives need not be plastered over. Rather, they can be acknowledged because they now no longer bind our future to the past. The assurance of grace makes the confession of sin honest. In this way, the process of human flourishing does not have to exclude our fallibility and our fallenness; it can accept them, recognize them and so become critical, even self-critical.

20. Cf. Miroslav Volf's illuminating remarks on the specter of nihilism in *Flourishing*, 197–201.

THE PROMISE OF PERFECTION AND THE MANAGEMENT OF OUR IMPERFECTIONS

Luther's formula of our life as God's matter for life in its future form, for its future glory states that God's fallen but reconciled creatures again brought on the way towards the future glory. Just as the Gospel is clear that God is the subject of reconciliation, so too God is the one through whom we are perfected. This is, on the one hand, a disappointment: humans are not the agents of their own perfection. The ideals of human self-perfection which, especially since the Enlightenment, motivate so many attempts to overcome the imperfections of life, from genetic technology to social engineering to achieve the perfect classless society, appear from this perspective as misdirected. If, however, one considers how much suffering has been caused by misplaced ideals of perfection, this disappointment is a liberating thought. How much injustice was committed to achieve the perfectly just society, peopled by ethnically, racially, genetically pure, flawless individuals? The idea of the perfect human being—the *Übermensch*, the superhuman—has been the background of so much inhumanity, as has been the idea of a perfect human society which can be used to justify countless victims on the way that leads towards its achievement. We are tasked not with our own perfection but with the management of our imperfectability; improvement in the participation in the goods of human life leads to the envisioning of humane goals that do not achieve perfect at the cost of the exclusion of the imperfect. The Christian confession of sin, even in the radical sense of original sin, means taking leave of ideals of human self-perfection and discloses them as examples of the very character of sin, of trying to be like God.

The liberating disappointment is only the critical side of the great promise that God will bring the will to be in communion with his creation to its promised end so that our present life will receive its future form in eternal communion with God. As much as we are now engaged in the management of our imperfections, this struggle is not motivated by the moral effort to try to avoid the worst, it is fuelled by the hope for the best, the perfected communion of God with the reconciled creation. The religious life in all world religions lives from the anticipation of the ultimate goal of our becoming as creatures and from the foretaste of the fulfillment of our relational being. It is because of that, as Volf rightly insists, that we must draw on the resources of the religious tradition if we want to develop effective visions of human flourishing. In Christianity, this vision has the concrete form of the New Jerusalem, the heavenly city where the dwelling of God is with humans (Rev 21:3). The apocalyptic envisions the presence of God as the end of death and mourning so that God will wipe every tear from human eyes (Rev 21:4). This vision is anticipated in the sacramental presence, which is characterized by the unity of being, meaning, and value that Christians hope for when they pray for the coming of the Kingdom of God. This resonates with the images of fulfilled life which constitute the energy field of the world religions. For Christian hope, this vision makes clear that the promise for our flourishing *is* becoming the matter for the formation which takes place when God makes our lives the matter from which the future form of our lives will be formed according to the fullness of God's love who, as Luther says in his seventh Invokavit sermon on the 15th of March 1522, is "a glowing oven full of love, reaching from the earth to the heavens."[21]

FLOURISHING TOGETHER?

The burning issue that Volf raises in *Flourishing* is no less than the question whether the religions can contribute to humanity's flourishing together in a globalized world. One starting point for an answer is to note that according to the self-understanding of the religions they are not the true sources of human flourishing and not the agencies of personal formation. They are ways in which we relate to God as the true source of all flourishing (or, as in Buddhism, the ultimate void as the liberation from all suffering). The mark of true religions is that they do not mistake themselves for the source of flourishing—that would be self-idolizing—but that they point beyond themselves to what they, in very different ways, believe to be the ground of meaning and truth. Could it be that in order to contribute to human flourishing in a globalized world we need to follow the direction the religions provide and not reflect on the religions but reflect on the source of all flourishing? Could it be that part of the answer why we need religion in a globalized world is that they lead us to do theology, together and in conversation with one another? After all, it is not the one who meditates on religion day and night who is like a tree planted by the water (Ps 1:2–3).

---

21. Newlands, "Luther's Ghost," 291. The original quotation is in WA 10/III, 56.

BIBLIOGRAPHY

Aristotle. *Metaphysics*. In *The Complete Works of Aristotle: The Revised Oxford Translation*, edited by Jonathan Barnes, 2:1552–1728.

———. *On the Soul*. In *The Complete Works of Aristotle: The Revised Oxford Translation*, edited by Jonathan Barnes, 1:641–92. Princeton: Princeton University Press, 1984.

———. *Physics*. In *The Complete Works of Aristotle: The Revised Oxford Translation*, edited by Jonathan Barnes, 1:315–446.

Ebeling, Gerhard. *Lutherstudien*. 3 vols. Tübingen: Mohr, 1971–1989.

Luther, Martin. *Career of the Reformer IV*, edited by Lewis W. Spitz. Vol. 34 of *Luthers Works*, edited by Jaroslav Pelikan and Helmut T. Lehmann. Philadelphia: Fortress, 1960.

Newlands, George. "Luther's Ghost—ein gluehender Backofen voller Liebe." In *Theology as Conversation: The Significance of Dialogue in Historical and Contemporary Theology, A Festschrift for Daniel L. Migliore*, edited by Bruce L. McCormack and Kimlyn J. Bender, 273–93. Grand Rapids: Eerdmans, 2009.

Schwöbel, Christoph. "God as Conversation: Reflections on a Theological Ontology of Communicative Relations." In *Theology of Conversation: Towards a Relational Theology*, edited by Jacques Haers, 43–67. Bibliotheca Ephemeridum Theologicarum Lovaniensium 172. Leuven: Peeters, 2003.

———. "Human Being as Relational Being: Twelve Theses for a Christian Anthropology." In *Persons: Divine and Human*, edited by Christoph Schwöbel and Colin E. Gunton, 141–65, Edinburgh: T. & T. Clark, 2000.

———. "The Justice of God and Justice in the World." In *Van God gesproken: over religieuze taal en relationele theologie*, edited by Theo Boer et al., 217–232. Zoetermeer, Netherlands: Boekencentrum, 2011.

———. "Promise and Trust: Lutheran Identity in a Multicultural Society." In *Justification in a Post-Christian Society*, edited by Carl-Henric Grenholm and Göran Gunner, 15–35. Eugene, OR: Wipf & Stock, 2014.

———. "Recovering Human Dignity." In *God and Human Dignity*, edited by R. Kendall Soulen and L. Woodhead, 44-58, Grand Rapids: Eerdmans, 2006.

Volf, Miroslav. *Flourishing: Why We Need Religion in a Globalized World*. New Haven: Yale University Press, 2016.

Weinrich, William C. "*Homo theologicus*: Aspects of a Lutheran Doctrine of Man." In *Personal Identity in Theological Perspective*, edited by Richard Lints et al., 29–44. Grand Rapids: Eerdmans, 2006.

Wendte, Martin. *Die Gabe und das Gestell: Luthers Metaphysik des Abendmahls im technischen Zeitalter*. Tübingen: Mohr 2013.

Wolterstorff, Nicholas. *Justice in Love*. Grand Rapids: Eerdmans, 2011.

———. *Justice: Rights and Wrongs*. Princeton: Princeton University Press, 2008.

5

The Theory of Five Forces
Rav Kook on Human Flourishing

Alon Goshen-Gottstein

THERE ARE MANY WAYS of honoring a scholar-friend. One way is to recall the good times. Miroslav and I have spent many beautiful hours together in group settings studying each other's texts, gleaning the wisdom of our traditions. What more beautiful tribute to such a friendship than sharing texts on a theme that lies at the heart of Miroslav's work—flourishing.

I would like to share a text by Rabbi Abraham Isaac Kook, a nineteenth-to-twentieth-century giant of Jewish mysticism, thought, and spirituality, who was also the first Chief Rabbi of then-Palestine. The text is a recently discovered one, unknown in the hundred years or so since its composition. It represents an early stage in Rav Kook's thought. It is taken from one of the only systematic works written by Rav Kook, a kind of contemporary *Guide of the Perplexed*, written in the late nineteenth century as a way of responding to various contemporary intellectual and social challenges. Its present day editor accordingly named it *To the Perplexed of the Generation*.[1]

---

1. Kook, *To the Perplexed of the Generation*. The editor devotes an appendix to an attempt to describe the work's particular character, to date it, and to contextualize it within Rav Kook's broader corpus.

The present contribution is probably the first attempt to translate any part of this work into English. What follows is by no means the most important part of the work. But it does give us a view into the typical thought patterns of Rav Kook, as these crystallized already in early stages of his thought. One of the many original contributions of the work is what may be called the "theory of five forces." I offer it to Miroslav because it speaks explicitly about flourishing and because it develops a theory of human flourishing that is worthy of engagement. For students of Rav Kook it is a theory worth engaging because it is distinct in relation to some of his later work. It puts forth a universal theoretical frame of reference from which a variety of issues, of relevance to the Jewish as well as the non-Jewish reader, may be engaged.

The theory appears first in chapter 24 of *To the Perplexed of our Generation*. It then makes secondary appearances in chapters 25 and 26, where we see how it goes beyond a simple theory of human flourishing and how it is integrated into other topics, particularly topics that were of contemporary public and spiritual concern. That the theory can be applied to contemporary challenges suggests it has broader potential. Perhaps making it the focus of the present contribution could lead to further reflection on how it might be put to practice and what contemporary issues it might address.

I will translate these texts for the first time. Let it be noted that Rav Kook is an extremely difficult author to translate due to the richness of his language and the density of his thought. I am increasingly confronted by present-day rabbis and teachers who feel his thought is inaccessible to them for these reasons. Translating Rav Kook involves one in working through multiple meanings at every turn of the phrase. The translation that follows is therefore heavily footnoted, in an attempt to capture that complexity and to be true to Rav Kook's text, even as I seek to make it address a new audience and a new intellectual setting.

CHAPTER 24:
A THEORY OF HUMAN FLOURISHING[2]

Text

There are five general[3] forces,[4] and one must see to it that they are made whole[5] in the life of the collective and the individual. In them will then be found the appropriate force for removing all harm and for the flourishing of life in the proper way.

The first: the health of body and soul[6] as a complete living being, delighting[7] in life.

The second: human forces[8] will be appropriately developed, sentiments of spiritual delights, beauty, poetry, healthy imagination, including the quality of attributes[9] that should be pleasant in social company, based on the principle that good traits precede the Torah.[10]

The third: a national sentiment must be sufficiently developed, according to the value of each person's nation and its needs, quality, and standing, so that one's heart should be awake and one's soul feeling with a healthy and courageous sense what is good for one's nation, desiring with living and natural love to increase its value[11] and success.

The fourth: the development of a religious feeling,[12] which is a lofty feeling, planted in a human being's soul [nefesh] by the maker of his soul [neshama],[13] in order to impress within him[14] the true relation between a

2. In Rav Kook's work this section is titled simply chapter 24.

3. *Kelaliyim.* Could also be translated collective, as the same word is used in the continuation of the sentence. General seems more appropriate, however.

4. Could also be translated as strengths or powers.

5. Or: reach their fulfillment.

6. Rav Kook uses multiple terms for soul. The Hebrew here is *nefesh*, referring to the vital soul, animating the body and its vitality. This is the lowest rung on the kabbalistic ladder of the soul.

7. Or: happy.

8. Or: powers, potentialities.

9. Personal behavioral traits and qualities.

10. This is a famous rabbinic maxim. See, for instance, *Vayikra [Leviticus] Rabba* 9.3.

11. Or: worth.

12. Or: sentiment.

13. Rav Kook uses two different terms for soul in this sentence. The former is *nefesh*, already used above; the latter *neshama*, designating the higher spiritual soul. The maker of the higher soul also plants the religious sentiment, situated in the lower soul.

14. This seems like the preferable rendering for *lehatbia bekirbo*. A less likely reading

person and his maker, as [that] relation ought to be between a creature and his creator. And this[15] embraces with its powerful arm[16] all the foundations of life and morality, collective and individual.

The fifth is the development of mind, knowledge of the world and reality, theoretical sciences, practical and abstract,[17] until one feels a natural need to delight in the splendor of abstract wisdom that speaks of divinity and all matters that are adjunct to its knowledge.

Now, every person has a natural disposition to acquire some part of these general acquisitions, everyone according to his quality and value. However, healthiness[18] is only found when all these forces will be well-balanced in a proper system, one in relation to the other, and one will not enter the domain of the other, growing at its expense. Now, gaining more[19] is never bad in and of itself, but sometimes excess[20] may be considered a bad thing, causing loss when valued relationally,[21] such as when it breaks the equilibrium by abnormal leaning.[22]

However, in order to restore the balance there are always two paths: to reduce the force of that which is excessive or to increase the other forces so that the excess is harmonized.[23] It is obvious that as long as there is even some possibility for increasing[24] the other forces in such a way that what has been gained[25] is (seen as) an excellent quality[26] as is appropriate for it, this is better than that simple path of diminishing that which has been gained, for

---

would construe *lehatbia* from *teva* ("nature"), rather than *matbea* ("stamp," "form"). The text would then read "to make natural within him."

15. The sentence could refer back to the religious sense, at the beginning of the paragraph, or to the appropriate relation between creature and creator, which is the foundation of life and morality. I prefer the former option.

16. Echoing Isa 62:8.

17. These either describe the theoretical sciences or are two additional types of science and wisdom.

18. The use of the term probably also includes dimensions of wholeness and sanity.

19. Or: addition, growth, excess, advantage, for the Hebrew *Yitaron*. In context the choice above seems most appropriate, while "addition" is the closest literal rendering.

20. Same term as above, adapted to the flow of the sentence.

21. Or: a loss in relation to the overall combination.

22. In other words, when one force is too dominant, causing an imbalance in the overall economy of forces.

23. Or: equilibrated.

24. Or: augmenting.

25. Or: added, increased.

26. Or: level; Hebrew: *ma'alah*.

in so doing he reduces the image[27] and dwindles life, whether individually, in the life of the person, or collectively, in the life of the collective and the nation.

However, where human society fails is when it places its trust and the solution to its questions in only one of these general forces, or even in some of them. For even if it has the strength to address a contemporary challenge[28] [brought about] by a lack resulting from a want in some particular force, due to which the felt evil has come about, nevertheless, as long as the forces are not all harmonized, the crisis will not be healed. For immediately many other disharmonies[29] will emerge[30] that sprout forth from the deficiency of destroying the general equilibrium that is required in order to harmonize all the forces according to their value and how many portions[31] of each one of them are required in putting together the web[32] of life.

Analysis

Let us consider the text in detail. One thing strikes us from the start: the dual perspective of individual and collective. As Rav Kook explores this issue he keeps the dual vision of relating to the individual and the collective simultaneously. This is a hallmark of his thought, which considers the individual from a broader collective perspective, but which never lapses into a kind of ideology that ignores the individual and his or her consciousness, processes, and flourishing. Beyond the general and repeated references to individual and collective, we note that the third force is national. We might have not considered this a foremost force to be reckoned with in accounting for broader human reality. Yet it is hard to overestimate the significance of the national dimension in Rav Kook's thought. Rav Kook was a prophet of the spiritual revival of the People of Israel in their Land, in the late nineteenth and early twentieth centuries. This prophetic dimension saw the larger whole, leading to the affirmation of the centrality of the national dimension. His thought was in no small measure influenced by nineteenth-century German idealism and the lofty place it allocated to national identity.

---

27. Echoing Bavli (i.e., the Babylonian Talmud.—Eds.), *Yevamot* 63b, where the divine image in humanity is dwindled and made small through wrongdoing.

28. Literally: to fence off a break (in the surrounding fence), felt in its time.

29. Possibly: confrontations; Hebrew: *sichsuchim*.

30. Literally: be born.

31. Or: shares; Hebrew: *menayot*.

32. Possibly: tractate.

Therefore, we should not be surprised to find the national sentiment as part of the image of the whole and integrated individual and collective.

What is surprising is the *ladder* of forces. There seems to be some kind of hierarchy, certainly where the first and last are concerned. The first force concerns the health of body and soul, clearly a foundation for anything that would follow. The final force is introduced in a later chapter with the introductory phrase "above all," thereby suggesting it really is the crowing force.[33] If so, are the five forces listed in a hierarchical order? Even if we do not assume an intentional hierarchy, the order in which they were introduced is still striking. One might have imagined the religious life and the religious sense would be the crowning force of the human person. This is not how they are portrayed. Moving from health of human body and soul to the development of human forces, Rav Kook then shifts to the national sentiment, only to return to the religious sense, which is nevertheless not presented as the most significant force. Rather, the fifth place is reserved for the cultivation of the mind in its fullness. Wisdom is the crown of human perfection, a wisdom sought in its fullness, a fullness that consists in knowing wisdom in its divine context. Thus, divine knowledge is the highest goal. Rav Kook does not state that all other forces are there to serve it and to point to it. We are left with room to reflect on whether ultimately all forces must lead to the acquisition of divine knowledge, or whether divine knowledge is only one of several perfections, but not one that subsumes the others. The emphasis on knowledge is very appropriate for a work that seeks to be a latter-day guide of the perplexed. As in Maimonides, knowledge is the crown achievement of the religious life, and, again like in Maimonides, this knowledge is comprehensive in scope, including all sciences, abstract and practical, all leading to divine knowledge.

Some additional points are noteworthy. The second force relates to the development of human capacities. I note with interest that the development of the affective life is absent or nearly absent. There is emphasis on social and moral attributes. There is reference to beauty, imagination, spiritual delights, and social qualities. Where does the development of human affective life come in? Perhaps this was included in the strength of soul in the first force and is seen as an extension of the health of body and soul. As noted in the translation, Rav Kook uses a term that relates to the lower aspect of the vital soul and that could therefore be identified with emotions.

In accounting for why the religious life is fourth and not fifth on the list, we do well to note the reference to religious *feeling*. Religious feeling grounds one's orientation within a relationship of creature and creator. It

---

33. See below in the text from Rav Kook's chapter 26.

(or this orientation)[34] also provides proper foundations for morality and for life itself. But it is still related to life. It does not go beyond the reality of the created order. Only the cultivation of the mind in knowledge of God takes one beyond that order to God himself. Religious sentiment is an important educational instrument of orienting a person, but ultimately it remains focused on the person and is therefore limited to the realm of the human. Only the quest for knowledge and wisdom takes a person beyond the human realm and into God's reality.

We note with interest that there is nothing particular to Israel or Judaism in this theory of five forces. Here too the early Rav Kook is remarkably Maimonidean. Knowledge of God cuts across religious difference and is integrated in a theory of human flourishing that is not specific to one nation or one religion. Throughout, Rav Kook refers either to the human person or to the generic national affiliation. Nothing is said about Israel or Judaism specifically. Just as the sense of nationhood is generic and applies to one and all, so religious sentiment is a human common. There is no suggestion that Jews have a finer or different religious sense. The fundamental religious sense relates to the relationship of creator and creatures and so cuts across any religious divides.[35] And so does the knowledge of God, which is not in any way circumscribed to Israel or even dependent on the Torah. Knowledge, science, and the cultivation of the mind are universals that apply to one and all as part of a theory of human flourishing.[36] What this suggests, in

34. See above note 16.

35. Indeed, *To the Perplexed of the Generation* has some of the most open attitudes to other religions, not only in comparison to some of Rav Kook's later works, but even in relation to most thinkers throughout the ages. In terms of contemporary pluralist sensibilities, this work is a treasure trove of resources and precedents.

36. The theory of five forces appears only in *To the Perplexed of the Generation*. Because it speaks of forces and their actualization it is particularly suitable for a discussion of flourishing. Later essays of Rav Kook maintain the same structure of core principles and the need for their integration. In these essays Rav Kook speaks not of the five forces but of "the broad spiritual horizon" or "the spirit of humanity," which then finds expression in four particular spirits: divine, moral, religious, and national. There is partial overlap with the theory of five forces, but the concepts are reconfigured, and different emphases are given. Emphases also change between different iterations of the later concept. See *Ma'amrei Reiya*, 21 and 102. The earlier articulation of *Talelei Orot*, published in 1910 seems to be more systematic, while there is more fluidity in the later articulation in 1933 in *HaTorah veHatarbut Haenoshit*. The discussion of the four spirits is also relevant to a discussion of flourishing, inasmuch as all four are required for flourishing. However, Rav Kook does not use the language of flourishing, possibly because the spirits are not spoken of as human potentialities, but rather as manifesting or revealing spirits, as if in a movement from above to below. Where our text may be read in an upward pointing hierarchy, the 1910 text at least seems to be based on a hierarchy based on divine revelation in a movement from above to below. These later texts are therefore

terms of human flourishing, is that the processes and the goals related to human flourishing are identical for all humanity, and possibly for all religions as well.

We have thus far two dimensions of human flourishing. The first concerns the cultivation to fullness of all forces of the human person. The second emerges from the structure of the list and how it points beyond the human to the divine, with knowledge of God as the crowning force of the human person. There is a third. The third dimension concerns the harmonious cultivation of all forces that form a whole, a web, a totality. Harmony, balance, and integration are hallmarks of Rav Kook's thought throughout his rich literary career. The key to flourishing is that all forces should be cultivated and that none should come at the expense of the other. Equilibrium, balance, and harmony are the keys to realizing how the forces interact with one another. Cultivating one force only—the body, feeling, imagination, national identity, a religious sense, or even the quest for wisdom—is a sign of illness. It leaves the person and the collective facing harm and spiritual ill. Only in their totality do these forces lead to human flourishing. Absent that and we are in the realm of illness and crisis. Indeed, as we shall see in other chapters, many contemporary crises and diseases can be attributed to the broken harmony that fails to integrate all forces into a sense of the fullness of the human person and society.

Simply calling for harmony and balance would miss an important aspect of Rav Kook's approach. Rav Kook's orientation is one of incessant growth, aspiration, and evolution. He is a powerful evolutionary thinker who always seeks the growth, augmentation, and increase of power, knowledge, life. In this light we should appreciate the final part of the presentation. Restoring harmony could take one of two forms. If one force has outgrown others, it may have to be curtailed, or others should be invited to grow and expand in a manner that is commensurate with the power that has grown. While recognizing the first possibility, Rav Kook clearly prefers the latter. Flourishing means ongoing growth to perfection. Where imbalances

---

closer to a notion of fullness or perfection than to a notion of flourishing, inasmuch as their starting point is the higher spirit, rather than the actualization of human potential. Both our text and the later texts share the view that the different forces or spirits must be harmonized, and therein lies perfection or flourishing. The later texts, however, do assign a more important place to Israel and the Torah in this process of harmonization. While the four spirits are universal, it is Israel that provides for harmonization of these spirits within humanity (1910 version), and it is the Torah that lifts all four spirits and brings their ultimate spiritual perfection (1933 version). While maintaining the same universal vision, the later theory stands in closer rapport to particular Jewish concerns, while the earlier theory of five forces is devoid of an attempt to tilt the universal ideals towards particular Jewish ideals.

between forces occur, the response should be more growth on other fronts, as a means of restoring lost harmony.

Rav Kook's reference to the diminishing of the divine image is an allusion to the possibility that the totality of the five forces is really what makes for the fullness of the human person and may indeed be one way of viewing man's (or humanity's) creation in the divine image.[37] And it would seem that the capacity to increase and grow in all these qualities is itself an expression of the divine capacity in humans, the capacity to increase and attain fulfillment and the fullness of human flourishing.

APPLYING THE THEORY
TO SPECIFIC THEOLOGICAL CHALLENGES

That Rav Kook considered this theory an important contribution of his philosophical tract can be seen by the fact that he appeals to it in subsequent chapters. These may shed further light on the theological foundations of the theory and on how it is to be applied. Chapter 25 is devoted to the great questions of life and being. The riddle of life can be tackled either through denial of faith or through the path of light that leads to the knowledge of God. This knowledge itself can follow two tracks. The first recognizes God as a great power who brought about reality, but remains outside it. The other is the recognition that in reality there is nothing but God. Rav Kook goes on to make one of the most striking and original statements made by any Orthodox author concerning Spinoza. He embraces Spinoza's pantheism and finds this view to be the heart of kabbalistic and hassidic teaching. All particular realities are but revelations and manifestations of the greater reality. Everything is a manifestation, a spark of divinity. The length to which Rav Kook goes in presenting this view shows he clearly identifies with it.

Given the choice between the path of light and the path of darkness, denial and faith, what would lead one to reject faith? Rav Kook attributes such rejection to the obligations that faith places upon one and that generate an internal resistance that causes one to "lose his normal path." It is confusion of thought that leads to rejection of faith, which is contrary to human nature and contrary to pure and still mental processes. The loss of such clear mental powers is due to the forces that ought to aid and fill the religious sentiment not having developed properly. Recognition that heresy is due to an imbalance of personal faculties, leading one to make an improper choice,

---

37. The concept is very present in *To the Perplexed of the Generation*, proportionately much more so than in most of Jewish literature. Significantly, here too we note echoes of Maimonides, who opens his *Guide* with a discussion of the image of God.

rather than an appropriate intellectual conclusion, brings Rav Kook back to the theory of five forces.

> Only full healthiness[38] in all five fundamental parts that are foundation stones for the construction[39] of the human person will provide control and protection[40] against the various imbalances[41] that we see in the condition of both our physical and spiritual lives. And only the pursuit and full accord, together with the well worked-out[42] knowledge of significant public actors, to unite specifically all these together in one complementary harmony, only thereby will be healed what was smitten in mankind, and in particular what was smitten in our people. However, the insistence[43] to hold on to one aspect[44] and to let go even of one part that is held together[45] in the entire web[46] that builds up the character of the person and of the nation, will only add negativity, by destroying the balanced equilibrium that it will cause.

In terms of the theory itself there is no major contribution beyond what we saw in chapter 24. Rav Kook does refer to "our people," but only in terms of applying the theory of harmony of forces. Our people as well as mankind were smitten, and harmony is required for all. The theory of five harmonized forces provides a basis for tackling heresy. Heresy, moving away from faith, is an illness, due to imbalance in the overall harmony between the forces of the person and of humanity. The harmony of the forces should be made manifest publicly by public actors, so as to serve as a model for human perfection and presumably as a basis for emulation by others.

Reading this recapitulation of ideas from chapter 24 at the end of the discussion of heresy and faith and the different paths of faith raises the question of how well this theory is integrated within the thematics of the present discussion. The immediate cause for appealing once again to the theory was the suggestion that faithlessness is a sign of imbalance within the internal

---

38. See above, note 19.
39. Or: building. The sense is: development.
40. Literal quote of Ps 32:9.
41. Hebrew: *Peraʾot*, destructions and break-ins.
42. Or: clarified, purified.
43. Closer to literal sense: adding force.
44. Literally: detail.
45. Less likely: one percent.
46. Or: tractate.

economy of the person.[47] The consequence of this recognition is that full harmonious cultivation of all human forces—full flourishing—is also the natural foundation for faith. In this way, the theory is not simply a theory of human flourishing but also a means of confronting a contemporary threat and challenge.

But the fact that this appeal to the theory of the five forces comes as it does after the discussion of true faith also raises another possibility for how the theory should be appreciated. Rav Kook clearly sides with the pantheistic view, according to which all of life's powers and realizations are but manifestations and sparks of the divine that is being known. This perspective might allow us to consider a pantheistic basis for the theory of five forces as a foundation for human flourishing. Seen in common perspective, these are five human forces that must be integrated for the sake of human perfection. This chapter teaches us that their integration is also a condition for gaining faith. Inasmuch as the fifth power, that of knowledge of God and the choice of how to come to know him, is dependent on the other forces, their integration is also a condition for the fulfillment of the most important force: knowledge of God, the grounds of faith. But placing this discussion after a discussion of divine manifestation in all forms of life leads to asking whether the ultimate grounds of the theory of five forces, and consequently of the theory of human flourishing, is not the recognition that all is divine. If so, the cultivation of the body, emotions, national identity, the religious life, and the quest for the knowledge of God are all expressions and manifestations of the divine life. The requirement of equilibrium and harmony between forces is a condition for gaining the recognition that it is the divine life that is manifesting through these five forces. And perhaps, though Rav Kook never states that much, the very drive for harmony is itself an expression of the drive for harmony that characterizes the divine reality that then manifests in the human person and in humanity.

We noted above an allusion to a rabbinic passage where God's image manifests in humanity. The specific reference refers not simply to the image of God in the individual person, but as *manifesting* in *each and every* person. These manifestations then make up and manifest the greater divine body. We might not be far off the mark in suggesting that in a similar manner the internal divine harmony and fullness is manifest in the fullness and harmony between the forces of the person and the collective. Flourishing, by this reasoning, is the realization of the divine image, which in turn is

47. Rav Kook returns to this theme at the beginning of chapter 26, where he speaks of the faithlessness of a Jew as an impairment of the soul that can be attributed to an imperfect national sentiment, sense of righteousness, and even possible bodily imperfection.

understood as a revelation of the all-pervasive reality of God that manifests through all of life's aspects and situations. The quest for harmony and fullness of the five forces is therefore nothing but the quest for manifesting the divine in humanity and recognizing the fundamental divine reality of everything.

FROM HARMONY OF FORCES TO HARMONY OF OPINIONS

Chapter 26 provides us with another way of engaging the theory of five forces and thereby allows us to uncover one further dimension of the theory. The chapter continues the discussion of heresy and explores the epistemological foundations of Jewish heresy and in particular the negative effects of biblical criticism and how it undermines healthy faith in biblical stories. Rav Kook considers that the ability to accept certain critical theories is grounded epistemologically in an unbalanced personality. A natural balance of all the forces would make it impossible for someone to accept a view that is belied from within a healthy, harmonious, and integrated view of reality. The following passage echoes once again the theory of five forces. However, it takes it in an unexpected direction that may shed further light upon the theory itself.

> Know and recognize that the power of understanding, the imagining of the critical mind,[48] can only proceed along its path to know truth, especially the truth that bridges the present to the past in this direction and to the future in this direction, when it has available to it all the forces required for the completion[49] of its images: health of the senses, fullness of feelings, sensitivity of spirit, and pure will.[50] The entirety,[51] the entire heart, all of life, must be attuned to provide the critical mind the wherewithal[52] for its judgment,[53] as true witnesses that support the throne of its judgment. Then will understanding be whole understanding, so that he may see with his eyes and hear with his ears, and his heart will understand, and he will return and be healed.[54] How-

48. Hebrew: *Shofet,* judging. Could also be "discerning."
49. Or: fulfillment, perfection.
50. Possibly: desire.
51. Or: the collectivity.
52. Literally: material.
53. Or: discernment.
54. Isa 6:10.

ever when will this be? Only when all five lights serve as one integrated light:[55] the health of body and soul; full force for righteousness and human justice; a living, awakened, and developed religious sentiment; a strong and healthy national sentiment; and above all the development of the mind that comes from the joining of the seeking[56] of the Torah in its practical and theoretical aspect together with the knowledge of the world and life and all the streams of inclinations[57] as is appropriate for an educated person who loves wisdom and knowledge. Only by an appropriate balance and complementary harmony of these healthy and fresh forces that construct matter and spirit together will there arise a generation full of courage, living a full life, a life of strength and power in the exaltedness of the name of God, the Lord of Israel.

And towards these quests[58] together we must fortify our forces and aspirations so that we attain them, because only then will we feel that we are turning towards God, and that we are aspiring to the goal that has been prepared from us from the beginning, from the lofty foundations, from the days of the youth of our people, when we came out of Egypt. Therefore, brothers, let us labor together the labor of our people. Let us all know that we must increase and not detract, build and not destroy. Let us feel, every one in himself, and every party as a whole, what it has that is of additional value in relation to the rest of our people, so that it can proffer of its talent upon those who are lower than it in its particular aspect.[59] At the same time, let it not forget also the quality of humility, to know what it lacks, so that it may aspire to become whole[60] by means of the influence of another party upon it.

Here the theory of five forces functions not simply as an ideal of human flourishing but also as a basis for a critical epistemology. The different forces provide the background for the critical mind, echoing what seems to be the primacy of the mental faculty within the five forces, as noted in the sequence of the list in chapter 24. Thus, harmony of all forces is a condition

55. Hebrew: *avuka*, a candle made of multiple wicks that join to a larger light.

56. Also: study or quest.

57. I understand by this inclinations to learn and understand reality, through a natural curiosity, even independently of systematized study of sciences.

58. Literally: requests, desiderata.

59. Literally: occupation or angle.

60. Or: perfected.

for proper knowledge. Absent such harmony, the mind is unstable and can be led to false conclusions.

The final part of the quote is a call to all parties within the Jewish people of his time to work together. Each party has what to give the other and they must join forces, proffering upon one another, in all humility, their special gifts.

This introduction then leads Rav Kook to a lengthy discussion of reconciling religious and theological differences. The example he offers is that of the conflict between hasidim and their opponents, a conflict that can be reconciled from the present vantage point. Rav Kook develops a religiously based theory of tolerance. According to this theory, which is representative of his lifelong quest for religious, spiritual, and social unity and integration, conflicting opinions and perspectives are partial and complementary visions of reality. Reconciling them in harmony provides us with access to a fuller vision of truth. The theory of harmony is thus extended from harmony between a person's different forces to harmony between conflicting opinions.

The thematic unfolding of the chapter is, then, the following. Following a debate with critical views of the Bible that are seen as signs of personal and epistemological imbalance, Rav Kook reiterates the need for harmony between forces. This, in turn, leads him to a discussion of harmony between conflicting legitimate opinions, which are to be reconciled within a broader theory of religious tolerance, based on a vision of inclusiveness and harmony that accommodates all.

The flow of the chapter gives pause for thought. There is obviously a difference between the first part and the latter in terms of Rav Kook's willingness to apply an accommodating perspective and a theory of tolerance. Critical views of the Bible are a sign of personal disharmony, not complementary expressions of a truth that have to be reconciled. One wonders whether a century later one might be able to incorporate such critical approaches within the same harmonious attitude that Rav Kook is willing to extend to internal Jewish divergences of spiritual path and practice. Some more recent rabbinic voices are willing to make that move.[61]

What is the meaning of moving from a discussion of the harmony of five forces to harmony of conflicting religious perspectives? One possible answer is that the harmony between these forces allows one to bridge differences between different legitimate religious paths. Epistemological correctness, based on harmonious flourishing of the different forces, opens one up to being able to recognize how divergent religious views are part of a

---

61. Notably Rabbi Mordechai Breuer. See Carmy, "Concepts of Scripture."

larger whole. Surely Rav Kook can be seen as an instance of someone who would have considered himself to have attained harmony of the five forces and who also practices harmonious reconciliation of conflicting legitimate religious world-views.

There is another way of understanding the sequence. We have here a move from harmony between a person's, or a community's, forces to harmony of ideas and religious tolerance. As we saw above, the practice of harmony brings to light the fundamental unity of being, grounded in the reality of the divine, which is made manifest through these different powers. The same may be true of diverging religious paths. Given the all-encompassing unity of the divine, the different religious approaches are harmonized and reconciled in the greater whole, emerging from the full knowledge of God. In this reading, a theory of tolerance is grounded in the divine being, source of harmony. The divine vision allows one to accommodate differences and to harmonize them through a vision that is grounded in the harmony of the one divine being, manifesting in the diversity of human and communal forces, as well as of different religious views. Both are reconciled through the harmony grounded in God's very being.

This leads us back to the question of limits of harmonization. The chapter opens with a very unharmonious treatment of biblical criticism, treated as a malady, a sign of personal, mental, and spiritual imbalance. It continues in a movement of great harmonious reconciling of different religious schools. Within this dual perspective, where might one situate the present-day dialogue between religions? Would a view of another religion be closer to that of biblical criticism or to legitimate religious diversity? Does a divinely rooted tolerance allow us to recognize in the theory of harmony of religious forces, which is really an expression of divine harmony, also a mandate for harmony of world-views of different religions? If so, then Rav Kook's theory of forces points us to a more fundamental ground of harmony that has huge implications both for a view of flourishing and for a view of dialogue between religions. Flourishing is to recognize how ultimately divine reality invites us to reconciliation, harmony, and tolerance.[62] In terms

---

62. One should recall that Rav Kook's theory of five forces, in and of itself, is universal and does not make a distinction between Judaism and other religions. In fact, even when speaking of the religious sentiment, Rav Kook makes no mention of religions as such. The criteria and view of flourishing are identical across religions. Even the later theory of four spirits leaves little room for religious difference. The earlier 1910 articulation makes no reference to religions. Only the later essay of 1933 refers to religions. "The spirit of faith is manifested in the foundations of religions, according to their distinctive characteristics" (102). Though acknowledging some difference, all religions are treated as equivalent and equally valid expressions of the spirit of faith. While Rav Kook does provide us with a theory of flourishing, it is based on fundamental commonality

of interreligious dialogue, when practiced at its best, grounded in an integrated personality, in light of the five forces and their integration, it would be a further expression of the recognition of the profound unity of all paths, grounded in divine unity and harmony.

I believe Rav Kook not only offers us the possibility of constructing such a view of interreligious dialogue, stretching the boundaries of tolerance to other religions. He also carries such a program out in this work. *To the Perplexed of the Generation* features some of the most radical and open views of other religions in the history of Jewish literature. As noted, these may be more radical than some later expressions of Rav Kook's thought. While not developing a full pluralist view of other religions, Rav Kook goes extremely far in validating all forms of religion, finding positive dimensions even in idolatry, let alone in religions that know the one God and spring from Judaism. It seems to me that Rav Kook's openness in this work may be closely related to the broader view of truth, its unity and harmony. If so, the theory of five forces and their harmony, as a program for human flourishing, is but one expression of a broader theory, which has direct consequences also for relations between religions. It is a theory of tolerance that is much more than simple tolerance of the being of other religions, and it is founded upon recognition of their place in the greater divine economy, grounded in divine unity and omnipresence.

I am deeply moved by how what started out as an exercise in understanding a text on a Jewish view of flourishing, presented in honor of Miroslav, ended up pointing us to the core concerns that have been shared by Miroslav and myself, concerns that seek to affirm the deeper bonds and unity behind our different religions.

---

and does not permit us to propose flourishing as a lens through which we might approach religious difference. The present argument extends internal religious diversity to diversity between religions and seeks to view both in light of the theory of five forces. The proposed theory of tolerance and accommodation would account for why religious difference does not feature in the theory of five forces. The 1933 article might, nevertheless, recognize a difference between Judaism, or Torah, and other religions. It is Torah that helps lift the four spirits, and by implication other religions, to their higher goal. If so, the later essay may be described as taking an inclusivist view of other religions, while the earlier statements are pluralist, inasmuch as they minimize religious difference and emphasize fundamental commonalities of spirit. Recognition that other religions lead to the flourishing of their followers can be justified on both pluralist and inclusivist grounds. The theory of five senses does not allow us to propose "flourishing" as a means of sidestepping issues of religious truth. The fifth force assumes commonality in the attainment of knowledge of God and its related truth value.

BIBLIOGRAPHY

Carmy, Shalom. "Concepts of Scripture in Mordechai Breuer." In *Jewish Concepts of Scripture: A Comparative Introduction*, edited by Ben Sommer, 267–79. New York: New York University Press, 2012.

Kook, Rav Avraham Yitzchak Hacohen. *To the Perplexed of the Generation.* Edited by Shahar Rahmani. Tel Avid: Yediot, 2014 [Hebrew].

6

Divine Beauty and Human Flourishing

Reflections on
Miroslav Volf's Vision of the Good Life

Reza Shah-Kazemi

IN THE EPILOGUE TO his latest work, *Flourishing: Why We Need Religion in a Globalized World*, Miroslav Volf outlines a vision of human flourishing based on Christ's two great commandments: "Love the Lord your God with all your heart and with all your soul and with all your mind," and, "Love your neighbor as yourself" (Matthew 22:37–39 NIV; based on Deut 6:5 and Lev 19:18). The vision he shares with us is indeed beautiful and inspiring. After asking us to adopt these two golden rules for ourselves, he proceeds with a globalization of the kind of world we would inhabit if all people did the same:

> Spread wide and boldly the wings of your fancy, and imagine that all your neighbors do the same, which is, of course, exactly how Christians have for centuries imagined the world to come—as the world of love. Each thing in the world is now a relationship marked by love. Each distant star and every gentle touch, each face and every whiff of the freshly plowed earth,

102

in sum, literally every good and beautiful thing shimmers with an aura both vibrantly real and undetectable to our five senses. Each thing in the world is more than itself and just so a source of deep and many-layered pleasure.[1]

With this vision in the back of my mind, I made the following notes on a two-day trip to Paris with my wife, visiting some of the most inspiring sacred places in Europe. After transcribing, annotating, and slightly editing these brief notes in the first part of this essay, I will offer in part 2 some more considered reflections on the theme of divine beauty in relation to prayer and virtue, the foundations for human flourishing, basing myself on mystical perspectives found within Islam and Christianity.

I. PARISIAN REFLECTIONS

April 4th 2016: La Sainte Chapelle

"God is the Light of the Heavens and the earth" (24:35).[2] These are the words of the Qur'an which come to my mind as I sit here in the Sainte Chapelle in Paris, the rays of the late afternoon sun streaming in through the western window of this spectacular testimony to the "good life," such as it was conceived by Latin Christendom in all its glory. The question I ask myself is this: am I, as a Muslim, capable of fully sharing this Christian vision of human flourishing, or am I compelled to "appropriate" the unsurpassable beauty of this place and "domesticate" it, by stripping it of its specifically and exclusively Christian content, and just marvelling at its beauty, meditating on the Qur'anic verse of light and repeating the words of the Prophet Muhammad: "God is beautiful and He loves beauty"?[3]

For a Muslim, or any non-Christian, there is certainly nothing wrong with this way of appreciating the beauty of the Sainte Chapelle; indeed, for most Muslims, this would be the only acceptable way of doing so: seeing the Face of God that is everywhere (2:115), but seeing it with particular brilliance through the art of the stained glass windows.[4] However, abstracting

---

1. Volf, *Flourishing*, 204–5.

2. All translations of the Qur'an are my own, based substantially upon the translation of M. M. Pickthall. [Throughout this essay, parenthetical citations with just chapter and verse are from the Qur'an.—Eds.]

3. We shall return to this fundamental saying in the second part of this paper.

4. Writing of the Sainte Chapelle, Jean Hani remarks, in his magnificent work, *Le Symbolisme du Temple Chrétien*: "This is the epoch when Hugo of St Victor and Suger said that the House of God must be illuminated, brilliant like Paradise. . . . In this perspective, perfectly in harmony with Scripture, God is Light; essential beauty is identified with Clarity which, with harmony and rhythm, reflects the divine Beauty"

from this beauty all of the Christian theology embedded within it, together with the conception of sacred history portrayed in the windows, must appear, to the Christian, as missing the entire point of the sacred art of this temple. The beauty of the place is there, the Christian may protest, precisely to adorn the truth of the message revealed by the narratives of the Bible depicted in the 1,113 stained glass windows.

The problem here touches on themes germane to Miroslav's quest for a vision of human flourishing, a vision that is at one and the same time rooted in a Christian philosophy of the good life, and yet appealing and attractive to all human beings in our contemporary globalized context. If we compare the vision of human flourishing given by the Sainte Chapelle with the vision adumbrated by Miroslav—the latter being distilled in the two "Great Commandments"—there appears to be a chasm separating the two. They may both be visions of beauty within a Christian context, but the one is saturated with quasi-exclusive Christian symbolism—fully intelligible only within a worldview utterly dominated by Christian dogma; while the other is rendered intelligible to all, but, it would seem, only at the price of a dilution of the richness, depth, and totality of the all-encompassing Christo-centric vision proper not just to medieval Christendom but also traditional Christianity.

April 5th, 2pm: Chapel of Our Lady of the Miraculous Medal

I am now sitting in the Chapel, having recited the *Fatiha*[5] at the side of the immaculately preserved body of St. Catherine Labouré. Herein, perhaps, lies one possible solution to the "problem" touched on yesterday at the Sainte Chapelle. However great be the theological differences between Muslims and Christians, blessings remain blessings, prayer remains prayer, grace remains always grace. If ever one needed an illustration of the meaning of human "flourishing," surely it is here: the body of a saint, found perfectly intact over half a century after her death, a physical sign of the eternal life awaiting the celestially embodied souls of the saved. Just as St. Catherine's body was "immortalized" by the power of grace—bestowed through her visions of the Blessed Virgin—so, it is to that same grace that we, as Muslims, have recourse when we recite the *Fatiha* "for" St. Catherine, but in reality

---

(143–44).

    5. This is the opening chapter of the Qur'an, consisting of seven verses, recited as an essential part of the canonical daily prayers. It is the central prayer of Islam, and thus the prayer most commonly recited for the deceased. See my *Spiritual Quest*, 15–40, for a translation and some reflections on the meanings of the verses of this prayer.

for ourselves: "Guide *us* along the Straight Path," we say, at the heart of this prayer. What is this Path, how is it described? "The Path of those whom Thou hast graced."

April 5th, 4:30pm: The Great Mosque

Completing the earlier reflection—now seated in the peaceful garden of this jewel of Islamic architecture, having performed my afternoon prayers—the birds chirping; the spring sun shining; smiling, appreciative visitors strolling through the garden, taking in its beauty and serenity: the verse which now comes to mind, linking the serenity of the mosque to the sanctity of St. Catherine, is this: "Whatever good thing ye have is from God" (16:53). The rather weak "good thing" translates the word *ni'ma* in Arabic, to which the word "yes," *na'am*, is related. It is most often translated simply as "grace" or "blessing," since all good things—according to this verse, and to Muslim spiritual sensibility—come from God as *al-Mun'im*, "bestower of grace." So closely associated are the notions of goodness and grace in the soul of the Muslim that no good thing, on any level, is perceived or experienced without seeing therein the trace of divine grace. As St. Ambrose said: "All that is true, by whomsoever it has been said, has its origin in the Spirit."[6] Muslim sensibility resonates deeply with this point of view, so much so that one might almost paraphrase this sentence as follows: wherever you find goodness—in whatever religion—it has its origin in God.

We return to the *Fatiha*, where as we noted earlier, the essence of the prayer is the supplication to be guided along the Straight Path, the Path of those "whom Thou hast graced." Most unfortunately, some Muslim exegetes interpret this category to be the path taken by Muslims, in contrast to that of "those upon whom is wrath"—glossed as "the path taken by Jews"; and in contrast to that of "those who stray"—glossed as "the path taken by Christians." Such an interpretation, however, flies in the face of the universal, supra-confessional conception of divine grace by which the message of the Qur'an is penetrated. To cite just a single verse in which the Straight Path is alluded to through mention of the categories of those "graced" by God: ". . . those whom God hath graced, among the prophets, the saints, the martyrs and the righteous—and what beautiful companions they are!" (4:69). There is no question here of any religiously defined boundaries in this all-encompassing evocation of those graced by God and thereby traversing the Straight Path. To look at the "prophets" (*al-nabiyyun*) alone: in addition to the twenty-five prophets named in the Qur'an itself, the

6. Cited by Coomaraswamy, *Figures of Speech or Figures of Thought?*, 27.

Prophet Muhammad tells us that God has sent one hundred and twenty-four thousand prophets to mankind. How many more must there be among the saints, the martyrs, the righteous—of *all* traditions? When asked which religion God loved most, the Prophet refused to name one religion to the exclusion of all others, and instead referred to a spiritual quality: "the primordial, generously tolerant faith," *al-hanifiyya al-samha*.[7]

The word *hanifiyya* can be translated also as "original monotheism," the *hanif* par excellence being the patriarch Abraham, who exemplifies primordial human nature, *al-fitrah*, the two notions coming together in a crucial verse alluding to the immutability and incorruptibility of human nature as the quintessence or infrastructure of religious consciousness: "So set thy purpose for religion as one by nature upright [*hanifan*]: the primordial nature [*fitrah*] established by God, according to which He created mankind. There is no changing the creation of God. That is the eternally ordained religion, but most people know not" (30:30). According to the Prophet, then, what makes a religion lovable to God is its capacity to generate in the souls of its adherents this spiritual quality which brings to fruition the potentialities implanted in the heart of every human being. This spiritual quality, *al-hanifiyya*, or Abrahamic monotheism, on the one hand, and *samha*, generous tolerance, on the other, synthesizes the Two Great Commandments at the heart of Miroslav's vision of the good life (and at the heart of the initiative, *A Common Word*, let it be noted).[8] Being an Abrahamic *hanif* implies unswerving love of God; and being generously tolerant implies love of the neighbor as oneself.

April 5th, 8:15pm: Notre Dame Cathedral

Omnia cum Domino dona redisse suo.

"Everything that comes from the Lord must go back to the Lord"— reads the translation in the programme for *Resurrectio: Chant grégorien*.

In fifteen minutes we will be listening to some of the most "enchanting"—in the literal sense—music on earth: Gregorian chants celebrating Easter. The Latin verse written above comes close to the end of the printed text of the programme. As my wife and I prepare for this spiritual feast, we are both struck by the number of phrases that echo Qur'anic formulae. But it is not only on account of these felicitous coincidences that we are already bursting with the spiritual joy of anticipation of the celestial harmonies by

7. *Sahih al-Bukhari: Arabic-English*, 1:34 (translation modified).

8. Arguably the most successful interfaith initiative in history. See www.acommonword.com.

which we are about to be regaled. Nor do we have any need to bracket out our "Muslim" beliefs temporarily (through a kind of "suspension of belief" rather than of "disbelief") in order to enter fully into the spirit of the sacred music. Rather, it is because of our concrete sense of the sacred that we are ready to be inspired, unreservedly and unconditionally, by the sacred substance of the music which, coming from God, leads back to God, as the Latin verse puts it; and as it is expressed, in a slightly different form, both in the Qur'anic verse which came to us this afternoon at the mosque: every good thing/grace is from God; and in the all-embracing truth expressed in this Qur'anic sentence: "We belong to God and we are ever returning to Him" (2:156).

II. DIVINE BEAUTY AND HUMAN VIRTUE: FOUNDATIONS OF FLOURISHING

In the Muslim call to prayer (*adhan*), we hear the following exhortations: "Hasten to prayer! Hasten to flourishing!" (*hayya 'ala'l-salah, hayya 'ala'l-falah*). The Arabic *falah* is most often translated as "prosperity" or "success." But these words do not do justice to the root-meaning, *f-l-h*, which means to cultivate, to plow or till the land. Thus, a farmer is a *falah*. The English "flourishing," itself etymologically rooted in the idea of something coming to "flower," is, I would argue, a better translation of *falah* than "prosperity/ success." The call to prayer invites us to come and perform the act which most effectively implants the seeds of our salvation in the Hereafter and waters the seeds of our sanctification in the here-below; the notion of "flourishing" embraces both kinds of fruition, so it appears to me as the most appropriate translation of *falah*.[9]

If we were to be asked what the connection is between prayer and flourishing, we would answer: divine beauty. In prayer—not just petitionary prayer, but also canonical prayer, meditative prayer, and, most especially, contemplative prayer, or invocation of the Name of God—we commune with the very substance of divinity, and this substance is infinitely beautiful.[10] The Prophet said, as mentioned above, "Verily, God is beautiful and He loves beauty."[11] Now, what God loves, He transforms and, in a mysterious

9. As it does to Nicholas Starkovsky, *Koran Handbook*, 153.

10. We totally agree, therefore, with Dostoyevsky's famous assertion, through Prince Myshkin, in *The Idiot*: "Beauty will save the world," if this beauty is seen as the substance of prayer, the link between the human and the divine.

11. *Sahih Muslim*, 1:53, saying no. 275. *Encyclopaedia of Hadith*. The saying is also found in the collections of al-Tirmidhi and Ahmad b. Hanbal.

sense, becomes. A mode of union (*tawhid,* in the literal sense of this verbal noun: "making one") is consummated between God as the Lover and His devotee as the beloved. This idea is stated in the following "holy utterance" (*hadith qudsi*), in which God speaks in the first person, through the tongue of the Prophet:

> My slave draws close to Me by nothing which I love more than that which I have made incumbent upon him [i.e., the obligatory rites]. My slave never ceases to draw near to Me through voluntary acts of devotion until I love him. And when I love him, I become his hearing by which he hears, his sight by which he sees, his hand by which he strikes, and his foot by which he walks.[12]

This saying, strongly authenticated in the Muslim tradition of hadith, describes a truly miraculous transformation: divine plenitude, source of all human flourishing, radiates through the devotee sanctified by divine love. "Slavehood," symbol of absolute humility and sincere self-effacement, becomes a transparent veil through which the light of the divine shines, giving life, light, and love to all that which it touches. The slave thus transfigured becomes a "friend of God" (*wali Allah*), a saint, reference to whom introduces this crucial saying in Islamic spirituality.

There is nothing mechanical about this transformation—no implication that mere performance of the canonical and voluntary prayers suffices to bring about this sanctification. For the Prophet made it clear that nobody enters Paradise on account of their deeds; it is solely through the grace of God that one enters Paradise.[13] The same applies to sanctification, that is, living in a paradisial manner already here on earth. No amount of action suffices; it is grace or, in the words of the *hadith qudsi,* love, which alone brings about this transformation. But since God is beautiful and He loves beauty, His love cannot but be attracted to a beautiful soul. One can therefore say that it is the magnetic beauty radiating from total, sincere, heartfelt prayer that attracts the divine love which transforms and sanctifies the soul. Herein lies a key to realizing that kind of human "flourishing" which is properly spiritual and not secretly materialistic. For, without this divine life, light, and love—and without the human poverty or transparency which predisposes the soul thereto—all talk of human "flourishing" is but a secular façade behind which human misery hides its shame. In such a context, the grace, or *ni'ma,* referred to above (16:53), which every good thing objectively constitutes by its very nature—"whatever *ni'ma* [good thing/grace] you

12. *Sahih al-Bukhari* (Summarized), 992, saying no. 2117 (translation modified).
13. There are various versions of this saying, in sources such as al-Bukhari.

have is from God"—this good thing embodying and expressing divine grace is subjectively stripped of its divine content. All that remains is a caricature: *na'ma* instead of *ni'ma*, that is, materialistic ease and indulgence, instead of the truly "good life," which is by definition a grace from God.

The Qur'an censures those who seek the *na'ma* of good things for their own sake (instead of being grateful for good things as so many gifts of *ni'ma* from God) as follows: "Leave Me [to deal] with the deniers, those of [i.e., those attached to] ease and comfort, and bear with them for a while" (73:11).[14] Therefore, any quest for the "good life" apart from God is, implicitly, a denial of God; and to deny God is to deprive oneself of the very essence of the "good life."

By contrast, when the quest for flourishing is motivated by the desire to give oneself to God as a pure slave, possessing nothing of one's own, seeking nothing for oneself, placing one's entire will and life at the disposal of God—then, whatever comes to the soul is assimilated as a mode of "flourishing," even if outward life be dominated by suffering. This self-emptying for the sake of God—or *vacare Deo*—defines the very essence of Sufism, insofar as the latter is identified with poverty (*faqr*), and consummated in "extinction" (*fana'*), which is the condition *sine qua non* for "subsistence" (*baqa'*): subsistence in God coming after extinction from self. To be filled with the plenitude of the presence of God presupposes a prior emptiness of self: it is this emptiness that makes one a Sufi or more literally, a *faqir*, one is "poor," aware of being permanently or ontologically in need of God. In the measure that one is a *faqir*, ever open to the graces of extinction from self and subsistence in and through God, one will flourish. The greater the spiritual poverty, the deeper the inward flourishing, whatever be the outward circumstances of one's existence.

In terms of the notion of flourishing, we can distinguish between three types, basing ourselves on criteria proper to Sufism (and, as we shall see in a moment, Eckhartian metaphysics). First, the category of those who believe that "flourishing" is all about material prosperity and comfort. They will find all talk about divine beauty, love, and beatitude as irrelevant: a waste of time and a diversion from the concrete requirements of human happiness. Then comes the category of believer who has spiritual aspirations, but these aspirations and ideals are accompanied by subtle worldliness. Piety may well characterize the soul, but flourishing and happiness will be *de*

---

14. This perspective, reminiscent of the Buddha's warning of the suffering (*dukha*) that inevitably follows any attachment to the impermanent (*anicca*), is also expressed at Q 100:8, where we read this censure of those who love good things, without being grateful to God: "Truly the human being is ungrateful; and he indeed is witness to that; and he is truly intense in his love of good."

facto dependent upon a worldly well-being: a "flourishing" according to the spirit, in principle, but according to the flesh, in practice. Finally comes the category of those whose well-being, whose "flourishing," is permanent, however much hardship they may be outwardly experiencing.

The difference between the latter two types of believer is made clear in the following exegesis of a Qur'anic passage by 'Abd al-Razzaq Kashani (d. 1330), one of the most important mystical commentators of the Qur'an. At Q 76:5–6, we read about a celestial fountain, named Kafur, from which the "slaves of God" drink, and the more they drink, the more copiously it flows. Kashani tells us that they make the fountain flow because, in essence, they are one with that fountain, having been liberated from their egos, their sense of separate selfhood, whence their designation as "slaves." They are one with the fountain of Paradise because they are one with Paradise, the divine life pulsating through their individual beings, according to the principle of subsistence (*baqa'*). The pious (*al-abrar*), are also said to drink from the fountain, but not directly: they drink from a cup whose liquid is only "flavoured" by the wine of Kafur. Why is it that the "slaves" are allowed to drink the flowing wine, undiluted, from the fountain itself, whilst the pious only drink from a cup of diluted wine?

Kashani's explanation reveals the distinction between a type of flourishing that flows permanently for the highest category of saints, permanently contemplating divine Beauty, and the type of flourishing that is *de facto* dependent upon the vagaries of phenomenal experience. The slaves of God, he writes, do not distinguish between such existential contrasts as "constraint and loving-kindness, pity and harshness, trial, destitution and prosperity." This is because "their love abideth in the face of opposites, and their delights continue amid graces and afflictions, mercy and oppression." As for the righteous, "though they love the Grace-Giver [*al-Mun'im*] and the Loving-Kind [*al-Latif*] and the Merciful [*al-Rahim*], yet at the manifestation of the Constrainer [*al-Qahhar*] and the Trier [*al-Mubli*] and the Avenger [*al-Muntaqim*], their love abideth not at all, and their delight is changed into revulsion."[15]

The "slaves" are those saints, in other words, who inwardly enjoy the beatific vision even while outwardly experiencing hardship. This perspective is concretely expressed by Zaynab, sister of Husayn b. 'Ali, martyred with seventy-two of his companions on the plain of Karbala in the year 680, in her famous utterance: "I saw nothing [at Karbala] except Beauty."[16] Having

---

15. Abu Bakr Siraj ad-Din, *The Book of Certainty,* 86. See, for the Arabic text, *Tafsir Ibn 'Arabi,* 2:360, on 76:5–6. The commentary is erroneously ascribed to Ibn 'Arabi, but was in fact written by 'Abd al-Razzaq Kashani.

16. Cited in Amuli, *Hamasah wa 'irfan,* 256. In similar vein, the father of Zaynab

such a metaphysical perspective is only possible as a result of divine vision replacing human vision, the saint seeing all things *sub specie aeternitatis*, God having "become" their seeing and their hearing. They have realized this spiritual rank through the "voluntary acts of devotion" which open them up to the miraculously transformative love of God. Since God creates through love,[17] all subsequent bestowals of love are to be interpreted according to the principle expressed in the verse of light (24:35); that is, "light upon light" implies "love upon love." According to a metaphysical interpretation of this *hadith qudsi*, the change of state in question pertains not to God—who, in objective reality, is the true, unique agent in all acts, and who is eternally radiating with love. Rather, it is the devotee whose state of consciousness is changed. By virtue of his ever deepening love, sincerity, and devotion— manifested by total dedication to prayer (over and above the obligatory, canonical requirements)—the veil of egotism is either lifted or gradually rendered transparent, that veil which had hitherto obscured the reality that God is eternally bestowing love, on the one hand, and is the eternally real, sole agent who acts, sees, and hears through all human beings, on the other. This perspective helps us to understand the esoteric meaning of the following highly paradoxical verse of the Qur'an: "Nothing is like Him; and He is the Hearing, the Seeing" (42:11). If we hear and see, are we not like Him? No, because He alone possesses the ontological substance of the faculties of hearing and seeing; in Sufi spirituality, all acts of human perception are seen as "metaphorical" (*majazi*), whilst divine consciousness is, alone, "real" (*haqiqi*).

This possibility of permanently enjoying a vision of divine felicity, even amidst outward suffering, opens up to a way of flourishing which is scarcely conceivable in our materialistic age. But it is an ideal whose influence is detectable among pious Muslims, and not just among the mystics. Most pious Muslims intone the Qur'anic prayer: "Our Lord, give us good [or beauty: *hasana*] in the world, and good in the Hereafter" (2:201), seeking to "flourish" in this world in the way that is normally understood from the notion of prosperity. But the more spiritually sensitive are at the same time aware of the higher ideal of experiencing a purely inward, spiritual sense of well-being, and possibly of "flourishing," despite outward hardship—even if this is only an ideal to which they aspire, rather than a spiritual condition characterizing their actual state. For traditional Christians, such an ideal

---

and Husayn, Imam 'Ali, some twenty years earlier, when hearing of the name of Karbala as he and his army were marching past it, said prophetically: "This is the plain of the lovers and the witnesses/martyrs ('*ushshaq* and *shuhada*')." Cited in ibid., 229.

17. According to the teachings of the Qur'an, as HRH Prince Ghazi bin Muhammad has comprehensively proved in his *Love in the Holy Qur'an*.

was so self-evident that it hardly needed to be stated. One only has to think of the early martyrs laughing at their Roman executioners before being killed. Such was the degree of certainty of eternal joy in the Hereafter that no amount of suffering here-below could detract from the consolation, and indeed laughter-producing happiness, bestowed on the soul by the spiritual anticipation of heavenly beatitude.

Meister Eckhart helps us to see how this inward state of beatitude can co-exist with outward suffering. Let us start with his astonishing interpretation of Jesus's words: "My soul is exceeding sorrowful, even unto death" (Matt 26:38 KJV):

> He did not mean his noble soul according as this is intellectually contemplating the highest good, with which he is united in person, and which he is according to union and person: that, even in his greatest suffering, he was continually regarding in his highest power, just as closely and entirely the same as he does now: no sorrow or pain or death could penetrate there.[18]

Eckhart says that the Blessed Virgin also—and indeed any "just" person—is capable of enjoying an inner vision of beatitude even while outwardly being subjected to suffering: he compares the "inner man," immutably fixed in contemplative felicity, to the hinge of a door; the "outer man," subject to suffering, is like the actual door itself. The door may swing this way and that, but the hinge is immobile. If one discovers this inner self, then there is nothing in existence but happiness. One is reminded of Kashani's descriptions of the slaves of God when Eckhart writes:

> Now observe what an amazing and blissful life this man must lead "in earth as in heaven"—in God Himself! Discomfort serves him as comfort, grief as well as joy—for if I have the grace and goodness of which I have spoken, then I am at all times and in all ways equally comforted and happy; and if I lack it then I shall do without it, for God's sake and by God's will.[19]

To enter into this perpetual inner joy, fruit of absolute submission to God's will, one needs to discover that "power" within the soul, the intellect, which is "neither created nor creatable": "There is one power in the soul to which all things are alike sweet: the very worst and the very best are all the same to this power, which takes things above 'here' and 'now': now meaning time, and here the place where I am standing."[20]

18. Eckhart, *Meister Eckhart*, 2:291.

19. Ibid., 3:71.

20. Ibid., 2:237.

Returning to the transformative love of God in Islamic spirituality, the key element in both the obligatory and voluntary acts of devotion—referred to above in terms of the divine utterance (*hadith qudsi*) so crucial to Sufi thought and praxis—is the revealed Word of God, whether in diversified form, as the Qur'an, or in essentialized form, as one of the Names of God. This revealed Word, according to Titus Burckhardt, "reverberates in the musical order, and this is most assuredly the firmest possible link between rite and art."[21] To recite holy scripture and to invoke the Name of God is thus to perform a sacred art, it is to open oneself up to infinite beauty, source of virtue and hence of the good life and human flourishing. As Ananda Coomaraswamy writes so perceptively: "Every mimetic rite is by nature a work of art; in the traditional philosophy of art the artist's operation is also always a rite, and thus essentially a religious activity."[22] Similarly, Martin Lings refers to the rites of religion as "symbolic acts or enacted symbols," and describes them as being "providentially endowed with wings for return to their Source, wings which the performer of the rite acquires by identifying himself with the act in question."[23]

The Revelation constituted by Divine Speech (*kalam Allah*) can be seen as the archetype of all musicality. So the recited Revelation—*al-Qur'an* in the literal sense: the recitation—is one of the most tangible and transformative modes of beauty in creation, being a crystallization of supra-formal, celestial melodies within the field of audible, terrestrial sound. The Shaykh al-'Alawi (d. 1934), makes a remark that is most pertinent here: "Music is not crippled with the dry bones of words. Liquid and flowing like a stream, it carries us into the Presence of God."[24] This in turn might be seen as a comment on the saying of the Prophet: amongst the greatest of the beauties of creation is "the fine intonation of a beautiful voice."[25] One can well imagine how much the Prophet would have appreciated the sacred harmonies of Gregorian chant, referred to above in our Parisian reflections. One is also reminded here of the view of St. Dionysius the Areopagite, expressing the interiorizing power of beauty:

> The super-essential Beautiful is called Beauty because of the beauty communicated by It to all beautiful things in accordance with their nature, and because It is the cause of the harmony and splendour in all things, flashing forth upon them like light,

21. Burckhardt, *Art of Islam*, 83.

22. Coomaraswamy, *Christian and Oriental Philosophy of Art*, 57.

23. Lings, *Symbol and Archetype*, 10.

24. Lings, *A Sufi Saint*, 115.

25. See for discussion Shah-Kazemi, *Spiritual Quest*, 6–8.

the beautifying beams of Its fontal Ray; and It calls all things to
Itself, whence It is also named Beauty, and It gathers all in all in
Itself.[26]

The Sufi would recognize here the power of *tawhid*, "making one,"
as the supreme function of divine beauty. Beauty unites within itself every
thing that is consistent with its own nature in the measure that the thing
opens itself up to the divine source of beauty. Ananda Coomaraswamy
demonstrates brilliantly how this unifying, interiorizing power of beauty
was perceived as such in all the sacred traditions of the world. For all these
traditions, "beauty has to do with knowledge and goodness, of which it is
precisely the attractive aspect";[27] "Beauty is . . . perfection apprehended as
an attractive power; that aspect of the Truth, for example, which moves the
will to grapple with the theme to be communicated. . . . Beauty adds to the
Good an ordering to the cognitive faculty, by which the Good is known as
such; beauty has to do with cognition."[28]

The Qur'an is not only sacred music revealing the beauty of God; it is
also a divine message disclosing the fact that the beauty of God is ubiqui-
tous, or rather, inescapable: "Everywhere you turn, there is the Face of God"
(2:115). Given that God "is beautiful and He loves beauty," the Face of God
that is there, wherever one looks, must be infinitely beautiful. This implies
that the whole of creation is beautiful, the whole of existence being a kaleidoscopic, perpetual, and universal disclosure of the beauty of God's "Face."
This is precisely why we find the Qur'an telling us: "He made beautiful everything that He created" (32:7). The phrase "made beautiful" translates the
Arabic *ahsana*, the root meaning of which, *hasuna*, denotes being in a state
of beauty, primarily, and then, by extension, being in a state of goodness,
virtue or excellence. It is therefore not surprising to find that the notions
of beauty and virtue are inseparable in Islamic sensibility. The *muhsin* is
the good or virtuous person, but also, and more fundamentally (and more
correctly, in strictly grammatical terms), "the one who makes beautiful" his
or her character. In the light of this relationship between beauty and virtue,
on the one hand, and the principle expressed in the hadith, "God is beautiful
and He loves beauty," on the other, we can see more clearly the profound
ethical as well as spiritual repercussions of the Sufi principle of *ta'alluh*, dei-
fication or theosis.

The Sufis use the following hadith as one of the foundations of their
spiritual method in this regard: "Adorn yourselves with the character-traits

26. Dionysius, *Divine Names*, 34–35.

27. Coomaraswamy, *Christian and Oriental Philosophy of Art*, 17.

28. Ibid., 77.

[*akhlaq*] of God."[29] The divine traits of character are expressed through the "Names" of God, such as the Merciful, the Loving, the Wise, etc. But there are also such Names—as cited above by Kashani—as the Avenger. Does the Sufi adorn himself with these names of wrath also? Yes and no. Yes, in terms of spiritual combat; that is, insofar as the qualities designated by these Names oppose and overcome the vices and faults of the Sufi's own soul. But no, in terms of ontological substance, for such attributes connected with wrath are described as "accidental," therefore unreal, in relation to those which pertain to mercy, love, and compassion, these latter being substantial, disclosing the intrinsic nature of the Real. In one of his many commentaries on the hadith, "My Mercy takes precedence over My Wrath," Ibn 'Arabi (d. 1240) writes: "He [that is, God] says: Mercy takes precedence over Wrath because the beginning was [engendered] through Mercy. Wrath is an accident, and accidents disappear."[30]

So, to "adorn" oneself with the characteristics of God means, essentially, to embody and realize the virtues which reflect, and participate in, the fundamental substance of the Real, this substance being itself defined in terms of the "most *beautiful* Names," *al-asma' al-husna*. The "accidental" Names of God describe the means by which disequilibria—on the human or cosmic level—are corrected; in other words, the Names of wrath describe the extrinsic, transient, and phenomenal consequences flowing from the lack of receptivity by human beings to God's "substantial" or principial radiance as infinite love and beauty. The "substantial" Names of God, by contrast, disclose the nature whence flows this infinite beauty. To see God is therefore to see absolute Beauty, and this takes us back to the relationship between the beauty of the divine nature and the virtue of the human soul, or the relationship between divine beauty and human flourishing. For the Prophet defined *ihsan* (which can be translated as "making beautiful," "excellence," or simply "virtue") as "worshipping God as if you could see Him."[31] We see why hastening to prayer is hastening to the source of one's capacity to flourish; for praying and flourishing are woven together by the virtues, graces, and beatitudes overflowing from the spring of divine beauty: "Hasten to prayer, hasten to flourishing!"

We may now understand better the significance of the hadith: "I saw my Lord in the most beautiful form."[32] The great Persian saint of Shiraz, Ruzbehan Baqli (d. 1209) comments on this saying as follows: "The mystery

29. See for discussion Chittick, *Sufi Path of Knowledge*, 283–88.

30. Chittick, *Self-Disclosure of God*, 225.

31. Ebrahim, *An-Nawawi's Forty Hadith*, 30.

32. *Encyclopaedia of Hadith*, Sunan al-Tirmidhi, 2:87–88, saying no. 3043.

of the Real is to be found in the self-disclosing theophany [*tajalli*] of beauty. The souls of the lovers perceive in the beauty of primordial human nature [*fitrah*] the reflection of eternal beauty, finding in this symbol the key to the science which was [hitherto] unknown."[33] He makes clear that without human virtue there is no question of appreciating that the "mystery of the Real" is to be found in the theophany of divine beauty: one must continue to repeat the hadith, "adorn yourself with the qualities of God," in order to assimilate the beauty of God within oneself, to thereby become properly virtuous, and thus participate in the theophany par excellence: the radiation of the divine self-disclosure as beauty, all of the "most beautiful Names" being comprised within this single, essential attribute. Human flourishing, predicated upon spiritual virtue, hence, beauty of soul, can be seen to be totally dependent on the transformative graces emanating from the power of love attracted to the magnet of beauty: "when I love him I become the hearing by which he hears, the sight by which he sees . . ."

The complementarity between beauty and virtue is implied within the sense of the sacred. In the words of Frithjof Schuon: "The sense of the Sacred, which is nothing other than a quasi-natural predisposition towards the love of God and a sensitivity towards theophanic manifestations or heavenly perfumes, essentially implies both a sense of beauty and a tendency towards virtue; beauty being so to speak outward virtue, and virtue inward beauty."[34]

Returning to the beauty of the divine nature, the Sufis assert that since there is only one reality (*la ilaha illa'Llah*: no god but God), if God is beautiful then reality can be constituted *only* by beauty. Anything that is not beautiful is by that very fact unreal. This vision of beauty reminds us of Miroslav's vision of human flourishing: "Every good and beautiful thing shimmers with an aura both vibrantly real and undetectable to our five senses. Each thing in the world is more than itself and just so a source of deep and many-layered pleasure."[35] To this, the Sufis would say: Yes, but how does one arrive at this vision spiritually, seeing with the eye of the heart, rather than just with the mind of the philosopher? The answer would be twofold. First it is necessary to know that, in fact, *everything* in existence does indeed "shimmer with an aura both vibrantly real and undetectable to our five senses," insofar as "the seven heavens and the earth and all that is therein praise Him, and *there is not a thing but hymneth His praise*; but ye understand not

33. Baqli, 'Abhar al-'ashiqin, 31. See Corbin's magisterial elucidation of Baqli's perspective in *En Islam iranien*, 3:9–146.

34. Schuon, *Esoterism as Principle and as Way*, 239.

35. Volf, *Flourishing*, 205.

their praise" (17:44; emphasis added). The aura that "shimmers" is precisely the "praise" of God radiating from each and every thing in the cosmos. In other words, it is not necessary to imagine a world in which everyone loves God and the neighbor for such a vision to arise: the world, in its objective reality, is already pulsating with the love that flows from the beauty and the praise constituted by everything in creation. As noted above (32:7), God "made beautiful" everything He created. It is all a question of spiritually perceiving the beauty and the praise which is already "given," objectively real. This leads to the second point the Sufis would emphasize: the indispensable methodic means by which the eye of the heart is opened up, granting a properly spiritual, rather than merely speculative, vision of universal and inescapable beauty.[36] The indispensable means? "Hasten to the prayer!" And here we have to take careful note of what the Qur'an tells us: while the canonical prayer "prevents lewdness and iniquity," the remembrance of God (*dhikr Allah*)—the quintessence of all possible prayer—"is greatest" (29:45). As noted above, the invocation of the divine Name and the recitation of the Qur'an are the chief ritual means of establishing the permanence of the consciousness of God; they are by that very token the central forms of sacred art in Islam, the means by which the beauty of God immanent in all things (in all *real* things) becomes supernaturally visible to the eye of the heart. The heart is purified and cleansed by prayer, allowing it to see the beauty of God: "For everything there is a polish," said the Prophet, "and the polish of the hearts is the remembrance of God."[37] One sees divine Beauty everywhere, if that Beauty is glimpsed, through contemplative concentration, or through an illuminating grace, at its source.

It would appear that Eckhart is referring precisely to the fruits of this mode of concentration on God when he says: "All things become simply God to you, for in all things you notice only God, just as a man who stares long at the sun sees the sun in whatever he afterwards looks at."[38] In Origen's terms, one who is in constant prayer is perpetually celebrating a divine feast: "He who is doing his duty is in reality keeping a feast; for he is always praying, continually offering bloodless sacrifices in his prayers to God."[39]

36. Indispensable, that is, for all those who have not had the eye of their heart opened by the grace of a sudden illumination (*fath*) or ecstatic "attraction" (*jadhba*). In Sufism, one who has been graced by such an illumination is called a *madhjub* (literally, "attracted" to God through an ecstatic grace); whereas one who traverses the Path methodically, stage by stage, having the eye of the heart open up gradually, is called a *salik*, "wayfarer."

37. This saying is found in Bayhaqi's *Shu'ab al-iman*, and other sources of hadith.

38. Eckhart, *Meister Eckhart*, 1:44.

39. Origen, *Contra Celsum*, 467.

This notion of continuous prayer, emphasised by St. Paul ("pray without ceasing": 1 Thess 5:17), resonates deeply with Sufi praxis, based on explicit Qur'anic texts, exhorting the believers to do "much remembrance" (33:41), to remember God "standing and sitting and reclining on their sides" (3:191), and describing believers who are "perpetually at prayer" (70:23); and based on the prophetic definition of spiritual virtue, excellence, or simply "making beautiful" (*ihsan*), as note above: "to worship God as if you could see Him, and if you see Him not, [be constantly aware that] He sees you." When Jesus, at the Last Supper, told his disciples to eat the bread "in remembrance of me" (Luke, 22:19; 1 Cor 11:24) we see the selfsame exhortation, for remembering Jesus—the Word of God (Q 4:171) breathed into Mary (Q 21:91 *et passim*)—is metaphysically identical to remembering a Name of God.

To make clearer the Sufi conception of the "ontological" nature of beauty, let us note the helpful exposition on this subject by 'Abd al-Karim Jili (d. 1428), a renowned authority in the school of Ibn 'Arabi. He asserts that there is in truth nothing in being except beauty, for the whole of creation is constituted by the theophany (*tajalli*) of the divine Names and Qualities; and since these are all beautiful, everything in creation is beautiful. From this point of view, ugliness (*al-qubh*) remains ugly, but its "reality" derives not from the Real, but from its negation of the beauty of the Real. It disfigures or corrupts the only substance that there is, the beauty of God. Ugliness does not possess an ontological essence, it has no root in true Being, and is therefore a kind of nothingness that only appears to be something. "Ugliness cannot be found in the cosmos except by way of relationship [with what can be found, namely, beauty], so, that which is ugly has no property of absoluteness [or nondelimitation, *itlaq*]. Nothing then remains in being except absolute [or non-delimited] beauty [*al-husn al-mutlaq*]."[40] The principle here in question can be seen more clearly with the help of the following passage of the Qur'an:

> He sends down water from the sky, so that valleys flow according to their measure, and the flood carries scum on its surface—such as also arises from that metal they smelt in fire to make ornaments and tools; thus does God strike [similitudes for the sake of distinguishing] the true and the false. As for the scum, it passes away as dross; but that which is of benefit to mankind, it abides on earth. Thus does God strike similitudes. (13:17)

Just as one does not confuse the scum for the water, so one does not confuse the ugly for the beautiful, or the false for the true: the scum is, as it were, generated by the water from which it is inseparable, and from which

40. al-Jili, *Al-Insan al-kamil*, 101.

it derives its insubstantial form; but, as an accidental disfiguration of water, the substance from which it momentarily arises, each bubble of its foam-like form passes away in the very instant after it appears. The scum disappears, the water remains;[41] the difference between the two things symbolizes, *mutatis mutandis*, the difference between the eternal reality of Beauty, on the one hand, and the illusory nature of ugliness, on the other.

The verse immediately following this description of the scum brings home the relationship of this analogy to the reality of beauty: "For those who answered God's call is that which is most beautiful [*husna*] ... " (13:18). We are given essentially the same message in this passage:

> The similitude of the life of the world is only as water which We send down from the sky, then the earth's growth of that which men and cattle eat mingleth with it till, when the earth hath taken on her ornaments and is embellished, and her people deem that they are her masters, Our commandment cometh by night or by day, and We make it as reaped corn as if it had not flourished yesterday. Thus do We expound the revelations for people who reflect. And God summoneth to the abode of peace, and guideth whom He will to a straight path. *For those who make beautiful is that which is most beautiful, and yet more.* Neither dust nor ignominy soileth their faces. Such are rightful owners of the Garden; they will abide therein. (10:24–26; emphasis added)

"And yet more," we return to Miroslav's vision: "Each thing in the world is more than itself and just so a source of deep and many-layered pleasure." Each thing, in other words, is a symbol of something much greater than itself, a symbol whose archetype is in Heaven. As the Qur'an says: "There is no thing but that its treasuries are with Us; and We only send it down in a known measure" (15:21). The beauty of these celestial treasuries—the archetypes—stands revealed to the eye of the heart in the measure that this heart is "polished" and purified by the permanent remembrance of God, this remembrance being the essence of *ihsan*, the "making beautiful" referred to in the verses cited above (10:24–26), and which the Prophet defined as "worshipping God as if you could see Him." So, the "yet more" that is given to the "makers of beauty," the *muhsinun*, the virtuous, is, in its essence, divine beauty: to those who are truly virtuous will be given, in proportion to the depth of their virtue, the gift of spiritual vision. On the one hand, "Everywhere ye turn, there is the Face of God" (2:115); and on

---

41. "Verily, the Truth [*al-Haqq*] has come, and the false [*al-batil*] vanishes away; truly the false is ever-vanishing" (17:81).

the other: "Is the reward of *ihsan* anything other than *ihsan*?" (55:60). We might rephrase this rhetorical question thus: is the reward of that form of beauty which spiritual virtue constitutes anything other than its own archetype, namely, celestial beauty? We can go further and say that God's act of creation is itself the ultimate archetype of all *ihsan*, all "making beautiful," for, as already noted, "He made beautiful [*ahsana*] everything He created" (32:7). And, according to another *hadith qudsi* central to Sufi metaphysics, God said, "I was a hidden treasure and I loved to be known, so I created the cosmos." Now a treasure is valued precisely on account of its beauty. The entire cosmos is thus a divine work of art, a manifestation of beauty, motivated by love, whence the Names of God, *al-Sani'*, "the Artisan," and *al-Wadud*, "the Loving," and the designation of the entire creation as the "handiwork," the *sun'*, of God, a term used in verse 27:88, ". . . the handiwork of God, who perfecteth every thing."

The question that might be posed here is this: do we disdain the earthly symbol once its heavenly archetype has been assimilated? Does the good thing on earth—the gift of God—in any way diminish in value because we see through it, contemplating the divine qualities of which it, the good thing, is but a transient reflection? We would answer: on the contrary, the good thing, the symbol, is immeasurably enriched insofar as we see the Sovereign Good, the supreme Archetype through the God-given form and symbolic qualities of the good thing. But this process of metaphysical enrichment of the symbol is strictly predicated upon a prior renunciation of the purely physical, material, temporal dimensions of the symbol. In the words of Eckhart, before we can see the creature as an image of God, we first have to see the creature as a "pure nothing." He tells us that "All creatures are pure nothing. I do not say that they are a little something, or anything at all, but that they are pure nothing."[42] He also says: "One is the negation of the negation and a denial of the denial. All creatures have a negation in themselves: one negates by not being the other . . . but God negates the negation: He is one and negates all else, for outside of God nothing is."[43] This negation of the negation—reminiscent of the Vedantic method of *neti, neti* ("not this, not this")—implies that, once the negation constituted by the creature as such is negated, then the negation of this negation amounts to a supreme affirmation of the One, of which the creature is an image. We thus return to a vision of the creature, now seen as a pure positivity, insofar as it is a manifestation of the One.

42. Eckhart, *Meister Eckhart*, vol. 1:l.
43. Ibid., 2:339.

This doctrine is found succinctly expressed in the double testimony of Islam, considered in metaphysical mode: first, one negates all that is other than God, "no god but God." In light of the Absolute, all relativity is reduced to the status of illusion, or "nothingness," in Eckhartian terms. But then comes the second testimony: "Muhammad is the Messenger of God," which we understand to be a restitution of the relative reality of the creature, grasped now as an image of God. In other words: first we see the distinction between the symbol and the symbolized, and then we see the symbol as being one with the symbolized. As regards the aspect of distinction, in Sufi metaphysics, and in Eckhartian "spiritual logic," what is distinct from God is other than God, and what is other than God is illusion: the creature *per se* is nothing. As regards the aspect of unity, by which the symbol is not other than the symbolized, the creature as image of God is perceived as a divine manifestation: the manifestation of the One stands revealed as the One, manifested.

We see the same two-step process of negation prior to affirmation in the sayings of Jesus, the same perspective of differentiation based on the transcendence, or all-exclusive reality, of God, followed by unification based on the immanence, or all-inclusive presence, of God. On the one hand: "Why callest thou me good? There is none good but one, that is, God" (Mark 10:18 KJV; Luke 18:19 KJV). On the other: "I and my Father are one" (John 10:30 KJV). Out of fidelity to the transcendence of the One even the phenomenon of Jesus Christ, supreme symbol of "the good life," must be "seen through" if the dimension of unitive immanence, the oneness of substance uniting him to the One, is to be properly assimilated. Again, let us turn to Eckhart to help us understand this.

With reference to John 16:7 (KJV), "Nevertheless I tell you the truth; it is expedient for you that I go away: for if I go not away, the Comforter will not come unto you; but if I depart, I will send him unto you," Eckhart says: "This is just as if he had said: 'You rejoice too much in my present form, and therefore the joy of the Holy Spirit cannot be yours.' So leave all images and unite with the formless Essence."[44] How does one unite with the Essence? Not just by knowing the Son, but through identifying totally with the Son; identifying with the Son, not as distinct from the One, but as nothing other than the One. Citing Matt 11:27 (KJV), "Neither knoweth any man the Father, save the Son," Eckhart comments: "If you would know God, you must not merely be like the Son, you must be the Son yourself."[45] To thus "be" the Son means to be at one with the Word eternally spoken by the Father, as op-

44. Ibid., 3:128 (translation modified).
45. Ibid., 1:127.

posed to being the man Jesus who was born in a particular time and place;
one must unite with the symbol insofar as it is one with the symbolized, not
insofar as it is distinct from the symbolized. "God took on human nature,"
Eckhart says elsewhere,

> and united it with His own Person. Then human nature became
> God, for He put on bare human nature and not any man. There-
> fore, if you want to be the same Christ and God, go out of all
> that which the eternal Word did not assume . . . then you will
> be the same to the eternal Word as human nature is to Him. For
> between your human nature and His there is no difference: it is
> one, for it is in Christ what it is in you.[46]

We return to the spiritual meaning of the *fitrah*, quintessential, universal and immutable human nature, within which God is immanent, every
soul being made, according to the Prophet, echoing Gen 1:27, "in the form"
of God. But, going back to the question posed above about the relationship
between the symbol and the symbolized (and to our earlier question about
Miroslav's essentialized vision of the "good life," in contrast to the heavily
Christocentric vision embodied in the Sainte Chapelle), one might ask: does
this universalization of human nature not diminish the particularities of
each human being? To put the question in Christian terms: does our view of
the universal principle of the Christic reality inherent in each human soul
not detract from the particularities, indeed the glories, of Jesus the man?
Schuon implicitly gives us an answer in his assertion that our consciousness of the universal and timeless reality of Christ, "far from diminishing a
participation in the treasures of the historical Redemption, confers on them
a compass that touches the very roots of Existence."[47] The spiritual logic
here can be applied to every divine Revelation, and indeed to every divine
manifestation, which is to say, to everything in creation: the particular good
is ennobled and transfigured, not diminished or degraded, by being assimilated as a symbol of an archetype subsisting on a higher degree of being; that
is, by being integrated into its own universal essence. Eckhart is employing
the same spiritual logic in his at first sight baffling denial that God is pure
Being:

> Masters of little subtlety say God is pure being. He is as high
> above being as the highest angel is above a midge. . . . When
> I have said God is not a being and is above being, I have not
> thereby denied Him being: rather I have exalted it in Him. If I

46. Ibid., 2:313–14. See my *Paths to Transcendence*, where I elaborate upon these
points in the context of a comparison with the doctrines of Shankara and Ibn ʿArabi.

47. Schuon, *Light on the Ancient Worlds*, 70

get copper in gold, it is there . . . in a nobler mode than it is in itself.[48]

A spiritual awareness that Being is transcended by the Godhead as "Beyond-Being" does not imply a degradation of Being; on the contrary, Eckhart has "exalted" Being by subsuming it within its own supra-ontological source. The same principle applies on the level of phenomena within Being: traces of copper are all the more precious for being present within gold: copper is there, in gold, "in a nobler mode than it is in itself." Inversely, to the degree that copper (or any particular good) is viewed apart from gold (or the Sovereign Good) it is in that very measure deprived of value.

Miroslav's reference to sexuality in the context of love gives us the opportunity to apply the metaphysical logic at work here to this important and, alas, much misunderstood dimension of human life. The sexual act is spiritually elevated in the measure that it is consecrated to God, and gratefully received as a gift of God, as Miroslav says; but let us go further, and add: the sexual act is ennobling and inspiring, insofar as it is experienced as a symbol of the bliss embedded within the infinite creativity of the divine Spirit. Ruzbehan Baqli alludes to the bliss inherent in spiritual creativity in the following passage on God's creation of the Spirit, through which all subsequent creation takes place:

> When God wished to create this subtle being [that is, the Spirit], he projected His Majesty . . . engendering therefrom all the differentiated atoms by means of the theophanic manifestation of His Essence and Qualities, doing so out of creative ecstasy [ladhdhata halati takwiniha], so that they all came into being as a result of the magnetic power of love [takawwanat bi-jadhbati'l-'ishq].[49]

Every single atom in creation is thus charged, or rather, "magnetized," by spiritual love, the love that is the very essence of the Spirit, the first creation of God, through which all subsequent acts of creation come about.[50] Everything in creation thus both attracts love, by its spiritual nature, and also yearns to return to that flow of divine Love, through the Spirit, which is the source of its creation. As Rumi (d. 1273) puts it in the opening passage

48. Eckhart, Meister Eckhart, 2:150–51.

49. Baqli, al-Misbah, 46–47. See Corbin's excellent discussion, En Islam iranien, 3:30–44.

50. There is a lively debate in Islamic thought on the question of whether the Spirit (al-Ruh) is created or uncreated.

of his poetic masterpiece, the *Mathnawi*: "Every one who is left far from his source wishes back the time when he was united with it."[51]

However, Rumi never lets us forget that everything in this world is but a shadow in relation to its celestial archetype, an archetype which can be found in all its splendour within the heart; the heart is understood by the Sufis as truly containing, here and now, the kingdom of God.[52] Again, to apply this concretely to the question of sexuality, what this means is that a Rumi or a Ruzbehan would doubtless see the creative bliss of the Spirit reflected in the sexual act, but would also know—through spiritual insight, not speculative thought—that sexual joy is infinitely transcended by the purely inward ecstasy of the Spirit. Again, we observe the application of the complementary principles of transcendence and immanence, principles without which the spiritual meaning of symbols is impossible to understand. These principles are well articulated in relation to sexuality by Schuon:

> What the human spirit needs is not the sexual element, it is the element of infinitude of which sexuality is the manifestation on the vital and psychic plane. Whereas intellectuality or spirituality comprises a supernatural element by definition—a permanent or incidental intervention of the Holy Spirit—sexuality is something simply natural: but since it reflects a divine reality, it becomes a quasi-sacramantal support for that experience of infinitude which is contemplative extinction.[53]

Finally, let us note how the Qur'an poetically expresses the complementary principles of transcendence and immanence proper to the metaphysical logic at the heart of spiritual symbolism, at the same time as revealing the connection between the good life here and now, and the beatific life in the Hereafter: "Every time they [the people of Paradise] are given to eat from the fruits thereof, they say: 'This is what we were given to eat before [i.e., on earth].' And they were given something like it" (2:25). The aspect of essential continuity between all good things on earth and all good things in Heaven is expressed by the statement "this is what we were given to eat before." From the point of view of divine immanence, the earthly symbol is one with the paradisial archetype; it is not other than it. But the divine words, "And they were given something *like* it," express the perspective of transcendence. They indicate that the good thing on earth is distinct from

---

51. Rumi, *Mathnawi*, 1:5, line 4.

52. "The heart of the faithful is the throne of the All-Merciful," says a hadith, which forms the title of Seyyed Hossein Nasr's essay on this subject in Cutsinger, *Paths to the Heart*, 32–45.

53. Frithjof Schuon, *From the Divine to the Human*, 15.

its celestial archetype as regards ontological degree of intensity; it is *like* it, but not identical in every respect to it. In other words, the earthly good is "less real" than its celestial archetype, the symbol is to be distinguished from that of which it is only a symbol. The good life on earth—the truth and virtue, beauty and love that are inseparable from goodness—is thus a foretaste of the "fruit" of paradisial beatitude; but the spiritual impact of this foretaste is deepened to the extent that we understand that "the Hereafter is better and more lasting" (87:17), on the one hand, and that, conversely, "the life of this world is nothing but distraction and play" (29:64). For, to continue with this verse, "and truly the Abode of the Hereafter—that is True Life, if only they knew."

BIBLIOGRAPHY

Abu Bakr Siraj ad-Din. *The Sufi Doctrine of Faith, Vision and Gnosis*. Cambridge: Islamic Texts Society, 1992.

Baqli, Ruzbehan. *'Abhar al-'ashiqin*. Edited by Henry Corbin and Muhammad Mu'in. Tehran: Intisharat-i Manuchehri, 2004.

———. *al-Misbah fi mukashafat ba'th al-arwah*. Edited Asim al-Husayni al-Shadhili al-Darqawi. Beirut: Dar al-Kutub al-'Ilmiyya, 1971.

Burckhardt, Titus. *Art of Islam: Language and Meaning*. Translated by J. Peter Hobson. London: World of Islam Festival, 1976.

Chittick, William C. *The Self-Disclosure of God: Principles of Ibn al-'Arabi's Cosmology*. Albany: State University of New York Press, 1998.

———. *The Sufi Path of Knowledge: Ibn al-'Arabi's Metaphysics of Imagination*. Albany: State University of New York, 1989.

Coomaraswamy, Ananda K. *Christian and Oriental Philosophy of Art*. New York: Dover, 1956.

———. *Figures of Speech or Figures of Thought? The Traditional View of Art*. London: Luzac, 1946.

Corbin, Henry. *En Islam iranien: Aspects spirituels et philosophiques*. 4 vols. Paris: Editions Gallimard, 1972.

Cutsinger, James S., ed. *Paths to the Heart: Sufism and the Christian East*. Bloomington, IN: World Wisdom, 2002.

Dionysius the Areopagite. *The Divine Names*. Fintry, UK: The Shrine of Wisdom, 1957.

Ebrahim, Ezzeddin, and D. Johnson-Davies, trans. *An-Nawawi's Forty Hadith*. Damascus: Holy Koran, 1977.

Eckhart, Meister. *Meister Eckhart: Sermons and Treatises*. Translated by Maurice O'Connell Walshe. Dorset: Element, 1979.

Encyclopaedia of Hadith. Liechtenstein: Thesaurus Islamicus Foundation, 2001.

Hani, Jean. *Le Symbolisme du Temple Chrétien*. Versailles: Guy Trédaniel, 1962.

Jawadi-Amuli, 'Abd Allah. *Hamasah wa 'irfan*. Qum: Isra Publication Centre, 1999.

Jili, 'Abd al-Karim. *Al-Insan al-kamil*. Cairo: al-Maktaba al-Tawfiqiyya, n.d.

Kashani, 'Abd al-Razzaq. *Tafsir Ibn ⬚Arabi*. Cairo: al-Maktaba al-Tawfiqiyya, n.d.

Lings, Martin. *A Sufi Saint of the Twentieth Century: Shaikh Ahmad Al-'Alawī: His Spiritual Heritage and Legacy*. 2nd ed. Berkeley: University of California Press, 1971.

———. *Symbol and Archetype: A Study of the Meaning of Existence*. Cambridge: Quinta Essentia, 1991.

Nasr, Seyyed Hossein. "The Heart of the Faithful is the Throne of the All-Merciful." In *Paths to the Heart: Sufism and the Christian East*, edited by James S. Cutsinger, 32–45. Bloomington, IN: World Wisdom, 2002.

Origen of Alexandria. *Contra Celsum*. Translated by Henry Chadwick. Cambridge: Cambridge University Press, 1980.

Prince Ghazi bin Muhammad. *Love in the Holy Qur'an*. Chicago: Kazi, 2012.

Rumi, Jalal al-Din. *Mathnawi*. Translated by R. A. Nicholson. London: Luzac, 1934.

Sahih al-Bukhari: Arabic-English. Translated by Muhammad Muhsin Khan. Chicago: Kazi, 1977.

Sahih al-Bukhari. Translated by Muhammad Muhsin Khan. Riyadh: Maktaba Dar-us-Salam, 1994.

Schuon, Frithjof. *Esoterism as Principle and as Way*. Translated by W. Stoddart. London: Perennial, 1981.

———. *Light on the Ancient Worlds*. Translated by Lord Northbourne. London: Perennial, 1965.

Shah-Kazemi, Reza. *Spiritual Quest: Reflections on Qur'anic Prayer According to the Teachings of Imam 'Ali*. London: I. B. Tauris, 2011.

———. *Paths to Transcendence: According to Shankara, Ibn 'Arabi and Meister Eckhart*. Bloomington, IN: World Wisdom, 2006.

Starkovsky, Nicholas. *The Koran Handbook: An Annotated Translation*. New York: Algora, 2005.

Volf, Miroslav. *Flourishing: Why We Need Religion in a Globalized World*. New Haven, CT: Yale University Press, 2016.

7

Expectations

Jürgen Moltmann

MIROSLAV CAME TO TÜBINGEN as my doctoral student and left as my friend. Coming from a Pentecostal family he introduced me to Pentecostal circles. Grown up in late Yugoslavia he turned my attention to the deadly situations in the Balkan war. I came to Zagreb, Croatia and Sarajevo, Bosnia and Herzegovina, and felt deep compassion for the Christian friends who worked for peace between peoples with wounded and bleeding memories full of hatred or apathy. Miroslav has experiences working in his heart for new theological expression. His spirit is full of ideas. It is always a joy theologizing with him. I therefore dedicate the following essay, originally written as a contribution at a Yale Center for Faith & Culture consultation on June 22, 2015, to my friend.

WAIT AND SEE—EXPECT—WATCH

a. *Waiting for Godot* (Samuel Beckett). The two beggars are waiting because beggars are always waiting for something. Mr. Godot should come, but doesn't come. There is no Mr. Godot. Their waiting is without sense. It is absurd. This existentialist play was written to show that human existence is fundamentally absurd, especially human expectations. In *Waiting for Godot* the two beggars Vladimir and Estragon are speaking and doing only absurd things. The waiting for Godot is without any consequence for them. The object is indeterminate, and the waiting means nothing to them. "Waiting for Godot" is at best a "wait-and-see," *ab-warten*.

b. *The expectation of a child* is determined and related to a distinct object. It is no "wait-and-see," *ab-warten*, but a waiting for something and this "something" determines the waiting to an expecting, *er-warten*. The time is also limited at nine months. The embryo is already there in the mother's womb. Sure there are also fears: Will a miscarriage come? Is the child healthy? Will the birth be without complications? But the people are calling a pregnant woman a "woman of good hope." The expectation of a child changes lives: the woman becomes pregnant, the man becomes a father, the siblings are no longer alone. To expect a child means to prepare for the birth and the life with the child. The expected child is not only the growing of a family, *Familienzuwachs*, but also the beginning of a new life. In the perspective of a trans-individual stream of life, one may say with Hannah Arendt: Life is taking a new start.[1] No child is as the other; every child is a unique birth of life. Most important is the social field of expectation, into which children enter with their birth—and actually already in their mother's womb. Are they welcome or unwanted? Are they expected with joy and then grow up in an atmosphere of appreciation? Are they unwanted or neglected and then have low self-respect all their lives? The field of expectation in a family can also depress the child: will the child ever meet the expectations of the father?

c. "The kingdom of God is at hand"; "is come nigh unto you" (Luke 10:11 KJV); "The Lord is at hand" (Phil 4:5 KJV); "The end of all things is at hand" (1 Pet 4:7 KJV); "For the coming of the Lord draweth nigh" (Jas 5:8 KJV). We shall deal here with the Greek word *eggys*. If the divine future is "at hand" or "nigh," it is a present future, but in terms of time and space this future remains undetermined: "Time and hour nobody knows" (Matt 24:36). But the expectation of the Kingdom of God, or the advent of Christ, or the end of all things already transforms the present with repentance and with joy and with the exodus out of the past. The expectant people prepare for the expected future. They open their senses for the near-expected future: they watch. The nearness of the divine future can't be calculated as with the expected child. You can also not react with a "wait-and-see." This nearness can't be measured in days or years, it cannot be measured in space, because there are no distances in time and space: the divine nearness is "now." It is

---

1. "It is in the nature of beginning that something new is started which cannot be expected from whatever may have happened before." See Arendt, *The Human Condition*, 178.

like the personal intimacy in which we say: she is near to my heart. Experience of divine nearness is always accompanied with repentance, joy, and a new beginning. I would summarize this under the word "watching": "Pray and watch," "watch and be sober," "watch and see." (cf. The parable of the ten virgins, five wise, five foolish [Matt 25:1–13]).

d. Attempt of a first definition:
Hope is anticipated joy; anxiety is anticipated terror. Both are undetermined. Expecting brings the determined into the undetermined of hope and anxiety. Waiting can mean simply to "wait-and-see," in which case we contribute nothing to the arrival of the expected. Waiting can also mean expecting, in which case we prepare for what we expect. The expected future is already determining the present. Waiting can also mean watching. I don't know when it is coming, but it is already at hand. I begin to live in the nearness of the expected and open all my senses to meet the coming. A field of expectation is emerging, in which the expected can always enter.

EXPECTING A GOOD LIFE IN CHILDREN

For me there are three reasons why children are incarnate hopes for a good life, and are also God's true promises:

a. Every child that is born and accepted represents a new beginning of life, a beginning that we do not immediately understand because it is original, unique and incomparable. It is true that we always ask whom this or that child resembles, but when we try to compare it with the mother or the father we come upon what is special in this child. We must respect this; it is always astonishing. But we can only do so if we love the child's own life and keep his or her future open. We must be prepared to be surprised by the new possibilities that are born with every child. We know a child in its unique character only to the extent to which we love and have patience with this child.

b. With every new beginning of life, the hope in the fullness of the good life—and the eternal life, which fulfills the promise of the good life—acquires a new chance. Every child is also a new occasion for the home of life in this unredeemed world. For Ernst Bloch, the philosopher of hope, this is the "home of identity, which shines in the childhood of all, and in which nobody so far was."[2] The new beginnings and the new births point

---

2. [This is Moltmann's gloss on Bloch's "homeland of identity, in which neither man behaves towards the world, nor the world behaves towards man, as if towards a stranger." See Bloch, *The Principle of Hope*, 209. –Eds.]

out beyond themselves to the new creation of all things to eternal life in the presence of the living God. Every fortunate birth of a child confirms the great hope in the victory of life over death.

c. The final reason for seeing the beginning of the life of a child as the beginning of something new lies not only in seeing children as incarnations of our expectations but also in perceiving in them the embodiment of God's expectations for us. We do not expect only; we are also expected. Human beings are God's great love, human beings are God's dream for God's beloved earth, human beings are created in God's image. They should correspond to God's goodness and resonate with God's mercy. But as human history shows, humankind is a deep disappointment for the "God of hope." God may repent and be sorry for having created these ambiguous and contradictory human beings (Gen 6:6). But God remains "faithful" to his own creation-will. God is still expecting the truly humane human being in every newly born child. This expectation of God must be the deeper reason why "we are not yet wholly cut off," but one generation after the other is born. We and our children are born in this transcendent field of divine expectation. We expect the good life, and we are expected. What does a good life look like which meets God's expectations?

d. Janusz Korczak was right when he demanded fundamental rights for children in his book *How to Love a Child* (1919):

> I demand the *Magna Charta Libertatis* as a constitutional law for the child. Perhaps there are further—but I have identified these three fundamental rights:

1. The right of the child to his or her own death [or the necessity to trust him/her in his/her own life].

2. The right of the child to the present day [or the blessing of the present moment].

3. The right of a child to be what he or she is [or the necessity to trust the child in his/her own nature].[3]

These rights lie behind the various specific rights enumerated in the United Nations Convention on the Rights of the Child in 1989. Korczak voluntarily left with the children of the Jewish orphanage in Warsaw in 1942 to the SS extermination camp Treblinka and died together with the children.

---

3. Korczak, *Wie man ein Kind lieben soll*, 40. [The translation is the author's, with some slight adjustments by the editors. The text in square brackets comprises the author's glosses on Korczak's text. –Eds.]

EXPECTING A GOOD DEATH IN THE OLD

Death is part of human life on earth, and dying belongs to the living. If there is a "good life," what does a "good death" look like? If there is a good living, there must also be a good dying—or is every death an enemy of life and the "living God"? How do we experience death and dying?

a. "Abraham died old and satisfied of life" (Gen 25:8). Luther's translation: "*alt und lebenssatt.*" One can only be "*lebenssatt*" if one has really lived. The unlived life, the voluntarily missed life or the involuntarily stolen years of life, causes pain and grief and hinders a "good death." However, more of the old are tired of life, *lebensmüde.*

b. "Lord, now lettest thou thy servant depart in peace . . . for mine eyes have seen thy salvation" (Luke 2:39–30 KJV). A "good death" is a death in peace with God, oneself, the family, friends—and foes. Expecting death, it is good to make peace and to pray for peace, to forgive guilt and to ask for forgiveness of one's own guilt. We have this mutual forgiveness in our burial ritual, but it is, however, better to seek peace before than after death. Whoever dies in discord dies no "good death."

c. Where do we experience death? At the end of my life I shall experience dying, but I don't experience my death, because on earth I don't survive it. But in the cases of people I love, I experience their deaths, for I have to survive and to mourn their loss, being bereaved. The poet Mascha Kaléko wrote in her "Memento" when her only child died:

> I am not afraid of my own death,
> Only of the death of those near to me,
> How long can I live when they are no longer there?
>
> Alone in the fog I grope deathlong
> And willing let myself float into the dark.
> The going hurts not half as much as the staying.
>
> He knows it well who confronted the same;
> And they who bear it may forgive me.
> Remember: with our own death we merely die,
> But with the death of others we have to live.[4]

4. Vor meinem eignen Tod ist mir nicht bang,
Nur vor dem Tode derer, die mir nah sind.
Wie soll ich leben, wenn sie nicht mehr da sind?

But before one has to live with the death of others, one has to live with the slow departure of a beloved person. With the long life–expectations in our countries, aging and dying can no longer be separated. Where ends the aging? Where begins the dying? Sometimes parts of the brain are dying, and this changes the whole person. I find it difficult to take then the attitude of the therapist. This distant kind of care should not replace the living community. It is also not right to say: "This is no longer the person I loved once." I am trying to hold onto the togetherness of our common life and feel this is a "good life" under changed conditions. The slow departure from the past in forgetting is part of a "good dying." In the trust to be present in God's memory eternally, we can accept our own forgetfulness. And old couples have a "common memory": what the one can't remember, the other remembers. With the same love with which we had built up our life when we were young, we must also surrender the things of our youth with grace when we are old.

d. In our epoch of objective palliative medicine, organized care, and hospices for the dying, we need a subjective spirituality of "good dying." Aging is for many a kind of anxious watching. They know what is coming but not when it is to happen: *mors certa, hora incerta*. In earlier times there was a special *ars-moriendi* literature. One knew how to prepare for dying, because the people could look beyond death into the judgment and the kingdom of God, or into purgatory and the happiness of heaven. Today many say: "With death it's all over." They don't expect something beyond death. There can't be any spirituality of dying apart, perhaps, from surrendering to annihilation, or *amor fati*. Aging is becoming like *Waiting for Godot*, day after day, night after night. When we expect something new to happen after our death, we don't die as a victim of death but as a child of that new something. *Ars moriendi* becomes a part of the *bene vivere*. A willing readiness toward dying is the first step toward resurrection into divine life—no matter

---

Allein im Nebel tast ich todentlang
Und laß mich willig in das Dunkel treiben.
Das Gehen schmerzt nicht halb so wie das Bleiben.

Der weiß es wohl, dem gleiches widerfuhr;
– Und die es trugen, mögen mir vergeben.
Bedenkt: den eignen Tod, den stirbt man nur,
Doch mit dem Tod der andern muß man leben.

[Translation is the author's and the editors'. The German text can be found in Kaléko, *Verse für Zeitgenossen*, as well as alongside English and Spanish translations (Kaléko, "Memento").—Eds.]

whether one wants to accept *Sterbehilfe* ("euthanasia"), as does Hans Küng,[5] or would reject this as I do. Then dying is like expecting the birth of a child, a determinate expectation.

I work with the threefold concept of life: life—the good life—eternal life.[6] But where will the eternal life be?

The Apostles' Creed says: "I believe in the resurrection of the dead and eternal life" (wherever that may be).

The Nicene Creed has it more precisely: "We must expect the resurrection of the dead and the life of the world to come."

Eternal life is lived not in heaven but in the new creation of heaven and earth, where righteousness will dwell.

5. See Küng and Jens, *Dying with Dignity.*

6. [This is an echo of Maximus the Confessor's trio of *being, well-being,* and *eternal being.* See, e.g., *Four Hundred Chapters on Love* 3.23. –Eds.]

BIBLIOGRAPHY

Arendt, Hannah. *The Human Condition*. 2nd ed. Chicago: The University of Chicago Press, 1998.

Bloch, Ernst. *The Principle of Hope*, Vol. 1. Translated by Neville Plaice, Stephen Plaice, and Paul Knight. Cambridge, MA: MIT Press, 1996.

Kaléko, Mascha. "Memento." *Sirena: Poesía, Arte y Crítica* 6 (2010) 50–51.

———. *Verse für Zeitgenossen*. Hamburg: Rowohlt, 1958.

Küng, Hans, and Jens, Walter. *Dying with Dignity: A Plea for Personal Responsibility*. Translated by John Bowden. New York: Continuum, 1995.

Korczak, Janusz. *Wie man ein Kind lieben soll*. Edited by Elisabeth Heimpel and Hans Roos. Göttingen: Vandenhoeck & Ruprecht, 2008.

Maximus the Confessor. *Four Hundred Chapters on Love*. Translated by George Charles Berthold. In *Maximus the Confessor: Selected Writings,* edited by George C. Berthold. Mawhah, NJ: Paulist, 1985.

8

Joy and the Experience of Love

Natalia Marandiuc

IN HIS RECENT WORK, Miroslav Volf points to joy as the mark of a flourishing, fulfilling life.[1] He argues that living a genuinely good life is intrinsically related to the experience of joy. Volf further shows that joy is the union of meaning with pleasure.[2] Yet what creates this union, and in what context does it occur? I will argue here that meaning meets pleasure most significantly, and consequently gives rise to joy, in the experience of love. I will show that the locus of the intersection between meaning and pleasure is the quotidian, ordinary life, where human relationships of love and attachment unfold in their tangled complexity. I will also show, primarily in conversation with Søren Kierkegaard, that finite human loves do not operate merely inter-humanly, but they mediate and participate in the infinite streams of divine love—the source of enduring joy—resulting in the actualizing and flourishing of the human self.

Reflection on the meaning of life is a thoroughly modern construct. Charles Taylor has argued that a defining feature of Western modernity is the human quest for a framework of meaning.[3] This quest is fundamental for human wellbeing, or in Volf's categories, it is necessary for human flour-

1. Volf, *Flourishing*, 206.
2. Ibid., 201–2.
3. Taylor, *Sources of the Self*, 17–18.

ishing, because it is a quest for the most basic sense of life. This is a very different kind of predicament than what past or present people outside modernity experience. For example, the spiritual crisis of Martin Luther, who lived in intense anguish and despair until he finally embraced salvation by faith, was a crisis caused by his inability to meet the demands of God as he understood them, and to escape damnation. Taylor thinks that Luther's fear and dilemma is rather typical for a non-modern context where the highest pressure under which people might crack is the prospect of irretrievable condemnation for not coming close enough to the given vision of what is good and being irrevocably relegated to perdition. Taylor argues that, by contrast, the danger is utterly different for the modern seeker whose fear is above all fear of meaninglessness.[4] Taylor warns that Luther, or anyone in his age, or in fact anyone outside the context of the modern West, would find such a fear unintelligible.[5] The meaning of life was not questionable for Luther or anyone else in his environment. Conversely, it dominates the contemporary West and defines it to a significant degree. Volf is right to invoke meaning as a needed ingredient in the experience of joy in the context of contemporary existence. He is also right to observe the pervasive pursuit of pleasure, which, while not a new element of contemporary experience, is nonetheless embraced today as a self-evident right and telos.

Taylor thinks that an additional novelty emerges in modern existence: an unapologetic affirmation of ordinary life and its goodness. Previous frameworks of life, for instance those rooted in Aristotelian categories, downplayed the importance of ordinary life or even of human life as such[6] and perceived it as a mere baseline support for superior forms of existence either in the form of civic action or contemplation, which would amount to the good life as a super-stratum over and above merely living. Of course the good life understood that way was only available to the aristocracy. Modernity has brought about a profound shift: the good life's locus has now become the ordinary life. Its central point has become quotidian mundaneness, where one negotiates one's loves to one's proximate neighbors. The quest for meaning and the pursuit of pleasure occur precisely in the context of ordinary, quotidian realities, which also form the stage on which human relationships of love and attachment develop in their goodness, messiness, and complexity. The good life is how one lives her loves on a daily basis.

4. Ibid., 18.

5. Ibid., 28.

6. Perhaps the most compelling modern account of life viewed as an end in itself is given by Immanuel Kant in, among other places, his *Groundwork of the Metaphysics of Morals*.

Clearly, this is accessible to all people, not just the elite.[7] The key point for which Taylor is arguing is that the good life in the modern West is not outside or above ordinary life but is instead defined by the manner in which one lives it.[8]

How do we then live the good life? Jesus' greatest commandment is a call to love God as well as human beings. Human desires then ought to be fundamentally oriented in the direction of love, both towards God and towards people. To be sure, a significant feature of human life is the presence of desire. Few would argue against this, particularly in the context of the consumerist contemporary Western culture; yet to channel desire so as to find lasting pleasure, let alone meaning, eludes one easily. The greatest commandment provides precisely the kind of directionality for human desires that incorporates them into the pathway that engenders meaning-making in tandem with the experience of pleasure. According to Jesus' commandment, the pleasure of love finds its meaning when love's telos redoubles so as to aim towards God as well as the human beloved or friend.

Yet, while this commandment purports to channel human desires towards the very source of love, God, as well as those whom God loves, fellow human beings,[9] our desires are matched by an equally powerful need. We need to experience being loved.[10] We need to be at the receiving end of others' love desire as much as we experience the outgoing, other-oriented nature of our own desire. The greatest commandment matches one of the most powerful human needs: the need to experience that we are loved, not only by God, but also by human beings.

Preceding the Christian gospels, Plato's *Symposium* invokes Diotima,[11] a wise woman whose understanding of love centers around the meeting of resource and need. Love is replete with resources of energy and desire, yet it is also hungry and needy. The need propels one forward in eagerness and longing, yet one is satiated and fulfilled only when the desire of another meets this needfulness in its concrete particularity. Both the fulfillment of need and the right orientation of desire interlace pleasure with meaning,

7. Taylor, *Sources of the Self*, 13–14.

8. Ibid., 23.

9. John Duns Scotus has argued that to love God can only mean to love all that God is, and that includes all that God loves. Because God loves human beings, to love God then means to love people. See John Duns Scotus, *Ordinatio III*, suppl., d. 28, in *Duns Scotus on Divine Love*, 45–47.

10. Attachment theorists have amply demonstrated this need for the formation and maintenance of the human self. See Mikulincer and Shaver, *Attachment in Adulthood*, 9–28.

11. Plato, *Symposium*.

hence creating the conditions for joy. Yet, while the meeting of need and desire does not straightforwardly map on the union of meaning and pleasure, these dyadic formulations are related descriptors of human love.

Luther argued that human beings are lovable because of God's own love for them. While we are tempted to love people in response to what we find desirable or pleasing in them, God's love is not reactive to anything that resides in creatures. Luther showed that God's creative love is doubly-aimed: in addition to bringing human beings into existence, God's love also creates human beings' lovability.[12] God's love is creative of the very possibility that human beings can love each other, since our loves are prone to respond to an existing positive good. God creates this possibility of human love responses by loving us with a creative love which generates our lovability. Human desire can be safely oriented towards loving other human beings in a reactive mode, because God gives each person this gift of lovability from the very beginning, together with the gift of life. By making us lovable, God also makes our joy possible. The seed of joy is present in us *qua* creatures, from our very origin. In other words, our created default is to live a good life and to flourish.

Kierkegaard appropriates Luther's thought that divine love is productive of human actualization and wellbeing but makes room for human loves to co-participate with God in the creation of the good life of flourishing. The role of human love is to cultivate the gift of lovability in others by fulfilling the greatest commandment and thereby rightly orienting one's desires in the direction of neighbor love. When we do that we "build up" the other.[13] This building up is Kierkegaard's language for human growth toward flourishing. However, human powers alone can never kindle any form of love in another person. While flourishing is the culmination of a life of love, and while human love interweaves with God's love to co-create another person's well-being, the human lover must always presuppose that a kernel of love is already present in the beloved. We need to assume that God's own love infuses a spark of love in each human being.[14] Kierkegaard thinks that even though human love has exceptional capacities to build up another person, no human being is ultimately able to "lay the ground of love in the other person."[15] God lays this ground in tandem with giving us the gift of having been born alive. We would simply embrace an illusion if we conceived of any human work that would be a substitute for God's own act of providing

12. Luther, *Heidelberg Disputation*.
13. Kierkegaard, *Works of Love*, 217.
14. Ibid., 216.
15. Ibid., 219.

the ground of love on the basis of which any "building up" would be possible. God's love implants the seed of love within the human person that makes it possible for love to be cultivated, grow, and flourish.

A human lover (whether in the sense of experiencing erotic love, or friendship, or adoptive or biological kinship, or any other form of love) can therefore cultivate this original seed of love and draw it forth from the ground because it was planted there from the start by God's own work. The person who loves builds up the other, yet not from scratch, as it were, but from a foundation that is already in place, even as it is invisible at times and always inchoate at the start. Human persons are fundamentally lovable because of this divinely infused spark of love that resides in each one of us *qua* creatures. Kierkegaard envisions human love in the form of an attunement between the lover and the beloved: when the lover's love meets the love kernel in the beloved, it results in a process of growth in the beloved. The beloved's love is being drawn out and she is being "built up." Yet the lover must presuppose that the seed of love is indeed present in the beloved. This presupposition is what enables the building up of the beloved;[16] love then becomes a conduit towards the beloved's good life of flourishing and well-being by drawing out and cultivating the inchoate form of love infused by God in her.

Using this Kierkegaardian imaginary, I suggest that while the lover responds to the kernel of love present in the beloved by presupposing it, the beloved responds in turn to the lover's own love. The two partners' love-desires resonate with one another in what attachment psychology calls attunement.[17] We must first receive another person's love, which draws forth our inner seed of love, in order to grow and respond in turn with our own love. Kierkegaard suggests that we must experience this exchange of love, which by its nature starts with the reception of another's desire, in order to live a fulfilled life and to flourish, or in Volf's terms, to live a life of joy. In Kierkegaard's terms the love exchange is conditioned by the assumption that the foundation of love is always present in embryo, yet it must be retrieved and enabled to grow. To love then is akin to doing the work of a midwife, bringing forth the other's love, and therefore bringing forth her well-being and joy. Indeed, Kierkegaard describes the lover's role as one who "loves forth." As Socrates perceived himself in the role of a midwife, dialoguing with others with the purpose of retrieving from the hidden spheres of their minds inchoate, pre-existent knowledge,[18] Kierkegaard too, argues that one

16. Ibid., 216.

17. Siegel, *The Developing Mind*, 84–85, 96–97.

18. Plato, *Phaedo*; *Meno*; *Phaedrus*.

co-participates in the other's upbuilding, therefore in the other's flourishing and joy, by bringing forth the other's hidden love.

I showed earlier how Jesus' double commandment to love God and to love human beings correlates with the intersection of human need as well as desire on one hand, and the union of meaning and pleasure on the other hand, therefore being generative of joy. Numerous theologies have been proposed concerning the relation of human and divine loves. Building on Kierkegaard's thought, I suggest that the overall relationship between God and creation may be understood as a complex love story. Kierkegaard starts from the premise, imported from Luther, that God is an ultimate giver. God's love is a continuous outgoing stream, which, as I showed earlier, creates both the recipients of God's love (human beings) and their lovability. God's love is not conditioned even remotely by any positive good characterizing the subjects of God's love. Instead, God's love creatively brings into being both the subjects of divine love and their lovability. By contrast, Luther observes that human beings love what pleases them. God does not need such a feature in the beloved, because God is the one who bestows the good and lovability upon people. In fact, for Luther, God's love for creation climaxes in the love manifested on the cross, where it confers redemptive good upon the worst and neediest people. God makes the human being attractive by pouring the outflow of divine love upon us, no matter what our state is.[19] Luther's main trope here is one of a love flow that stems out of God towards human beings unidirectionally, with the productive power of creating goodness in the human receivers. However, Luther also thinks that human recipients of such lavish divine love should not hoard it for themselves but enable the love flow to continue to other human beings, or neighbors. We are channels of transmission through which the stream of love which God pours forth and which transforms our lives ought to flow further from us to our neighbors. Our task is to enable the flow of divine love to continue on from us to other human beings.[20]

Kierkegaard presupposes Luther's framework in his own understanding of how human and divine love dovetail. He builds on the assumption that God is the ultimate lover who always gives. However, Kierkegaard ascribes a more complex role to human love as co-partaker with God in the shaping of human life so as to propel it towards fulfillment and joy. The right orientation of human love is to be primordially toward God, as the first half of the greatest commandment calls for. Yet our love for God, while rightly directed toward God, is being re-circuited so as to reach other human

19. Luther, *Heidelberg Disputation*, 57.
20. Luther, *The Freedom of a Christian*, 371.

beings. The big love story between God and creation, of which God is both the author and the main subject, is complex. It is not reduced to either a God-to-human love move or a humanity-to-divinity love trajectory. To be sure, God is always a giver of love. Because of that, even as we are called above all to love God Godself, God resends our love for God to those whom God loves. These include all human beings across the whole creation.

In Kierkegaard's imaginary, our love for God is like a letter sent with a forwarding address. While we send our love letter to God, which we indeed ought to do, God forwards it to a new destination, which is another human person. Our love for God then does not stop at the divine address, so to speak. It is readdressed to the human neighbor, who is always God's beloved as much as we are. Kierkegaard agrees with Kant that the self is also always a neighbor. Although God asks for complete human devotion, Kierkegaard believes that God does not absorb in Godself human love and human giving. The moment we incline ourselves towards loving God we "immediately receive . . . a notice designating where it should be delivered further because God does not ask for anything for [God]self."[21]

Kierkegaard's premise is that the relationship between God and the human person is far removed from an I-Thou form.[22] Such a form would be impossible, since God is far removed from the spectrum of human existence that we experience in our quotidian lives. The gap between God and human existence is unspeakably enormous. God has no need whatsoever, and therefore God's love is the love of an ultimate giver. Human love can never be so, because we are creatures of need. Simultaneously we are also creatures of desire, who desire to love. God unites our need and our desire in that even when we love God, God transforms this love desire into a gift that meets human needfulness by redirecting the love flow from Godself to human creatures. Kierkegaard thinks that this is a feature of divine mercy as much as it is a feature of divine creative love; God continually points away from Godself.[23] Consequently, while Kierkegaard takes seriously Jesus' imperative that human beings must love God above all other loves, he interprets it to mean that God's reception of human love is yet another mode in which God loves, points away from Godself, and gives God's own self to us.

Kierkegaard translates the greatest commandment into a double mediation. One mediation is the forward move of our love for God, towards other human beings. On the other hand, our love for God cannot be direct. It is always mediated through our love for our neighbors. While we rightly

21. Kierkegaard, *Works of Love*, 161.
22. Cf. Buber, *I and Thou*.
23. Kierkegaard, *Works of Love*, 160.

relate to God by directing our love towards God, God remains unseen by human eyes. We cannot love the invisible God in any other way except when our love for God finds concrete particular embodiment in love relations with people in our proximity. We would delude ourselves to imagine that we can love the unseen God while excluding from that love disposition the earthly relationships with people with whom our lives are intertwined. Kierkegaard thinks that there must be a direct proportionality between how much one loves the unseen God and how much one loves the people one sees. It would be a complete farce and illusion to postulate that we are to distance ourselves from and reject our immediate human companions who are visible to us for the purpose of loving the God whom we do not see.[24] The delusion Kierkegaard worries about would allow one to think that God can be loved directly by human beings. Kierkegaard emphasizes that such a direct love of God would be impossible for humanity. "God is too exalted to receive a person's love directly."[25] The gap between God and human beings is impassable from the human end. As such, our love for God can only be indirect, reaching God through loving the people we see, our neighbors. Now, we should start with loving the unseen God, as the greatest commandment calls us to do, because this is how we learn to love. Yet, such a movement of ascent of the human heart into the darkness of the unseen would be fanatical if it were not redoubled by extending ourselves in earthly loves towards the very visible, embodied, needy, and particular people who surround us.[26]

In fact, according to Kierkegaard, when we love other people, we help them to love God. Similarly, we are truly loved when others, by their love, help us to love God.[27] We are always helped to love God through the direct experience of human loves. Our love for God remains indirect, while this human mediation enables it to be the only kind of love that we actually can give to God, because of our finitude and temporality. Our love for God, while having the right telos, passes through the mediating experience of loving fellow humans.

Yet the other mediation, which I described earlier, has to do with God's forwarding motion of our love toward another human person. The love flow between one person and another therefore includes God as a middle point through which it passes, since God does not absorb our love for Godself but rather sends it on to our neighbor. Since God receives and

24. Kierkegaard glosses on 1 John 4:20.
25. Kierkegaard, *Works of Love*, 160.
26. Ibid., 159.
27. Ibid., 107.

further channels human love toward other human beings, God is present within the love flow thereby created at a human level, starting with one human being, including God as the "middle term,"[28] and landing in another person's life. God becomes structurally part of human loves. Human love then does not stand in a vacuum; God holds love relations together by forwarding the lover's love flow to the human recipient and uniting it with God's own love for her. In between human lovers there is a divine presence which indwells the love arch thus formed. I suggest that this divine presence as a middle term in the interstitial space among human beings is a pneumatological indwelling which sanctifies human love and increases its power of shaping human life toward its flourishing. As God is present pneumatologically within human loves, such loves are sacramental and mediate human participation in God's own love for humanity. Natural human loves can be then supernaturally elevated into the love of God via God's own pneumatological inclusion in them.

I suggested above that there is a double mediation at play with respect to human love for God. On the one hand, our love for God is indirect and mediated by human loves, while on the other hand, God is forwarding our love for God to other human creatures, thereby becoming internal to human loves as their sanctifying middle term. Another Kierkegaardian image brings these two mediations together. Kierkegaard envisions a lake with a hidden spring at its bottom which supplies fresh waters continuously, while a stream of water flows from the lake and carries the water forward, keeping the water continuously fresh and in motion.[29] Kierkegaard uses this trope as an analogue for how God's love is always in motion. Furthermore, as the water in the lake is not simply moving but as it is carried by the stream it has a definite direction, God's love also has directionality. God's love is always in motion towards God's creatures, and it also moves human love for God toward the aim of God's own love: other people. To love God, then, means to enter the divine love stream that already has an established direction and telos of reaching other human lives. Human loves engender human participation in God's flow of love towards humanity while God is structurally part of human loving. Although all human beings are intended recipients of the replenishing streams of divine love, each human person can only partake in a finite number of such streams, as we are creatures of embodied finitude and temporal limitations. Yet God indwells this very finitude and elevates it by uniting it with God's transcendent and enduring love.

28. Ibid., 67, 107–9, 260, 301, 339, 450 among others.
29. Ibid., 10.

As human beings are creatures of need as well as desire, the need for love is met when the love they receive fits the particular nuance of their need. Human desire to love, which originates from the inner seed of love implanted in us by God, finds its right directionality when it ascends toward God, who redirects it to the needful beloved, friend, or any other receiver of love in the particular, unique form that fits that person's concrete life. Using Kierkegaard's framework, I propose that the kind of love that fulfills the greatest commandment and builds up the good life includes God as its middle term between human persons engaged in a rapport of love and places them within the love stream of God for creatures, which lifts them up to become participants in and mediators of the same stream of God's love. The union of human love goes beyond attaching the partners to each other. It also attaches each to God's love for them while this interweaving of human and divine loves meets both human need and human desire. Correlatively, it brings forth the intersection of meaning with pleasure, hence giving rise to joy.

I showed thus far that our love for human beings and our love for God are inextricably interwoven. We can only properly love God by also loving human persons, and we can only love human beings the right way by directing our love toward God in tandem with our horizontal love toward people. Simultaneously, God indwells pneumatologically the inter-human attachment space which unites both the lovers and their mutual love with the love of God. These two sorts of love are not the same, but they co-participate in the creation of human joy. At the same time, human and divine loves are not on the same plane. God's love is poured forth in infinite, unquenchable streams. Human beings instead cannot love other humans infinitely. Nor can they love in abstraction from their own neediness to be loved. Human love is only sustainable when it partakes in and is nourished by divine love. We cannot engage in infinite outpouring of love to another human person as if the beloved would be a terminus point able to absorb such extreme devotion. Neither infinite giving, nor infinite receiving of love is possible on a purely human plane. Only God can give infinitely and receive absolutely while also forwarding the received love in super-abundant extra giving to creatures. Overextending human loves would be destructive, because to give absolutely to a finite recipient extinguishes the giver. The receiver, too, would be insufficiently dependable on her own to absorb absolute love. It would be even more injurious to attempt to extract ultimate love from another person; it would colonize one into the other by absorbing the other's unique subjectivity into one's own desires, plus it would create a despot conditioned by such colonizing tendencies—a far removed picture from anything related to human flourishing and joy. It would be equally pernicious to withdraw from loving others in fear. Such a closing up to love would, in fact, confirm how undependable human loves are when they attempt to unfold operating on the basis of human power alone. Human love is an inescapable need as much as it is the channel of our desire, but it is not able to run on its own steam without partaking in the love flow that originates in God, who infuses us with a spark of divine love from our inception, and is a love that also passes through God en route to the human beloved. God as middle term within human loves creates the possibility of sustainable human loving in which the lover neither absorbs the beloved nor is lost in her, and nor does one run away in fear of such a loss from the other. Even though God does not absorb in and for Godself our love for God, our God-relationship[30] remains both primordial and ultimate in order for human love to be maximally expansive and therefore maximally conducive to joy.

In Kierkegaard's thought, the outcome of human non-participation in the divine love streams is despair. If we attempted to love infinitely a finite creature, which is what any earthly beloved would be, we would not only delude ourselves, but we would be in despair. The real source of despair in human life is not trouble within a love relationship or friendship or any other love attachment, or even the breaking of such relationships. Love woes might make manifest the underlying despair in one's life, but in themselves, they do not constitute despair. In Kierkegaard's framework, despair is the lack of what he calls the eternal ingredient in love,[31] or as I have depicted it in this essay, the lack of a pneumatological dimension in human loves. When human love is not sustained by the eternal streams of God's love, despair is bound to emerge. This kind of despair is not a feeling but "a misrelation in a person's inner being."[32] Despair is a misrelation within the self in the sense that the self is not primordially relating to God and nourishing human loves through their participation in God's love streams.[33]

Kierkegaard could be critiqued here for appearing insensitive to the grief of loss in love, unrequited desire, or bereavement. Yet he is conscious that it is nearly impossible to find comfort in such sorrows. His solution parallels Immanuel Kant's ideas about a heart revolution, which is only achievable with God's assistance. In Kant's case, the logic is that because God commands us to fulfill the moral law, it is our duty and it follows that God

---

30. Kierkegaard refers to the human rapport to God in love and faith with the term "God-relationship" throughout *Works of Love*. See for example 114, 128, 140–42, 143, 152–53, 190, 230, 320, etc.

31. Ibid., 40–41.

32. Ibid., 51.

33. For a more complex Kierkegaardian discussion of despair see Kierkegaard, *Sickness unto Death*.

must also provide what it takes for us to be able to do it. Since we are unable to fulfill the moral law on our own, God is faithful to God's own command and gives us God's own help which increases human powers to rise to the level of what God asks for. Yet we are riding on God's assistance and not on human ability.[34] Kierkegaard's move is analogous: "When eternity says 'you shall love,' it is responsible for making sure that this can be done."[35] Kierkegaard is aware that a commandment of love is a humanly impossible endeavor. However, the command carries within its own imperative the divine provision for the possibility of it being fulfilled. Of course, requiring love out of a person in despair would be mocking, yet Kierkegaard's response is that the impossibility of fulfilling the commandment with human power only shows its divine origin and that God provides help to actually live the commandment. As such, the right kind of love, which builds up human beings and therefore opens the gateway of joy in their lives, is not a mere earthly love experience, but it is permeated sacramentally by God's pneumatological presence. The Holy Spirit is the source of help that enables human loves to be rightly directed, to mediate and participate in the enduring streams of divine love, and thereby to be the source of human joy.

34. Kant, *Religion Within the Boundaries,* 66.
35. Kierkegaard, *Works of Love,* 51.

BIBLIOGRAPHY

Buber, Martin. *I and Thou.* Translated by Walter Kaufmann. New York: Scribner's, 1970.

John Duns Scotus. *Duns Scotus on Divine Love: Texts and Commentary on Goodness and Freedom, God and Humans.* Edited by A. Vos et al. Burlington, VA: Ashgate, 2003.

Kant, Immanuel. *Groundwork of the Metaphysics of Morals.* Translated and edited by Mary Gregor and Jens Timmerman. Cambridge: Cambridge University Press, 1998.

———. *Religion Within the Boundaries of Mere Reason.* In *Religion within the Boundaries of Mere Reason and Other Writings,* translated by Allen Wood and George Di Giovanni, 31–192. Cambridge: Cambridge University Press, 1998.

Kierkegaard, Søren. *Sickness unto Death.* Translated by Howard V. Hong and Edna H. Hong. Princeton: Princeton University Press, 1980.

———. *Works of Love.* Translated by Howard V. Hong and Edna H. Hong. Princeton: Princeton University Press, 1995.

Luther, Martin. *The Freedom of a Christian.* In *Luther's Works,* edited by Harold J. Grimm, vol. 31, 333–77. Philadelphia: Fortress, 1957.

———. *Heidelberg Disputation.* In *Luther's Works,* vol. 31, 39–70.

Mikulincer, Mario, and Philip R. Shaver. *Attachment in Adulthood: Structure, Dynamics, and Change.* New York: Guilford, 2007.

Plato. *Meno.* In *The Collected Dialogues of Plato Including the Letters,* edited by Edith Hamilton and Huntington Cairns, 354–84. Princeton: Princeton University Press, 1989.

———. *Phaedo.* In *The Collected Dialogues of Plato Including the Letters,* edited by Edith Hamilton and Huntington Cairns, 41–98. Princeton: Princeton University Press, 1989.

———. *Phaedrus.* In *The Collected Dialogues of Plato Including the Letters,* edited by Edith Hamilton and Huntington Cairns, 476–525. Princeton: Princeton University Press, 1989.

———. *Symposium.* In *The Collected Dialogues of Plato Including the Letters,* edited by Edith Hamilton and Huntington Cairns, 551–63. Princeton: Princeton University Press, 1989.

Siegel, Daniel S. *The Developing Mind: How Relationships and the Brain Interact to Shape Who We Are.* New York: Guilford, 1999.

Taylor, Charles. *Sources of the Self.* Cambridge: Harvard University Press, 1989.

Volf, Miroslav. *Flourishing: Why We Need Religion in a Globalized World.* New Haven: Yale University Press, 2016.

9

Theology, Violence, and White Spaces

Nancy Bedford

IN THE "EPILOGUE" TO his book *Flourishing*, Miroslav Volf invites us to join in a "vital exploration" of flourishing, paying particular attention to the witness of various religious perspectives to the unity of meaning and pleasure.[1] He suggests that such a unity, expressed as joy, is vital in pushing back against the specters of nihilism, both in its world-denying and its world-destroying forms. I think that it is important to note that, as in other books he has written, in this project a backdrop of violence is clearly discernible: religiously motivated or justified violence in particular. His work resists the prevailing logic of that violence and proposes ways to foreground love, joy, peacemaking, abundant life, and flourishing in its stead. As a way to take Volf up on his call to focus on God's invitation to joy and flourishing, in this essay I will explore a dimension of violence that gets in the way of theology's ability to help people of faith resist forces that are destructive to a "good life." I am referring to the way in which Christian theology sometimes functions as a "white space."

---

1. Volf, *Flourishing*, 206.

TOWARD A DEFINITION OF VIOLENCE

Etymologically, our word "violence" comes from *violationem* and *violatio*.[2] It is connected to injury, dishonor, and profanation. I find the idea of profanation as a dimension of violence theologically suggestive. *Profanus* refers to something not consecrated, something unholy, which is out in front of (*pro*) the temple (*fanum*), and not welcomed into the realm of the sacred. It presupposes a kind of violence that treats another as if that other were by definition outside the circle of God's holiness and love. It thus entails the diminishment of the other and the reduction of the other to a mere "thing" that can be manipulated, harmed or even destroyed at will. It also involves an impoverishment of the idea of God, as if some creatures or some dimensions of reality were somehow outside of God's purview.

I understand violence as a misuse of power that either intends to inflict harm or does effectively inflict harm on human and/or non-human creation, detracting from its flourishing and ignoring its sacrality. The harm perpetrated can be psychic as well as physical, though most often the two are connected. By definition, violence involves an imposition or coercion, often justified by the perpetrator as "necessary." Indeed, intrinsic to explicit and consciously chosen forms of violence is the notion that the ends justify the means.[3] However, not all forms of violence are even acknowledged or recognized by those involved in them; some forms of violence have been "naturalized" to the point that they are accepted as a norm by the majority in a given society.

Some kinds of "violence" fall outside of the above definition. For example, there is a "violence" that seems built into the natural world, as can be seen for instance, in the shattering effects of earthquakes. In this sense, "as historical and cross-cultural records demonstrate, our evolutionary history is laced with examples of violence."[4] However, the violence of "natural" disasters can be compounded by human violence as understood above ("misuse of power"), as evidenced in the present cycle of violent weather events aggravated by humanly induced climate change or indeed in the phenomenon of earthquakes triggered by the waste-water produced by fracking, as

2. The gendered dimension that is so often present in violent acts can be seen in the Spanish word *violación*, which means "rape."

3. As Duane Cady points out, those who argue that violence is justified, generally "do not value it in itself, but as a means to an end sufficiently good to outweigh the evils of the injury or violation involved." Cady, "Violence," 677–78.

4. Guerra and Knox, "Violence," 1650.

is happening in Oklahoma, a formerly seismically dormant area that is now experiencing tremors almost daily.[5]

Given the present physical reality of the world, including natural cycles of birth and death, it is probably not possible to live in absolute non-violence, though some religious traditions do make serious attempts in that direction, such as Jainism with its principle of *ahimsa* or non-violence toward all living creatures. It seems to me that even with the best of intentions, realistically preserving the life of one creature (for example, a human baby) may sometimes mean killing another creature (for example, an *aedes aegypti* mosquito that can carry a number of viruses deadly to humans). Still, that does not justify the kinds of human habits that make our species massively deadly to other creatures, decimating entire species and changing climate in detrimental ways. In a rather hopeful twist, the social sciences teach that human "individuals are biologically and socially capable of peaceful coexistence" (with humans and with other creatures) given "effective prevention and control."[6] So we do seem to have some non-violent or anti-violent options as humans, even if we don't achieve total non-violence. At the very least, human choices do make a difference when it comes to the exercise and the degree of violence.[7]

If we approach the question from a Christian faith perspective, we find that the point made repeatedly in the New Testament is that God's logic is not the logic of violence. For God, "good" ends do not justify violent means; as I read Scripture, violence is not God's proposed method of conflict resolution. On the contrary, Christ arguably comes to put an end to the logic of religiously justified sacrifice and violence.[8] Paradoxically, God does so by suffering the violence of our world in God's own incarnate self in order to subvert the logic of violence; God does not overcome violence by applying even greater violence, as we tend to want to do.[9]

5. Cf. TG, "Energy Extraction."

6. Guerra and Knox, "Violence," 1654.

7. Stephan and Chenoweth ("Why Civil Resistance Works") actually seek to prove (and to my mind, do so effectively) that non-violent methods are more effective than violent means such as warfare in achieving policy goals.

8. The author of Hebrews, for instance, seems to argue that though Christ does indeed function as a sacrifice as well as a priest, his action puts an end (or should put an end) to a religious economy of violent sacrifice; cf. Heb 9:26, 10:5–18.

9. This is not to deny the fact that violent apocalyptic imagery does appear in the New Testament, but it seems to me that such themes are usually depicted as the result of human violence as it is perceived from the perspective of the oppressed, not as a justification of violence as God's *modus operandi*; on this, cf. the essays in Grimsrud and Hardin, *Compassionate Eschatology*, especially Finamore, "A Kindler, Gentler Apocalypse?"

The emphasis in Scripture seems largely to be for followers of Jesus to understand the scope of violence and to learn to outwit its logic in multiple creative ways.[10] We are not expected to achieve an ultimate victory over violence in this "evil age" (Gal 1:4), but we can hope and act for God's peace and justice, not allowing the logic of violence and counter-violence (revenge) to colonize us. To outwit violence also means to curtail it, contain it, and reverse it whenever possible. Such a way of life requires epistemological agility, a capacity for discernment in many different material situations, and a non-violent exercise of power, all of which require reliance on the Holy Spirit.[11]

OBJECTIVE AND SUBJECTIVE DIMENSIONS OF VIOLENCE

Violent ways and means are so entrenched in our ways of being in the world that it can be difficult to grasp violence in all its complexities. Slavoj Žižek makes the point that in order to understand violence we need to look at it "sideways" or "awry"; said otherwise, we need to take a step back from it in order to really *see*.[12] He suggests that there is more to violence than initially meets the eye: in fact it has a threefold dimension. First of all there is what he calls *subjective* violence, "performed by a clearly identifiable agent" or subject. But if we respond only to that dimension, which is so to speak in the foreground, we miss the backdrop of the violence we have perceived, which is also involved in its generation. Žižek calls that backdrop the "objective" side of violence, which he further divides into two: *symbolic* violence (which is embodied in our languages and functions in our universes of meaning) and *systemic* violence (resulting from the way our economic and political systems work).[13]

The reason I find Žižek's categories useful is that they help us contextualize violence when it flares up. Subjective violence does not "come out of nowhere" against a "normal" background of peace and absence of violence.

10. Cf. Wink, *Jesus and Nonviolence.*

11. That is one reason I don't find Arendt's influential notion that power and violence are opposites particularly helpful. She holds that power is acting in concert with others, whereas violence requires acting "with implements" against others. She denies that that power also has to manifest itself "with implements," that is to say, in some material fashion, even if it is not a strictly technological one. One might even argue theologically, however, that the incarnation itself is a particular "implement" of God's power. Cf. Arendt, *On Violence*, 4 and 56.

12. See Žižek, *Violence.*

13. Ibid., 1–2.

Rather, the "norm" is already systemically and symbolically violent.[14] If we only take into account the "subjective" dimension of a violent act and forget the systemic and symbolic depths whence violence arises, our responses to particular instances of violence will be fairly useless. At most they will "treat the symptoms" without really getting a handle on the disease itself.[15] We can see this for instance in the killings at Mother Emmanuel AME church in Charleston, SC on June 17, 2015. A white man called Dylann attended Wednesday evening Bible study and was welcomed into the group. At one point, he said: "Y'all want something to pray about? I'll give you something to pray about." He then pulled out a gun, insulted the people present in racist terms, and killed nine of them, including the pastor. All of them were Black. If only the "subjective" dimension of this act of violence is taken into account, the analysis is limited to the violent "subject," Dylann Roof, and what aspects of his particular psyche would lead him to murder nine people.[16] That would miss the "objective" (systemic and symbolic) dimensions that grounded his violence. It was embedded in a white supremacist understanding that Roof holds in common with many other people in the United States and it was meant as a reminder to all Black people everywhere that there is nowhere in this country they are ever safe, even if they are at prayer in their houses of worship (symbolic dimension).

In her critique of white feminism (or as she puts it, of *whitefeminists*) at the intersection of race and gender, Ellen Armour makes a similar point, speaking of the problem of the oppression of women: "to attempt attacks against women's oppression *without* attending to the systemic violence at work in the discourse that inscribes the institutions and individuals we hold responsible—*and ourselves*—is to risk following false exits that either leave the system in place or reinstate it on new ground."[17]

We should also not fall prey to what Žižek calls the "anti-theoretical edge" of the urgent injunctions to action that emerge every time we feel outraged by violence; we need not only to act, but also to *discern* and *understand*.[18] Jesus tried to get his disciples to do just that and to realize that discernment is itself a *praxis* linked to prayer. We see this for instance in the story placed just after the transfiguration, when the disciples have difficulties in curing a young boy afflicted by a demon (Mark 9:14–29 and par.).

14. Ibid.

15. Ibid.

16. See, for example Bauerlein et al., "'Loner' Held."

17. Armour, *Deconstruction*, 184.

18. It would be a false binary to oppose "symbolic" and "physical" violence: they coexist and reinforce each other; they must be discerned and opposed jointly.

When they ask Jesus privately why their attempts had failed, he responds that in such difficult cases what is needed is prayer. In the face of knotty situations of violence affecting individuals and systems simultaneously, what is required is not mere activism, but considered action accompanied by the kind of *theoria* ("contemplation") that only prayer provides.[19]

Žižek writes about the "obscene underside" of US culture as it is exemplified in the Abu Ghraib tortures.[20] Something similar might be said of the killings of Black boys and men by policemen in the United States. Officially sanctioned torture and killing illustrate how systemic and symbolic "objective" violence undergird the "subjective" action of individual agents of violence. From Žižek's perspective, to be submitted to humiliating torture by officials of the United States is not a strange aberration. Rather, it marks for the victims an effective initiation into US culture, which accommodates violence as a spectacle alongside (or as the underside of) its discourse about tolerance, personal dignity, democracy and freedom. As Žižek puts it, to see the humiliation of the prisoners at Abu Ghraib is to see "the very core of the obscene enjoyment that sustains the US way of life."[21]

The videos posted on YouTube of the killings of Eric Garner, Laquan McDonald, and Tamir Rice function much in the same way.[22] The murders happened within a few weeks of each other in the summer and fall of 2014. They are representative of many more instances of mistreatment and violence inflicted on Black bodies in the United States, some known widely, others known only to a few people. The video footage of these incidents on the one hand has forced public discussion of such killings. On the other hand, they can easily become a voyeuristic exercise that reinforces the principle that Black lives don't matter: lethal, racist violence as spectacle, in the tradition of the public lynchings of the past. Eric Garner was a forty-three-year-old Black man suffocated by a police officer who put him in a chokehold in Staten Island, New York on July 17, 2014. The police had accused Garner of peddling cigarettes on the street and he had complained, claiming harassment. He repeated the phrase "I can't breathe" eleven times, before finally losing consciousness and then dying.[23] Laquan McDonald was a seventeen-year-old Black youth who was shot sixteen times by a police officer and killed in Chicago on October 20, 2014. He had a small knife in his

19. As Ignatian spirituality has it: *contemplativus [contemplativa] simul in actione.*

20. Žižek, *Violence*, 176.

21. Ibid., 176–77.

22. These incidents were caught on video respectively by a cell phone camera, a police car dash cam, and a security camera. The recordings are widely available on the internet.

23. See Williams, "Summer of Hate," 10.

hand and was walking away from the police. The policeman who shot him was standing about ten feet away.[24] Tamir Rice was a twelve-year-old Black boy shot and killed by a policeman in Cleveland, Ohio on November 23, 2014, after he was seen playing in a park with a toy gun.[25] The gratuitous and unnecessary killing of these human beings made in the image of God brings to mind the tremendous surge of violence recounted in Genesis 4, first with the killing of Abel by his brother Cain and later with the cry for vengeance multiplied by Lamech, the descendent and symbolic heir of Cain's violent choices. The blood of the victims, then and now, cries out to God from the earth (Gen 4:10).

According to Žižek, the "heart of darkness" habits that led to the Abu Ghraib tortures can be seen in the underbelly of many institutions. This includes the Church with its systemic problems with pedophilia and other forms of sexual abuse. He thinks that the Church should be "investigated with regard to the way it systematically creates conditions for such crimes."[26] Constantly to say that a certain kind of violence is an "aberration" rather than a predictable effect of particular structures and of the logic of ongoing violence may serve to deflect our attention from understanding the backdrop for individual violent acts. It is necessary to see what elements in a society, a culture, a religion, or an institution *create the conditions* for a given form of violence, even if they simultaneously state that such violence is abhorrent, the opposite of the values for which they stand.

The question that emerges for me is whether (or perhaps when) theology contributes to the creation of conditions that lead to certain forms of violence, even while we as theologians may state that violence is the opposite of the values for which we stand. Feminist and womanist theologians have explored the matter of violent tropes within Christian doctrines, focusing especially on the knotty question of the theological interpretation in the New Testament and beyond of the violent execution of Jesus of Nazareth.[27] Certain applications of Christology do seem to be good candidates for what Žižek calls "subjective" violence, i.e. violence carried out by recognizable agents. Even though most theological constructions do leave some wiggle room for a variety of possible interpretations, a Christology that holds, for instance, that native peoples must be subjected by force because they are enemies of Christ and worship "bad demons," fits quite clearly in such a category. Such was the reasoning of Hernán Cortés as he justified the invasion

---

24. See Friedersdorf, "Corrupt System."
25. See Smith, "Why Video Evidence Wasn't Enough."
26. Žižek, *Violence*, 168.
27. Cf. Bedford, *La porfía de la resurrección*, 87–156.

and despoiling of Mexico, a thought process justified by christologically by theologians such as Juan Ginés de Sepúlveda.[28]

What I'd like to reflect upon here, however, is a little different. I want to ask not what happens when theology sins by commission (that is, by embracing doctrines or interpretations that easily lend themselves to coercion and violence), but what happens when it sins by omission. As a teaching and writing theologian, I must ask myself to what degree I am embedded in practices that create conditions for violence, in Žižek's "objective" sense, i.e. one that operates at the systemic and symbolic level and sometimes makes itself almost invisible. Is there something I need to change in the way I approach the theological task?

WHITENESS AND VIOLENCE: THE PROBLEM OF THEOLOGY AS A WHITE SPACE

Because at this time I live and work in the US context, I am particularly interested in working to find ways for theology to disarticulate its complicities with the violence of white racism, the "original sin" of the United States, which continues to manifest itself in many ways, including some that are ignored and sometimes even justified by dominant Christian theological thought in this country. The violence of white racism and white privilege works against flourishing and joy. It is urgent that not only theologians and communities of "color" push back against the logic of white privilege, but also—with particular responsibility—theologians and communities who for whatever reason benefit from "whiteness" as it functions in US society.

I am embedded (by virtue of the tonality of my skin) in the systemic violence of white privilege in this imperial nation. White privilege also functioned in the other two countries I've lived in, Argentina and Germany, but in a different way, since each culture contextualizes its racism and other injustices a little differently. The fact is that I am white and also straight, married, a mother, highly educated, employed, tenured, hyper-documented (i.e., I have more than one passport and nationality), bearer of an Anglo-Saxon surname and to top it all off, Christian. There is nothing intrinsically problematic with any of these factors. I need not renounce them or be ashamed of them. The violence comes, however, when they work together in toxic ways to the detriment of others. One example of this is when the matter of white obliviousness gets the upper hand in a theology. Immersion in white privilege can obscure my ability to see and to respond to the world as it really is. Jon Sobrino calls the ability to see things as they really are

28. See Mires, *En nombre de la cruz*, 30–32.

"honesty with the real" and argues that such honesty is a vital part of doing theology in Spirit-led ways.[29] There is a real sense in which complicity in white racism and privilege can threaten to undo my very vocation as a theologian, by blinding me to what is going on outside of the cone of protection provided by my white privilege.

Sociologist Elijah Anderson describes what he calls "white space" as it functions in US society. By this he means public spaces such as schools, neighborhoods, stores, restaurants, or workspaces populated primarily by white bodies. He argues that Black people often receive the message, directly or indirectly, that they are either not welcome in those spaces or must justify their presence in them.[30] As he puts it:

> When present in the white space, blacks reflexively note the proportion of whites to blacks, or may look around for other blacks with whom to commune if not bond, and then may adjust their comfort level accordingly; when judging a setting as too white, they can feel uneasy and consider it to be informally "off limits." For whites, however, the same settings are generally regarded as unremarkable, or as normal, taken-for-granted reflections of civil society.[31]

There often is, in other words, a profound difference in the experience and thus in the perception of reality of people coded as white and people not coded as white in US society. People not coded as white are often obliged to answer questions as to what they are doing in a white space, for instance when a store clerk says pointedly "May I help you?" or when police officers stop a person to require an explanation about what they are doing. This happens to Black people of all backgrounds and socio-economic levels. For instance, Black colleagues and students from the seminary where I teach have told me many stories of how they are stopped and questioned by the campus police of the university where our institution is located. This can happen when they are getting into their cars, walking across campus, or even sitting quietly on a bench outside. They are asked questions such as "Are you in the right place?" or "Is this your car?" And it is not only the police who assume the right to question the right of a Black person to be in a "white" space. As Anderson stresses, "almost any white person present in

---

29. See Sobrino, *El principio-misericordia*, 16–25. [This text is available in English translation: Sobrino, *Principle of Mercy.*—Eds.]

30. See Anderson, "White Space."

31. Ibid., 10.

the white space can possess and wield [the] enormous power" of requiring another person to justify his or her presence in a given space.[32]

As Anderson explains, the accumulation both of micro-aggressions and of overt hostility makes it in many ways exhausting for Black people to be in white space, as they come to the realization that "being white is a fundamental requirement for acceptance and a sense of belonging in the white space."[33] People react in different ways to this realization: trying to avoid the white space altogether, or entering it fleetingly and leaving it with relief. The problem is, however, that "the white space is where many social rewards originate, including an elegant night on the town, or cultural capital itself—education, employment, privilege, prestige, money," and many other possibilities.[34] So in some very real ways, engagement with that space is a necessity, even while entering into the space and experiencing its codes can be deeply alienating for anybody not coded as white.

The notion of "white spaces" is a helpful heuristic tool in thinking about the theological task and indeed about many Christian institutions, including churches. If we consider the fact, for example, that mainline Protestant denominations in the United States are made up in their great majority by white people, we begin to see that though mainline Protestant-ism includes many people of color, such denominations and many of their institutions function in practice as white spaces.[35] This allows them to treat the hard theological questions that emerge from taking seriously the experi-ences, questions, and reality of Black and Brown bodies in this country as an optional exercise.

Ironically, mainline Protestant spaces have been some of the most pro-ductive for academic theology. In theory, they value academic freedom and make space for a number of different perspectives. If I think back on my own life as a theologian, institutions emerging out of the mainline have been consistently welcoming to me in the three (majority white) countries in which I've lived.[36] Mainline Protestants have generously supported me with

32. Ibid., 15. Cf. Willie Jennings on the theologically conditioned creation of a "public black body" regarded (by whites) as a commodity in US public space, in his essay "African American Theology and the Public Imaginary."

33. Anderson, "White Space," 16.

34. Ibid., 16.

35. In 2014, 86 percent of mainline Protestants were non-Hispanic Whites. The degree of "whiteness" among mainline Protestant denominations is greater than in any other Christian grouping, including Mormons and Orthodox Christians. See Pew Research Center, "Racial and Ethnic Composition of Religious Groups."

36. As a Latin American theologian who is also "white" I should note that Latin American liberation theology, especially in its first years, also suffered from the prob-lem of theology as a "white space," though some of the theologians who would be

scholarships, provided mentoring, and later offered places to work in which I've felt a great deal of academic freedom to pursue my theological interests, even though I do not strictly "belong" to them, given my Argentine Baptist roots and current US Mennonite affiliation. All of this kindness should not blind me, however, to the ways in which these institutions function as white spaces or the ways in which the theology we teach and produce in them is often also reflective of a "white" *locus theologicus*. Because I am coded as white in this society, it is much too easy for me to overlook this kind of institutional and ideological bias, and the ways that it is alienating to people who are not white. It is also much too easy to transfer to Black and Brown colleagues and students the theological work of bringing the gospel to shed light on the workings and consequences of racism and white privilege.

When I speak of theology as a white space, I don't necessarily mean that it is overtly demeaning to people not coded as white (though that, too, can happen). I mean that the theological task can be carried out with impunity by those coded as white as if the questions emerging from non-white spaces and actors were *optional*. These questions are not optional to the God who liberates and transforms us, and so they should not be optional for any theology that cares about God. Said in a slightly different way, Black history, Black experience, and Black thought (including Black and womanist theologies) point us all (Black or not) to constant engagement with the reality that at every level of this society the game is rigged in the favor of those coded as white. The implications of this kind of realization are profoundly theological and draw our attention to *loci* such as theological anthropology (who do we believe is truly human?), the theodicy question (how can a good God permit this injustice?), as well as to the need for conversion (to the way of Jesus) and discernment (by the work of the Spirit) in our theological pursuits.[37]

Rather than targeting the work of particular "white" theologians to illustrate my point, I'd rather ask myself—and by extension other theologians coded as "white"—a series of questions for us to carry with us into our work: What are we reading and discussing in our classrooms? What are the burning questions in our theological work? What haunts us? Do Black

---

considered "white" in Latin American would be thought of as "Brown" in the United States. Dwight N. Hopkins tells the story of James Cone and his encounter with the problem of the "whiteness" of early Latin American theology in *Introducing Black Theology of Liberation*, 167–72.

37. It is no coincidence that a Black theologian such as James Evans puts loci such as theological anthropology, theodicy and the nature of God at the center of his theological system. See Evans, Jr., *We Have Been Believers*; the same goes for Womanist theologian Diana Hayes, *Standing in the Shoes My Mother Made*.

lives truly matter to us? Do we knowingly or unknowingly create conditions for epistemic violence in our work? Are we hard at work in undoing our complicities with a racist system? How would our work have to shift for our theologies not to inhabit and embody "white space?" How do people of color feel when they are invited into our habitual workspaces? Which bodies are present in our spaces of worship? Why? In what ways do we need to change our habits of thought and of action? How does our "conversion" manifest itself?

TOWARD DISARTICULATING
THE HEGEMONY OF WHITE SPACES

Just as it is irresponsible for male theologians to persist in theological moves that are directly hurtful to the flourishing of women, so also is it unconscionable for theologians who benefit from white privilege to continue to cultivate theological habits that are harmful to people of color, whether directly or indirectly. An example of the first is easy to find in the theology underlying the many Bible translations that turn the apostle Junia, a woman mentioned by Paul in Rom 16:7, into "Junias," a (non-existent) man. An example of the second, also found in many Bible translations, is the infamous "I am black yet comely" of Song of Songs 1:5. The presuppositions behind these mistranslations are respectively that no woman in the early church could possibly be designated an "apostle" and that no dark-skinned woman could be considered "beautiful" without further clarification. Both examples may seem at first glance quite trivial, and yet both point to a deeply flawed theological anthropology in which light-skinned people, and particularly males, are the norm and the standard for the true, the good, and the beautiful. All others fall short of the mark. Again, this illustrates how a theology can create conditions at a symbolic level for certain forms of (sexist and/or racist) violence to emerge.

Disarticulating theology as white space requires us (by "us" here I mean especially "white" theologians) to pay systematic attention to questions that emerge existentially from non-white spaces. This includes careful consideration of the contribution of "non-white" theological sources, but also a persistent focus on the infinite value for God (and therefore for theology) of Black and Brown lives, and the constant threat that the violence of white racism, white privilege, white spaces and white logic constitute for those lives.[38]

---

38. Frederick Herzog was a theologian who took this kind of approach seriously; I well remember the impact on my life of reading his book *God-Walk,* after stumbling

As a theologian coded as "white" in this society simply to accept white privilege as a given is by definition violent because it makes me an accomplice in cementing an unjust *status quo*. The work of knowing, engaging, and interrupting such violence necessarily entails a journey of self-knowledge, of epistemological ruptures, and of transformation by the Spirit of God, whose desire it is that *all* might live abundantly, not just a few. Part of that journey is to learn that God is no respecter of white skin—much less of people (as Ta-Nehesi Coates would put it) who "believe they are white."[39] A theology that seeks to be true to God's character cannot be a respecter or enabler of white privilege, implicitly or explicitly, by omission or by commission.

Those of us who do theology while coded as "white" are challenged to work out our liberation (or our salvation) in fear and trembling (Phil 2:12; see also 1 Pet 1:17). We need to focus on disarticulating our complicities with a systemic violence that has been structured to benefit the likes of us. There can be no true joy and no genuine flourishing in a theology oblivious to the violence and pain inflicted systemically, symbolically, universally, and particularly on Brown and Black bodies in this country. Only if the theology produced by "white" people ceases to function as a white space will its discourse about sin and grace contribute to the unity of meaning and pleasure, as well as discovering the joy found in learning to tread a stony road alongside beloved sisters and brothers.

BIBLIOGRAPHY

Anderson, Elijah. "The White Space." *Sociology of Race and Ethnicity* 1 (2015) 10–21.
Arendt, Hannah. *On Violence*. New York: Harcourt, 1970.
Armour, Ellen T. *Deconstruction, Feminist Theology, and the Problem of Difference. Subverting the Race/Gender Divine*. Chicago: University of Chicago Press, 1999.
Bauerlein, Valerie, et al. "'Loner' Held in Charleston Church Killings." *The Wall Street Journal Eastern Edition*. June 19, 2015.
Bedford, Nancy Elizabeth. *La porfía de la resurrección: Ensayos desde el feminismo teológico latinoamericano*. Buenos Aires: Kairós, 2008.
Cady, Duane L. "Violence." In *Encyclopedia of Philosophy*, edited by Daniel Borchert. 2nd ed., 9:677–78. New York: Macmillan, 2006.
Coates, Ta-Nehisi. *Between the World and Me*. New York: Spiegel & Grau, 2015.
Evans, James H., Jr. *We Have Been Believers: An African-American Systematic Theology*. 2nd ed. Minneapolis: Fortress, 2012.

---

upon it by chance in the library at ISEDET in Buenos Aires. More recently, Perkinson, *White Theology*, is an example of the attempt of a "white" theologian to think through the discipline with that kind of persistent focus in mind. The themes of theological anthropology come to the fore because he emphasizes the questions posed to people coded as white by Black experiences and lives in this society.

39. See Coates, *Between the World and Me*, 7 et passim.

Finamore, Stephen. "A Kindler, Gentler Apocalypse? René Girard, the Book of Revelation, and the Bottomless Abyss of the Unforgettable Victim." In *Compassionate Eschatology: The Future as a Friend*, edited by Ted Grimsrud and Michael Hardin, 196–217. Eugene, OR: Wipf and Stock, 2011.

Friedersdorf, Conor. "The Corrupt System that Killed Laquan McDonald." *The Atlantic*, November 27, 2015. Online: http://www.theatlantic.com/politics/archive/2015/11/protesting-the-corrupt-system-that-killed-laquan-mcdonald/417723/.

Grimsrud, Ted, and Michael Hardin, eds. *Compassionate Eschatology: The Future as Friend*. Eugene, OR: Wipf and Stock, 2011.

Guerra, Nancy, and Lyndee Knox. "Violence." In *Encyclopedia of Crime and Justice*, ed. Joshua Dressler. 2nd ed. New York: Macmillan Reference, 2002.

Hayes, Diana. *Standing in the Shoes My Mother Made: A Womanist Theology*. Minneapolis: Fortress, 2010.

Herzog, Frederick. *God-Walk. Liberation Shaping Dogmatics*. Maryknoll, NY: Orbis, 1988.

Hopkins, Dwight N. *Introducing Black Theology of Liberation*. Maryknoll, NY: Orbis, 1999.

Jennings, Willie. "African American Theology and the Public Imaginary." In *The Oxford Handbook of African American Theology*, edited by Anthony B. Pinn and Katie G. Cannon, 468–78. Oxford: Oxford University Press, 2014. Online: http://www.oxfordhandbooks.com/view/10.1093/oxfordhb/9780199755653.001.0001/oxfordhb-9780199755653-e-033.

Mires, Fernando. *En nombre de la cruz: Discusiones teológicas y políticas frente al holocausto de los indios*. San José, Costa Rica: DEI, 1989.

Perkinson, James W. *White Theology: Outing Supremacy in Modernity*. New York: Palgrave Macmillan, 2004.

Pew Research Center on Religious and Public Life. "Racial and Ethnic Composition of Religious Groups." *America's Changing Religious Landscape*, May 12, 2015. Online: http://www.pewforum.org/2015/05/12/chapter-3-demographic-profiles-of-religious-groups/.

Smith, Mychal Denzel. "Why Video Evidence Wasn't Enough to Get Justice for Tamir Rice." *The Nation*, December 29, 2015. Online: http://www.thenation.com/article/why-video-evidence-wasnt-enough-to-get-justice-for-tamir-rice/.

Sobrino, Jon. *El principio-misericordia: Bajar de la cruz a los pueblos crucificados*. Santander: Sal Terrae, 1992.

———. *The Principle of Mercy: Taking the Crucified People from the Cross*. Maryknoll, NY: Orbis, 1994.

Stephan, Maria J., and Erica Chenoweth. "Why Civil Resistance Works: The Strategic Logic of Nonviolent Conflict." *International Security* 33 (2008) 7–44.

TG. "Energy Extraction: Man-made Quakes?" *ASEE Prism* 22 (Summer 2013) 16.

Volf, Miroslav. *Flourishing: Why We Need Religion in a Globalized World*. New Haven: Yale University Press, 2016.

Williams, Patricia J. "Summer of Hate: Eric Garner's Death in July 2014 Marks String of Hate Crimes Fifty Years after Freedom Summer." *The Nation*, September 1, 2014.

Wink, Walter. *Jesus and Nonviolence: A Third Way*. Minneapolis: Fortress, 2003.

Žižek, Slavoj. *Violence: Six Sideways Reflections*. New York: Picador, 2008.

10

Human Flourishing and Art that Enhances the Ordinary

Nicholas Wolterstorff

MOST PEOPLE, WHEN REFLECTING on the contribution of art to human flourishing, have in mind absorbed attention to some work of the arts: attentive viewing, attentive listening, attentive reading. The question they address is how that activity promotes the flourishing of those who engage in it.

Absorbed attention to some work of the arts is a distinct and complex activity. It requires leisure, respite from one's ordinary activities. To do it well requires training, both informal and formal. A great deal has been written about what goes into doing it well and about the rewards of doing it well.

In this essay I want to explore a very different way in which art contributes to human flourishing. Instead of taking us away from our ordinary activities, art often enhances those activities. I am well aware of the fact that many lovers of art are disdainful of such art; they dismiss it as "functional," art in the service of interests outside itself. In this essay I will not challenge that put-down.[1] My goal will be achieved if, by the end of the essay, the reader has some glimpse of how impoverished our flourishing would be if our lives were devoid of art that enhances our ordinary activities.

---

1. I have addressed it at length in my *Art Rethought*.

A general analysis of the ways in which art enhances our ordinary activities would necessarily operate at a high level of abstraction. I think it better to analyze in more detail and with greater specificity just one art. For no particular reason, I have chosen music. Even within music I will not attempt a general analysis of how music enhances our ordinary activities. Instead, I will first analyze how, in work songs, music enhances manual labor; I will then take and expand what we have learned for an analysis of liturgical singing.[2]

There are, of course, many different understandings of human flourishing, the differences due, in good measure, to different worldviews; naturalists understand flourishing very differently from how humanists understand it. So before I set out, let me briefly explain how I understand flourishing.

My understanding is a Christian understanding. Even among Christians, however, there are different understandings of flourishing; so let me be more specific. I understand flourishing to be what the writers of the Hebrew Bible/Old Testament called *shalom*. An entire essay could be devoted to analyzing the concept of shalom in the Hebrew Bible/Old Testament. Here let me just say that shalom consists of being rightly related to God, to one's fellow human beings, to oneself, to the natural world, and to society and culture, and of finding joy in being so related.

In English translations of the Hebrew Bible/Old Testament, "shalom" has traditionally been translated as "peace." If shalom is what I have just now said it is, "peace" is obviously a very poor translation. In some recent translations it is translated as "welfare." That's better, but still inadequate. "Welfare" has economic connotations; we speak of "the welfare state." I think "flourishing" is the best translation. Shalom is flourishing in all one's relationships: to God, to one's fellows, to oneself, to the natural world, to society and culture. It has both a normative component, being *rightly* related, and an affective component, finding *joy* in being so related.

SUNG WORK

Songs *about* work are sometimes called "work songs." By the term "work songs" I will not mean songs *about* work but songs sung as an *accompaniment* to work, specifically, manual work.[3]

---

2. In this essay, by the term "ordinary activities" I mean activities not focused on some work of the arts. In that sense of the term, praising God is an ordinary activity. In other ways it is, of course, not at all ordinary.

3. Some of what follows is taken from my discussion of work songs in chapter 16 of my *Art Rethought*.

The labor that work songs accompany can be performed without the songs: spinners can spin and rowers can row without singing. Sometimes the singing establishes a rhythm that is essential for coordinated activity by the laborers; but there are other ways to establish a rhythm for the work than by singing. From the standpoint of getting the work done, the singing is unnecessary. It's an addition, an excess. Except for those atypical cases in which some overseer orders the workers to sing, it's a gratuitous excess.

Just as the work can be done without the singing, so too the singing can be done without the work; that's what happens when work songs are performed in concert. With respect to the work, the singing is an excess; with respect to the singing, the work is an excess.

The situation is not entirely symmetrical, however. Usually the work is already there; the singing is not. Though the singing and the working are each an excess with respect to the other, usually the workers feel that the singing accompanies the work, not that the work accompanies the singing. In the term "work songs," the word "work" is the modifier and the word "songs" is the substantive. Our terminology would better reflect the typical reality of things if, instead of speaking of work songs, we spoke of *sung work*.

I spoke above of the singing as *accompanying* the work; I might also have spoken of the work as accompanying the singing. We can describe what takes place either as singing while working or as working while singing. Either way however, the word "accompany" is misleading. It suggests mere simultaneity. The singing and the working do, of course, occur simultaneously; but their relation goes beyond that. It's integral. Music piped into a factory as background music would be a mere accompaniment to the work.

When workers sing while working, they create an entity of a new genre. There is now neither ordinary work accompanied by singing nor singing accompanied by ordinary work. There is now *sung work*, an entity of a different genre, a hybrid, a blend of singing and working in which the singing and the working "coinhere"—to borrow a term from theology of the Trinity. Ted Gioia, in his fine book *Work Songs*,[4] remarks, "The work of the poorest laborer is still a process of creating and of making something where before there was nothing."[5] Singing while working is a manifestation of human creativity; the gratuitous excess represented by sung work is a *creative* excess.

In situations of labor under duress, this creative excess is the manifestation of a spirit that refuses to be reduced to mere utility—refuses to be reduced to a mere hoer of cotton or a mere splitter of rocks. By singing

4. Gioia, *Work Songs*.
5. Ibid., 257.

while laboring under duress, the workers manifest an indomitable sense of their ineradicable dignity. Speaking of some work songs from the country of Georgia, Gioia remarks that their spirit "was not all that different from work songs [from] the American state of Georgia. Both groups of workers managed to capture the strange, paradoxical combination of a wail of misery and an uplifting statement of human dignity as expressed in labor. Such music simultaneously complains and exults, denies and accepts, pushes forward and holds back."[6] One can understand why overseers in prisons sometimes refused to allow the prisoners to sing.[7] They wanted to crush their spirit. The singing was an indication that they had not yet succeeded. It was an act of resistance on the part of the workers to the attempt to crush their spirit. So the overseers forbade singing. They preferred sullen silent acquiescence. *Prison Songs* is a recording made by Alan Lomax in 1947–48 of songs sung by prisoners in the Parchman Farm prison in Mississippi.[8] In 1996 a researcher played this recording for a group of ex-prisoners living in the South Bronx and asked them what they thought about it. One said, "They sing for inspiration, survival. They were uplifting themselves." Another said, "You're trying to save your sanity. . . . You'd lose your spirit if you didn't sing." A third said that the songs were a manifestation of the "will of the human spirit. That will is something within me. It says that I have something that I can do to get myself out of this, too, or get through this day, or cope with tomorrow, and not just lay back and hope that someone else will come to my rescue. So I think these songs have a great value, a great lesson: the will of the human spirit—the will to survive and go on, no matter what, and in spite of everything."[9]

THE SINGING FITS THE WORK

If the singing and the labor are to coinhere, the singing has to fit the work.[10] Thus it is that

> the work song follows musical rules of its own, far distant from the cultural and formal considerations that hold sway in virtually all other types of performance art. Indeed, in almost

6. Ibid., 257–58.

7. See ibid., 207.

8. The full title of the CD is *Prison Songs: Historical Recordings from Parchman Farm 1947–48, Volume One: Murderous Home*. The CD is available as Rounder CD 1714.

9. These comments are to be found in the booklet accompanying the CD.

10. In my *Art in Action*, 96–121, I develop a theory of fittingness.

every regard the work song defies our conception of an "artistic performance." Its pace can be repetitive and predictable; often it strives to achieve effects that, in other settings, would be dismissed as merely monotonous. The time and setting of the performance, the number of singers—these factors and others are usually determined by external forces. No artists have less control over their "medium" than do the singers of these songs. The rhythms are typically slower than most other types of traditional songs, sometimes positively sluggish.[11]

Gioia quotes what Richard Henry Dana wrote in his 1841 memoir, *Two Years Before the Mast,* about the difficulty sailors sometimes experienced in finding the right shanty for certain shipboard tasks. "Two or three songs would be tried, one after the other, with no effect—not an inch could be got on the tackles—when a new song struck up, seemed to hit the humor of the moment, and drove the tackles 'two blocks' at once."[12] For simpler tasks

> the crew might be forgiving of a less-than-ideal shanty: "Tom's Gone to Hilo" (or "John's Gone to Hilo") was simply too slow to serve as a proper tops'l halyard song—it invariably took ages to hoist a yard given its languorous tempo; but nonetheless it was popular with sailors, who liked its melody and often put it to use despite this functional limitation. Other songs only found their true calling over time, such as "Santa Anna," . . . which started life as a pumping shanty and gradually made its way to the capstan where it served yeoman's duty.[13]

Not only must the tempo of the song fit the tempo of the work. The rhythm of the song must likewise fit the rhythm of the work. Or in case the work does not have an inherent rhythm, the rhythm of the song has to be a rhythm that can be imposed on the work. For some types of work it was important, or even indispensable, that the actions of the individual workers be synchronized; in those cases, the singing had to have a rhythm that could serve that function. Track 2 on *Prison Songs*, "No More, My Lord," and track 13, "Early in the Mornin'," are fascinating examples of the point. Both are songs sung to the action of chopping wood; and in both cases, not only does the rhythm of the singing establish a rhythm for the swinging of the axes but the ringing percussive sound of the axe-blows is an integral part of the music.

---

11. Gioia, *Work Songs,* 60–61.

12. This is a quotation from Dana by Gioia, *Work Songs,* 121.

13. Ibid., 122.

If the song is to fit the work, another requirement is that the expressive character of the song fit the nature of the work and the mood typical of those who perform the work. Gioia remarks that "no listener can hear the music of . . . traditional hunting cultures without sensing . . . joy and exultation, [the] expression of intense connection with the surrounding environment. The songs of herders and farmers are, by comparison, pensive and sober, only rarely achieving the vivacity that is a constitutive element of the hunter's daily music."[14] In pastoral music, he says, "we can sense a plaintive, melancholy tone—perhaps inculcated by the long lonely hours spent by the herder with only the company of sounds."[15] Lumberjack songs, like hunter songs, are joyful; their "general tone of gaiety puts lumber camp songs almost in a class by themselves in the area of work-related music."[16] Writing about the music of African tribes, the ethnomusicologist Rose Brandel observes that these peoples do "not deliberately project the 'work music' upon the scene in the manner of modern factory psychologists. Rather, the music seems to be an expressive outgrowth of the labor itself."[17]

SINGING WHILE WORKING MAKES THE WORK GO BETTER

Those who sang while working obviously found this new creation, sung work, to be more gratifying than the same work done without singing; that's why they sang. What was it about this new entity that they found more gratifying? The name of one of the inmates in the Parchman Farm Prison whom Alan Lomax interviewed was "Bama." When Lomax asked Bama why he and his fellow inmates sang, Bama said, singing makes the work "go so better."[18] Singing changes the work, modifies it, modifies it for the better; singing enhances the work, elevates it. Gioia sometimes describes the singing as "transforming" the work.[19]

The counterpart thing can be said about the effect of the work on the singing. The work modifies the singing, modifies it for the better, enhances it. About the seaman's shanty Gioia says, "Cut off from the activities that gave it meaning, the shanty has become just another song. This transition can only be lamented, for the work-a-day circumstances that gave birth to

14. Ibid., 26.
15. Ibid., 66.
16. Ibid., 141.
17. Quoted in ibid., 56.
18. Track 12.
19. Gioia, *Work Songs*, xi, 4ff.

the shanty also imparted the rough-and-ready beauty that made them so inspirational and this charm all but disappears when the music is brought inside the concert hall or recording studio."[20]

Let's set off to the side the enhancement of the singing effected by its combination with the work and reflect on the enhancement of the work effected by its combination with the singing. What is it about sung work that makes it more gratifying for the workers than work of the same sort performed without singing? In what way does the work "go so better"?

We have already taken note of one of the ways in which the singing makes the work go better: the rhythm of the singing coordinates the activity of the individual laborers. In addition, singing often energizes the workers. In Gioia's words, the songs "impart vitality and energy to an undertaking."[21] When accompanied by singing, tasks "have a stronger and more insistent force of momentum behind them."[22]

Singing enhances not only the work itself but the workers' experience of the work. The creative excess of the singing blurs the distinction between work and play by introducing a dimension of play into the work; this enhances their experience of the work. And when the singing is not solitary, as, for example, the singing of herdsmen often was, but is done together with others, the singing together heightens the workers' sense of solidarity.

Working together rather than individually—rowing a boat together, setting sails together—requires that each adjust what he or she is doing to what the others are doing; it requires mutual responsiveness. A sense of solidarity emerges. Singing together while working together adds a new level of responsiveness; now each participant must not only adjust his or her work to the work of the others but his or her singing to the singing of the others. From this new level of responsiveness an even stronger sense of solidarity emerges. Add to this that in singing the same words they are voicing the same sentiments. Is it fanciful to see in this heightened sense of solidarity a sign of shalom, using 'sign' in the sense in which the word is used in the Gospel of John? The signs that Jesus performed were samples of shalom that pointed to a shalom beyond themselves.

In these ways, and no doubt others, singing enhanced the experience of the work, whether or not the work was pleasant. It was especially when the work was unpleasant, however, that singing was important. Much of the work that human beings have performed while singing is tedious or laborious. The singing alleviates the unpleasantness; it makes the time go

20. Ibid., 136.
21. Ibid., 178.
22. Ibid.

faster. It does this not by distracting the workers from the work, in the way that reading a gripping novel distracts one for a while from the pain in one's foot; the workers still attend to the work. But their attention is now divided between the work and the singing. I quoted three words from what Bama said to Lomax when Lomax asked him why he and his fellows sang while working. Here is more of what Bama said in answer to Lomax's question:

> When you singin', you forgit, you see, and the time just pass on 'way' but if you just get your mind devoted on one something, it look like it will be hard for you to make it, see, make a day. The day be longer, look like. So to keep his mind from being devoted on just one thing, why he'll practically take up singin', see.

In short, singing while working leads the workers no longer to focus exclusively on the tedium and laboriousness of the work.

SINGING WHILE WORKING IS AN INTRINSIC GOOD

I posed the question, what was it about sung work that made it more gratifying than the same work done without singing. The answer I have offered thus far took its cue from a comment made to Alan Lomax by Bama: singing makes the work "go so better." Singing has the effect of modifying the work, modifying it for the better, enhancing it; and singing has the effect of modifying the workers' experience of the work so that it feels less tedious and laborious. Singing coordinates the activity of the workers, energizes them, and makes them no longer preoccupied exclusively with their work.

These are functional considerations, beneficial effects of the singing on the work and on the workers' experience of the work. Gioia doubts that such functional considerations exhaust the matter; I think he is right about that.[23] His guess and mine is that the workers often found this expression of creativity on their part, this *gratuitous excess* as I have called it, intrinsically good. Yes, singing together while working does have the effects mentioned. But the workers also sang for the sheer joy of creating sung work; sung work was an end in itself in the structure of their activities. The labor as such was not an end in itself for them—not usually, anyway; it was the sung work that was an end in itself. Gioia quotes from Charles de Rochefort's 1666 publication, *The History of the Caribby-Islands,* "They do also by singing alleviate the hard labour they are addicted unto and yet what they do, seems to be done rather out of divertisement, and to avoid idleness, than out of

23. See especially ibid, 56–59.

any considerations of advantage that they make thereof."[24] Like artists in general, the workers found joy in their act of creation. Is it fanciful to see in that joy a sign of shalom?

AN EXCURSUS ON JOY

How can prisoners experience joy in creating sung work when their overall condition is miserable, something they would never choose? To understand this apparently paradoxical situation, we need a brief excursus on joy.

Joy is an emotion. I judge that the best philosophical account of emotion currently available is that by Robert C. Roberts in his 2003 treatise, *Emotions: An Essay in Aid of Moral Psychology*.[25] Let me present the core of Roberts' theory without, on this occasion, defending it.

Emotions always have an object: if one fears, there is something that one fears; if one envies, there is someone that one envies; if one grieves, there is something over which one grieves; and so forth. Emotions are in this way different from sensations: a tingling sensation in one's finger has no object, nor does a burning sensation on one's tongue. Sensations are, as it were, non-referential.

Roberts' central claim is that emotions are *concern-imbued constru-als*.[26] Here's the idea. An emotion incorporates a certain construal or interpretation of some segment of reality; if I construed that segment of reality differently, or not at all, I would not have the emotion in question. When I fear, I construe something as threatening my life or well-being; when I envy, I construe someone as superior to me in some way.

Construals are not sufficient for emotions, however; what is also required is concern. What one construes as so-and-so must concern one. My construal of something as threatening my life must concern me or I won't feel fear; my construal of Michael as superior to me in a certain way must concern me or I won't feel envy.

Concerns vary in how important they are to the person—to put the same point in other words, they differ with respect to their depth of ingression into one's personality. Some are so important to one that one cannot imagine oneself not having that concern; they are constitutive of one's

24. Ibid., 59.

25. Roberts, *Emotions*, 2003.

26. The term that Roberts most often uses is "concern-*based* construals." His thought is not, however, that the construal is somehow *based on* the concern but that it is *imbued* or *infused with* the concern. He himself sometimes uses the term "imbued."

identity. Relative importance is determined by which member of some pair one would choose to give up, if one could choose and had to choose.

Concerns also typically vary with respect to intensity, with the result that emotions typically vary with respect to intensity. Depending on the intensity of my concern over Michael's perceived superiority to me, I may feel intensely envious of him or only mildly envious.

Where, within the panoply of concern-imbued construals of reality, is joy located? Joy, I would say, occurs when it's important to one that things be a certain way and one construes them as being that way. Roberts gives a nice example of joy; let me quote what he says.

> I am surrounded by my children, who are playing hap-
> pily . . . showing signs of flourishing, of growing well in body,
> mind, and spirit. As I contemplate this goodly scene, I am
> filled with joy. On my analysis of emotion, my joy amounts to
> a concern-based construal of my children: I "see" them in terms
> of their well-being, and this term impinges satisfyingly on my
> concern for their well-being. If I do not see them in terms of this
> or some similar aspect of the scene (let us say I merely perceive
> the noise and motion as an impediment to my reading), then
> I will not feel joy; or if I perceive them in terms of their flour-
> ishing but without this perception impinging on my concern (I
> am assessing them clinically, with perfect detachment, and give
> them a high grade), then likewise I do not feel joy.[27]

The linguistic connection between the English terms "joy" and "enjoy-ment" leads one to think that these are basically the same phenomenon. If Roberts and I are right in holding that joy is an emotion, then clearly they are not the same. Enjoying something—enjoying the taste of the ice cream, enjoying the display of aurora borealis—is not having an emotion. One "feels" joy, grief, pride, guilt, and so forth; one does not "feel" enjoyment. So, too, one does not "feel" happiness. One can, of course, feel happy. But happiness is unlike joy in that often it has no object. One just feels happy. Feeling happy has causes but not an object. Feeling miserable is like happi-ness in that regard.

The fact that joy always has an object, whereas feeling miserable does not, explains how one can be miserable and yet experience joy. A passage in

---

27. Ibid., 279. The passage continues: "Let us say, then, that joy is a construal of something in terms that satisfy one or more of one's concerns." Thus joy, as Roberts understands it, does not require that the concern in question be important to one. I doubt that one would naturally call it "joy" if the concern in question was unimportant to one; calling it "joy" would seem excessive.

Paul's Second Letter to the Corinthians offers a vivid example of the same point:

> As servants of God we have commended ourselves in every way: through great endurance, in afflictions, hardships, calamities, beatings, imprisonments, riots, labors, sleepless nights, hunger, by purity, knowledge, patience, kindness, holiness of spirit, genuine love, truthful speech, and the power of God, with the weapons of righteousness for the right hand and for the left; in honor and dishonor, in ill repute and good repute. We are treated as imposters, and yet are true; as unknown, and yet are well known; as dying, and see—we are alive; as punished, and yet not killed; as sorrowful, yet always rejoicing. (2 Cor 6:4–10 NRSV)

Often miserable—hungry, beaten, deprived of sleep, imprisoned, maligned—yet always rejoicing. To rejoice is to express one's joy. No matter how miserable he often was, joy was a constant in Paul's life. In the passage quoted he does not say what it was that gave him joy no matter what his condition. We know from other passages what it was; he found joy in knowledge of the salvation that had come to humanity and to himself in the crucifixion and resurrection of Jesus Christ.

LITURGICAL SINGING

Work songs have virtually disappeared from modernized societies; for most of us, they are a thing of the past. Elsewhere I have explored why that is.[28] Liturgical singing has by no means disappeared. Almost all enactments of Christian liturgies include singing. From Paul's letters we learn that this was true already in his day; he speaks of "psalms, hymns, and spiritual songs" (Col 3:6).[29] From its earliest days, the church has broken out into song.

Liturgical singing takes a number of different forms: the form of chanting a penitential psalm, the form of singing a prayer of confession, the form of singing the creed, the form of singing a hymn of praise or thanksgiving. It's important to recognize the variety. Nonetheless, I think there will be no harm if, on this occasion, we simplify our discussion by focusing on hymns of praise and thanksgiving. Almost everything that I have to say about such hymns applies to the other forms of liturgical singing as well.

28. Wolterstorff, *Art Rethought*, 269.

29. "Spiritual songs" may well have meant *inspired songs,* that is, songs inspired by the Spirit.

What we have learned from our analysis of sung manual labor applies, *mutatis mutandis*, to hymns of praise and thanksgiving. Hymns are sung work, the "work" in this case being praise and thanksgiving addressed to God.

Just as workers can perform manual labor without singing, so too we can praise God without singing. We can praise God in spoken prose; often we do. With respect to the action of praising God, singing is an excess, a *gratuitous* excess; it's not necessary.

The musical excess is not just tacked on; it does not merely coexist with the praise. The singing and the praising are fused; they coinhere to create an entity of a new genre, namely, *sung praise*. In this fusion, the praise is altered, changed, transformed. Compared to prose praise, sung praise is an enhancement of praise in much the same way that sung work is an enhancement of manual labor. Singing elevates our praise, ennobles it, makes it more fitting to the one to whom it is addressed, namely God. Singing makes our praise "go so better."

Just now I contrasted prose praise with the sung praise of a hymn. To describe the situation that way, while not inaccurate, nonetheless ignores an important complexity. The text of a hymn is typically not prose but poetry, often not poetry of a sort and quality that would qualify it for inclusion in an anthology of poetry, but poetry nonetheless.[30] (The same is true of the text of most work songs.) It's a work of one of the arts, a poem.

The full structure of the situation is thus as follows. With respect to the action of praising God, the poetry is a gratuitous excess; it's not necessary. The poetry is not just tacked on to the praise, however; it does not merely coexist with it. The poetry and the praise are fused; they coinhere to create an entity of a new genre, poetized praise. In this fusion, the praise is altered, transformed. Compared to prose praise, poetized praise is an enhancement of praise. Poetry elevates our praise, makes it more fitting for addressing God. The poetry makes the praise "go so better."

The music is then, in turn, a gratuitous excess with respect to spoken poetized praise. But it is not just tacked on to the poetized praise; it is fused with it. The music and the poetized praise coinhere to create an entity of yet another genre, namely, sung poetized-praise. When a hymn is sung in praise of God, the praise, the poetry, and the music, all coinhere; there is a trinity of coinherence. And in this trinity of coinherence, the poetry elevates the praise and the music elevates the poetized-praise, ennobles it, makes it more

---

30. Some of the sung hymns in the Orthodox liturgy have prose texts. And the Creed is, of course, not poetry.

fitting for addressing God. In the presence of God, the angels sing poetry; they don't speak in prose.

There is no such thing as generic praise of God. Whether the praise be in prose or poetry, the praise is concrete, specific. And it can always be interpreted in somewhat different ways. Thus it is that every musical setting of a text is an interpretation of the text. In his *Aesthetics*, Monroe Beardsley gives an interesting example of the point. He cites the musical phrase to which Palestrina, in his *Pope Marcellus Mass,* set the words of the Credo, *"descendit de caelis,"* and the musical phrase to which Beethoven set the word *"descendit"* in the Credo of his *Missa Solemnis.* The phrase in Palestrina descends gradually over an expanse of nine notes from F above middle C to A below. The phrase in Beethoven plunges abruptly over the expanse of three notes from B above high C to F above middle C. Beardsley remarks: "These are two descents, so to speak, but what different descents they are! In Palestrina the coming of Christ is a serene passage into the world from a realm not utterly remote; in Beethoven it is a dramatic plunge."[31]

The fusion of the music with a text alters our *experience* of the text, partly, but by no means only, because of how the music interprets the text. To sing a poem or to hear it sung is to experience it very differently from reading or reciting it, and also very differently from hearing it read aloud by someone else. Vivien Schweitzer is one of the regular music reviewers of *The New York Times*. In *The Times* of March 7, 2014, she reviewed a performance of Franz Schubert's *Die Schöne Müllerin* by Matthias Goerne and Christoph Eschenbach. Schubert's work is a setting of a cycle of poems by Wilhelm Müller. In the course of her review, Schweitzer quotes something that Müller wrote in his diary in 1815, before Schubert had set the poems: "I can neither play nor sing, and my verses lead but half a life until music breathes life into them. But courage! A kindred soul may yet be found who will hear the tunes behind the words and reflect them back to me." Müller was convinced that his own experience of his poems, not to mention that of the public, would not reach its full potential until they had been appropriately set to music. I do not know whether Müller ever heard Schubert's settings; but I think anyone would agree that Schubert's settings alter and enormously enhance our experience of the poetry.

My thesis has been that poetized praise is an enhancement of praise in prose, and that, in turn, sung poetized-praise is an enhancement of spoken poetized praise. Not always, of course; sometimes poetry deadens the praise, sometimes music deadens the poem. But it's the experience of all of us that, very often, the enhancement happens. So we continue to break out in song.

31. Beardsley, *Aesthetics*, 347.

What is it about singing our praise, whether poetized or not, that enhances and elevates the praise? What is it about singing that makes the praise "go so better"? What is it about singing "Oh come all ye faithful, joyful and triumphant" that makes our praise so much better than just saying the words together? What it is about singing "A mighty fortress is our God" that makes our praise so much better than just saying the words together?

I apprehend what it is about singing our praise that makes it intrinsically better than speaking our praise; but I find myself incapable of describing it. Singing gives to our praise a certain lift; but I am incapable of describing that lift. And in any case, to say that it gives to our praise a certain lift is not to say anything different from saying that it elevates our praise. There have been studies by cognitive psychologists of the changes that occur in the brain when people sing together.[32] But knowledge of those changes in the brain is of no help in describing the enhancement of our praise that we *experience* when we sing a hymn together.

What I can do is put into words some of what makes praising God *together* better than praising God alone, especially when we praise God together in song. When discussing work songs, I noted that, in order to work together, each worker must adjust what he or she is doing to what the others are doing, and that singing together while working requires an additional level of mutual responsiveness. This additional mutual responsiveness both expresses and intensifies the workers' solidarity; they're in this together.

The same points apply, *mutatis mutandis*, to singing together hymns of praise and thanksgiving: mutual adjustment and responsiveness is required. This is especially true when the singing is in harmony. In Stacy Horn's book, *Imperfect Harmony: Finding Happiness Singing with Others*, there is a fascinating discussion of the mutual adjustment required for choral singing. Here is one passage in which she describes her experience of singing in a choir.

> You make a contribution of sound waves and airwaves, and something more complex, something you couldn't possibly produce on your own, comes back to you. You constantly adjust your contribution. . . . It requires more concentration than if you were producing sound or singing on your own, say, in the shower, and thus you really do get lost—in the sense that you can't worry about anything else in your life at that moment. . . . I've loved being able to listen to individual voices singing right next to me on parts other than my own. It's both energizing and stabilizing to be surrounded by all four parts. . . . After all, there aren't too

---

32. See the discussion and references in Horn, *Imperfect Harmony*.

many chances in ordinary life to be in perfect cooperation with other people. Singing fulfills that need.[33]

Good congregational singing requires the same sort of mutual responsiveness that Horn experienced in singing in a choir. The theologian David Ford makes the point well in a chapter that he calls "Communicating God's Abundance: A Singing Self": "The specific contribution of music to [the] building up of community in worship includes its encouragement of alertness to others, immediate responsiveness to changes in tone, tune and rhythm, and sharing in the confidence that can come from joint singing. Singing together embodies joint responsibility in which each singer waits on the others, is attentive with the intention of serving the common harmony."[34] The mutual responsiveness required by *together* praising God in song both expresses and intensifies the participants' solidarity, what Ford calls "community." Liturgical singing is a sign of shalom: it's a sample of shalom that points to a shalom beyond itself.

Singing hymns together not only enhances solidarity by virtue of the mutual responsiveness required for singing together. It also enhances solidarity by unifying the participants around what they are saying in their singing, sometimes leading them to say what they would not previously have said. I think here of a paragraph in the book by the African-American theologian James Cone, *The Spirituals and the Blues*:

> Black music is unity music. It unites the joy and the sorrow, the love and the hate, the hope and the despair, of black people; and it moves the people toward the direction of total liberation. It shapes and defines black existence and creates culture structures for black expression. Black music is unifying because it confronts the individual with the truth of black existence and affirms that black being is possible only in a communal context.[35]

For many members of the African-American community, singing spirituals in church and elsewhere not only expressed and intensified their solidarity but was an act of defiance on their part. It was a declaration that their spirit had not been crushed, just as the singing of work songs by prisoners was a declaration that their spirit had not been crushed. The singing of their spirituals by African Americans was, in this way too, a sign of shalom.

---

33. Ibid., 120–21.

34. Ford, *Self and Salvation*, 122.

35. Cone, *Spirituals and the Blues*, 5.

JOY IN LITURGICAL SINGING

Let me conclude with a few comments about joy in liturgical singing. When discussing work songs, I took note of the fact that workers sang not only for the beneficial effects on the work and their experience of the work but also, sometimes at least, for the sheer joy of singing while working: the joy of creating this new entity, sung work. Singing while working was an end in itself for them. The same is true for liturgical singing. We sing hymns for the sheer joy of creating together with our fellow congregants this new entity, sung poetized-praise. But I suggest that there are, in praising God in song, two other sources of joy as well.

Praising God is "work" that most liturgical participants find joy in doing. When discussing work songs, I noted that the manual labor that work songs accompany is often tedious and onerous, not something that the workers would do if given a choice. Not always, of course. No doubt sailors sometimes found joy and satisfaction in setting sails; they would do it even if they didn't have to. No doubt weavers sometimes found joy and satisfaction in weaving. But typically the work was tedious on account of its repetitiveness, and onerous. By contrast, believers find joy in praising God—not only joy in praising God in song, but joy in the very act of praising God. It's not tedious or onerous. It's something they want to do, not something they would rather not do.

For the third source of joy in praising God in song, think back to the passage from St. Paul that I quoted earlier, in which he writes that, no matter how miserable and unhappy he often was, joy was nonetheless a constant in his life. No matter what afflictions and hardships he was undergoing, he found joy in the salvation that had come to humanity and to himself in the crucifixion and resurrection of Jesus Christ. When Christians sing hymns of praise and thanksgiving to God, they are singing of that which gives them deep joy. It is for this reason, especially, that they find themselves capable of singing hymns to God in times of adversity—or better, it is for this reason that they find themselves *impelled* to sing hymns to God in times of adversity. In this way, too, liturgical singing is a sign of shalom—a foretaste.

THE LARGER POINT

In this essay I have analyzed the contribution that work songs and liturgical singing make to the flourishing of the participants. The overarching concept that I have employed is *enhancement*: singing while working enhances the work; singing our praise and thanksgiving enhances our praise and thanksgiving. It is primarily by this enhancement that the singing contributes to the shalom of the participants. The fact that the enhancement is a creative gratuitous excess means that there is more to the worth of those who sing than their utility: they are creators.

In my introduction I indicated that I intended my analyses to call attention to, and illuminate, a larger point. That larger point is this: art in general contributes to our flourishing by enhancing our ordinary activities. To cite just one example in addition to music: architecture enhances the activities that we perform within our architectural enclosures. To this should be added the related point that art contributes to our flourishing by enhancing nor only our ordinary activities but also the objects that we use in our ordinary activities: visual decoration enhances our books, our buildings, and so forth; ceramic art enhances our vessels. There can be no doubt that art that rewards absorbed attention contributes to human flourishing. I am inclined to think that, all in all, art that enhances the ordinary makes an even greater contribution. Might it be that, in general, human flourishing is best advanced by enhancing the ordinary rather than by trying to deny it or in some way to transcend it?[36]

36. I thank Matthew Croasmun and Ryan McAnnally–Linz for their helpful comments on an earlier draft of this essay.

BIBLIOGRAPHY

Beardsley, Monroe. *Aesthetics: Problems in the Philosophy of Criticism*. New York: Harcourt, Brace and Company, 1958.

Cone, James H. *The Spirituals and the Blues: An Interpretation*. Maryknoll: Orbis, 1992.

Ford, David. *Self and Salvation: Being Transformed*. Cambridge: Cambridge University Press, 1999.

Gioia, Ted. *Work Songs*. Durham: Duke University Press, 2006.

Horn, Stacy. *Imperfect Harmony: Finding Happiness Singing with Others*. Chapel Hill: Algonquin, 2013.

Roberts, Robert C. *Emotions: An Essay in Aid of Moral Psychology*. Cambridge: Cambridge University Press, 2003.

Wolterstorff, Nicholas. *Art Rethought: The Social Practices of Art*. Oxford: Oxford University Press, 2015.

———. *Art in Action*. Grand Rapids: Eerdmans, 1980.

11

Flourishing in Tito's Yugoslavia

Miroslav Volf—A Theologian in the Evangelical-Pentecostal World of Tito's Yugoslavia

Lidija Matošević

INTRODUCTION

In the aftermath of World War II, a state emerged that was known as Tito's Yugoslavia. Its official name was the Federal People's Republic of Yugoslavia (1945–1963) and then the Socialist Federal Republic of Yugoslavia (1963–1991). The present-day Republic of Croatia (since 1991) was one of its six constituent republics under the name Socialist Republic of Croatia.[1] The state of Yugoslavia is often nicknamed "Tito's Yugoslavia" because of the extraordinary impact of Josep Broz Tito's (1892–1980) personality not only during his lifetime, but also after his death, until the very moment of

1. The other constituent republics being (in alphabetic order) the Socialist Republics of Bosnia and Herzegovina, Macedonia, Montenegro, Serbia (with two Socialist Autonomous Provinces of Kosovo and Vojvodina), and Slovenia.

Yugoslavia's dissolution in 1991. The breakup of Yugoslavia, a consequence of, among other things, the inadequately solved issue of national relations within the state, began with the proclamations of independence by the federal republics of Slovenia and Croatia (1991) and continued with those of Macedonia (1991), Bosnia and Herzegovina (1992), and Montenegro (2006), as well as the emergence of the Kosovo Republic in 2008. This series of independence proclamations resulted in a prolonged war in the territories of Croatia (1991–1995) and Bosnia and Herzegovina (1992–1995), followed by the Kosovo war (1998–1999), during which time the newly formed states had to defend themselves by arms against Serbian aggression, motivated by the ideology of "Greater Serbia," and, in the case of Bosnia and Herzegovina the collapse of the state into a complex multi-party civil war.[2]

Tito's Yugoslavia was one of the Communist states created in the wake of World War II, yet it was also a peculiar formation as it developed its own, unique type of Communism, known as "self-management socialism." This type of Communism evolved during and especially after the so-called "Informbiro crisis" (1948–1955).[3] Its main feature was considerable autonomy with regard to both Eastern and Western blocs, which went hand in hand with the ideology of political non-alliance.[4] Another important feature was a considerably "softer" version of internal governance with regard to the states of the Warsaw Pact. The legal framework of self-management socialism was provided by the Constitutional Law of 1953 and the Constitution of 1974, as well as the Law on Collective Labour (1976). In 1976, a course on the "Theory and Practice of Self-Management Socialism" was introduced to all public schools in order to popularize the idea of self-management among the young. The decline of self-management socialism began only with Tito's death (1980) and was finalized in 1991 with the dissolution of the state itself.

One of the consequences of this softened internal politics was the relative freedom of religious orientation. The turbulent period immediately following the end of World War II—a period that took the lives of many and in which the property of religious communities was partly confiscated—was followed by one in which the Constitutions of 1946, 1963, and 1974 made it possible for religious communities in the territory of Yugoslavia to exist and operate, under the condition that they would not intervene in the public or political sphere. Among the communities that continued their existence

2. On the dissolution of Yugoslavia, see among others Banac, *Raspad Jugoslavije*. [The Dissolution of Yugoslavia].

3. This was a crisis caused by Yugoslavia's resistance against the introduction of Soviet Communism and the corresponding Stalinization. Cf. Banac, *With Stalin against Tito*.

4. Cf. Jakovina, "Tito's Yugoslavia," 389–404.

within this legal framework were the two majority confessions—Roman Catholicism and Eastern Orthodoxy—as well as Islam. However, Tito's Yugoslavia also housed a small group of Protestants, among them members of various free churches or Evangelical Christianity.[5] Besides the Baptists and the Free Brethren, these churches included the members of various Pentecostal churches. As early as the seventeenth century, following the Reformation period in which the Protestant movement flourished in the Croatian lands, albeit in limited numbers, and left an important trace in Croatian and Slovenian cultural heritage, Protestantism was practically erased from the area of later Yugoslavia. Its reemergence began in the eighteenth and nineteenth centuries, primarily with the immigration of Lutheran Germans to the regions of Banat and Bačka, facilitated by the Edict of Tolerance issued by Holy Roman Emperor Joseph II in 1782, as well as the Patent on Protestantism (1859). Following World War II, in the context of the massive exodus of Germans from Yugoslavia, the Protestant Germans left the region as well. Evangelical Christians did not appear in Yugoslavia—with the exception of the Baptists documented in the late-nineteenth century—before the twentieth century. They link their beginnings to the German influence (Lutheran "Volksdeutschers"), and in most organized form to the return of economic emigrants from North America, as well as the activity of a number of foreign missionaries.

Tito's Yugoslavia presented a wider geographical, political, and cultural context both for the early years of Miroslav Volf and for his early writings. He was born in 1956 in Osijek (present-day Croatia) soon after the Informbiro crisis, in the very beginnings of self-management socialism. He attended primary and secondary schools in the period when self-management socialism was in its heyday—according to his own words, he sang "long live, long live our work" at the top of his voice together with other schoolchildren.[6] He wrote his first essays in the period of decline in self-management socialism. He left the country, more or less for good, in 1990, when self-management socialism de facto ceased to exist.

The world of Evangelical Christianity was the immediate context both of Volf's youth and of his early works. He was born as the son of "twice born" parents,[7] a Pentecostal father and a mother who was primarily Baptist. Thus, Volf first experienced the world of Pentecostalism in his parental home, which was for him a "beautiful and nurturing social microenvironment,"

---

5. Hereafter I will use the term "Evangelical Christians" for the free churches.

6. Volf, "Umro pos'o, crko trud?," 10 ["No pain, no gain?"]

7. Volf, Flourishing, 7.

some sort of a "faith island."[8] He embarked on his theological studies at a small school, which was nevertheless exceptionally important in the wider context of Evangelical Christianity in Tito's Yugoslavia, founded in 1972 by the Pentecostal Church of Christ: the Biblical-Theological Institute in Zagreb. Having completed his course of studies there and continued at Fuller Theological Seminary, Volf became involved as a theologian in the life of young Pentecostal communities and also in the activities of the school of theology, which had meanwhile moved from Zagreb to Osijek and changed its name to Evangelical Theological Faculty. It was during this period of intense involvement in Yugoslav Pentecostalism, especially at the Osijek school of theology, that Volf began writing his first theological works in the Croatian language.

In this article, I will offer an overview of Volf's Croatian writings during the time he was theologically active in Tito's Yugoslavia, namely 1981–1990. This means that I will not focus on those works that he wrote abroad during the same period, or those written in English and German, or even translations of these writings (or excerpts) into Croatian. My aim here is primarily to see how Volf functioned as a young "prophet in his own hometown." Starting from the fact that two contexts have essentially defined Volf's thought in the given period, namely the world of self-management socialism and that of Evangelical Pentecostalism, I will present the main features of these two worlds in the first two sections, with a focus on their multi-layered nature. In the four following sections, I will seek to answer the question of Volf's theological position. Thus, the first of these four sections speaks of Volf as a theologian who was "strengthening" his community of Evangelical Christians, the second of the theologian as a mild critic of his community, the third focuses on Volf as a theologian who found a Biblical hope in a world determined by the Marxist worldview, and the fourth section speaks of the theologian in encounter with authentic Christian faith beyond his small community of Evangelical Christians. The focus of these four sections is not on sequential development of various accents in Volf's theology, but rather, on different, sometimes contradictory, but nonetheless coexistent, accents in his theology during the time of his engagement in Tito's Yugoslavia.

8. Ibid., 7.

THE WORLD OF "COMRADES" IN SELF-MANAGEMENT SOCIALISM

Tito's self-management socialism was an attempt at creating a human society in which people would have a good—one may even say "flourishing"—life. That was supposed to happen by liberating the country from the remnants of the overly totalitarian Soviet regime and by returning to the values of original Marxism in order to develop a form of socialism in which people would have the duty and the opportunity to influence the working process and to make decisions in evaluating the products of their labor. However, self-management socialism was still a part of the global Communist project, which rendered it problematic in the same way as all global projects tend to be. It was burdened by many unsolved or hidden problems, such as the lack of civic, religious, and national/ethnic freedom, and generally the lack of democracy, as Yugoslavia was still a largely authoritarian state and directed its economy in a rather authoritarian way. For these reasons, many suffered in this context: individuals or members of specific national or religious groups. Memories of this suffering, where the all-powerful state robbed people of their civic freedom and freedom of religion occur regularly in Volf's texts written after the dissolution of Yugoslavia.[9]

However, self-managing socialism was also in some respects a successful project of creating a society where people would have a good life. A rather poor society and largely illiterate society, as Yugoslavia had been before World War II, had become a society where almost nobody was hungry, freezing, or deprived of medical care, in which everyone not only learned to read and write, but also had the opportunity to attend school for free, to the highest degree. It was a society where everyone had access to work and could also live decently from their salary. It was a society where one lived unburdened by fear: a society with safe streets, where many did not lock their doors by night, and—equally importantly—where one did not fear a precarious future in which one could easily lose one's job, one's home, and the basic means of existence. Eventually, it was a society where people seemed somehow happy and relaxed: at least judging from the insignificant amount of signals of unhappiness in human being and the society, such as the number of drug addicts, users of antidepressants, violence rate, and so on.

One could thus say that self-management socialism was truly ambivalent. On the one hand, the moderate oppression and the attempt to impose "socialist ideological sanctities"—which could not pass without a

9. See, for instance, Ibid., 5.

considerable number of victims, especially in the period immediately following World War II. On the other hand, "self-management" opened up
space for diversity, creativity, personal and social responsibility, and humanity. Thus, self-management socialism was a system whose repressive-
ness and monotony, with all its atheistic ideology, was curiously permeated
by a sort of silent and persistent prayer, a primordially human, religious,
and biblical hope of a different, better world. That hope, like a flame that
could not be extinguished by any social systems managed to survive in the
self-managing vision of the world. It was a vision of the world in which
people did not address each other as "comrades"—a somewhat worn-out
address—merely because it was politically or ideologically "in," but because
they genuinely cared for each other and were truly comrades. And that vision was something that many took along on their life journeys from those
certainly problematic times, something that would continue to motivate
and determine them long after the collapse of self-management socialism.

THE WORLD OF BROTHERS AND SISTERS: "FAITHFUL" IN AN "UNFAITHFUL" WORLD

The Evangelical world in Tito's Yugoslavia was likewise an attempt of creating a human society, by creating a community of believers in which true
life flourished. The community came into existence primarily as individuals
were "born again" from God. It was only and exclusively after this that they
could join the community of believers, freely and willingly, as it was a voluntary association in itself. This means that they did not become believers
or members of a believing community because their parents were believers, or because they belonged to a particular geographic area or cultural
circles dominated by a specific Christian confession, or even because being
a believer was politically "in" or for any other reason or interest. A community consisting of such individuals became a place ruled by love, creativity,
and joy: a place in which the transformation into a new world of God had
already begun and which thus represented an anticipation of the heavenly
Jerusalem with the gates that never closed, shining powerfully and powerfully attracting its surrounding.[10]

    The Croatian Evangelical churches faced the same questions as other
Christian communities that have imposed such high criteria of member-
ship: how can one determine who was born from God, on the basis of what
manifestations of religious experience? The consequence of this confusion
was sometimes that such religious communities, instead of being attractive

10. Cf. Rev 21:25.

cities with open gates, would turn into small fortresses or even small ghet-toes, which created the corresponding systems of "patterns" and "thresh-olds" for becoming and remaining a member of the community of believers. Such patterns and thresholds were, in their own turn, a result of narrow-ing, arbitrary interpretations of the universality of the Christian message and the richness of Christian religious experience. This narrowing, again, was a consequence of the long and weary way in which the message of the importance of "being born again"—be it through foreign missionaries or through the local people who returned from guest labor in the US—was tossed and jolted along the way from the American continent to Europe, where it settled down—not always for the best or most favorably—in the exceptionally specific religious and cultural area of Yugoslavia. Those who fitted in such patterns and crossed such thresholds considered themselves "faithful." Those, however, who did not pass the thresholds or fit the pat-terns, were called or at least considered "unfaithful." Considering the fact that the entire world of evangelical churches in Yugoslavia did not number more than a few thousand people, this meant that, according to the convic-tion of the majority of the "faithful," almost the entire population of Tito's Yugoslavia, which at that time amounted to approximately twenty-two mil-lion persons, belonged to the group of "unfaithful," who were "unsaved" and as such lost and eternally damned. This firm conviction of the small herd of "faithful" could not be shattered by the fact that Tito's Yugoslavia did not consist of atheists alone: the majority of the population belonged to the Roman Catholic or Eastern Orthodox faith, and a significant percentage of the population belonged to Islam. And the least of all it could be shattered by the fact that even the world of "atheists" in Tito's Yugoslavia was not entirely monolithic, but rather a world from which individuals emerged, again and again, who showed a considerable level of interest and sensibility for religion and religious issues.

The representatives of both state power and the majority confessions considered these communities of "faithful" to be "sects".[11] Despite this occasional pejorative nomenclature, the "sects" regularly, in accordance with the New Testament mandate (e.g., Romans 13), offered prayers and thanks for all people, especially the secular government. In addition to

11. To be sure, they overlooked the fact that they were thus complimenting the minority religious communities in a way, as an understanding of the relations between religion and the state according to which the state should not be biased towards any religious group, as an understanding endorsed by sects in general (including these Yugoslav sects, albeit mostly implicitly) became the foundation for understanding the relations between religion and the state in modern democracies. On the significance of the term "sects," see Troeltsch, *Social Teaching*, 1:331–43.

the New Testament, the community of "faithful" had another good reason for this: Tito's government treated all religious communities in the same way—allowing all of them to live in peace. Of course, under the condition that they stayed away from public and political life. Contrary to the majority confessions, which were at loss with regard to the earlier periods and which stood in an open conflict with the regime (at the beginning of the Communist rule) or in a latent one (during the entire Communist rule), for the "sects" this situation was more than satisfactory. The regime's attitude offered the "sects" an opportunity to exist in peace and actually gave them a favorable status with regard to the previous periods in the territory of Yugoslavia. They could now establish and register their communities without hindrance, erect buildings, open theological schools, invite numerous missionaries from the "West." The state did not intervene in their business and they did not intervene in politics.

All those who spent at least a part of their lives in any of the Evangelical churches remember very well the term "friends." "Friends" were all those who were preparing to join the community, but had not yet been baptized.[12] Friends could include people who found the group of "faithful" appealing, in the manner of Zacchaeus (Luke 19:1–10),[13] perhaps because they could identify themselves neither with the world of "atheism", nor with the form of Christianity that existed in Yugoslavia, which seemed too burdened with the national question and the traditional forms. On the other hand, they could not make a decision to join the community of the "faithful," often because of its unnecessarily narrow interpretation of the Christian message.

It is only logical that many suffered in these small and closed communities, and that many found them too "suffocating," which is why they abandoned them or distanced themselves in one way or another in order to seek a more universal expression of Christian faith. Thus, the group of "friends" could include the children of the "faithful" or even some formerly active and fervent community members.

However, this does not change the fact that these communities were places where people were seeking to integrate in their lives the primordial biblical hope in the world to come, by living the experience of powerful nearness of God in their earthly lives, by caring for each other regardless of all social or national differences and, while doing that, constantly expecting Christ's Second Advent and the arrival of God's New Jerusalem.[14] This primordial biblical hope that these pious, honest, and persistent people lived,

---

12. See Volf, "Crkva zajednica prijatelja," 6. ["The Church: Community of Friends"]

13. Cf. Halik, *Patience with God.*

14. Rev 21.

and which they truly emitted—despite the sometimes awkward language they used to articulate or explain it—that is something that many took along on their life journeys and what defined them for life as an extraordinarily precious token and an undying inspiration.

VOLF'S POSITION

The Theology of "Strengthening" the Community of the "Faithful"

It is striking with how much love and devotion the author whose theological language would later conquer the hearts and minds of many with its range and universality in most of his Croatian theological texts articulated, explained, and largely defended the way of life of his small community of the "faithful." For this reason, I have termed this aspect of Volf's theological thought the theology of "strengthening" of the community of the "faithful." I am referring here primarily to some fifty articles that he wrote in the 1980s for the Pentecostal journal *Izvori* [*Sources*].

The first thing that the reader of these articles will notice is that the world of Tito's Yugoslavia is viewed in a rather simplified manner. This world consisted of their own small community on the one side, and the "unfaithful" on the other, or—as Volf wrote in an article titled "What about the Weekend?"—it consisted of "us" and "our unfaithful neighbors."[15] The community of the "faithful" was in a situation that was analogous to that of the Christians in 1 Pet 3:13–16. Contrary to the world flowing into the river of debauchery and perdition, it was basically on the right way and had to explain its beliefs and its lifestyle to the unfaithful world, as well as live consistently with what it professed.[16] This accommodation to the community of the "faithful" is also reflected in Volf's imitation of the homiletic style that was common in Evangelical churches in Tito's Yugoslavia. Thus, some of his articles were written in the tone of assurance, optimism, and moderate triumphalism, whereby he interspersed his opinions with numerous quotations from the Scripture, generally briefly yet accurately explained. In this way, some of his articles reveal the almost perfected style and manner of preaching in Evangelical churches in Tito's Yugoslavia.[17]

---

15. Volf, "Što s vikendom?"
16. Volf, "Obrazloženje nade" ["Hope explained"].
17. Cf. Orčić, *Ludost propovedanja*. ["The Foolishness of the Preaching"]

In most of his articles from this period, Volf devoted himself specifically to the issues related to the dynamics of life in these communities of the "faithful." This tendency started with the article titled "Spiritual Pulp," in which he defended the Pentecostals from the works of "pulp fiction,"[18] and continued with a series of articles called "The Spirit in the Life of a Christian,"[19] in which he—in order to secure for the Pentecostals in Tito's Yugoslavia an equivalent position among the Evangelical churches, whose members occasionally derided them as "spiritualists"—elaborated on the gifts of the Spirit. The Pentecostals were here presented as appropriately living out the Biblical experience of ecclesiality[20] and as continuing Christ's mission of liberating the oppressed and the needy.[21] The experience of the Spirit also meant partaking in Christ's filiality with regard to God the Father, as well as partaking in His suffering in the world and for the world, which therefore amounted to partaking in the life of the Triune God himself.[22] In a series of separate articles, Volf elaborated on the relationship between spiritual gifts and the development of human personality, the equal dignity of all gifts of the Spirit, and on the task of pastors to recognize the believers' potentials.[23] In an interview with Jürgen Moltmann, he indicated the advantage of small communities, since they were—contrary to the *Volkskirche* (People's Church)—more suitable for bringing charismatic powers to the fore.[24]

Another contribution to Volf's struggle for the equivalent position of the Pentecostals among the Evangelical churches was his series on articles on "God's Will, Illness, and Healing."[25] The practice of praying for healing in the Pentecostal communities was seen as a sign of faith in the living God[26] and a sign of denunciation of fatalism and determinism, so foreign to the Christian faith.[27] However, concerning the self-image of the Pentecostals, Volf considered it equally important to indicate that God sometimes allowed evil and suffering to happen, including illness. Using the arguments

18. Volf, "Duhovni šund."

19. Volf, "Duh u životu kršćanina."

20. Ibid., I.

21. Ibid., IV.

22. Ibid., III and II.

23. Volf, "Svi su nadareni" ["Everyone is gifted"]. Cf. Volf, "Svatko treba svakoga" ["Everyone needs everyone else"]. Cf. Volf, "Starješine i vjernici" ["Elders and believers"].

24. Volf, "Razgovor s profesorom Moltmannom."

25. Volf, "Božja volja, bolest i izlječenje."

26. Ibid., I and III.

27. Ibid., V ; cf. Volf, "Ričući lav" ["The roaring lion"], 1/86.

of theodicy concerning God allowing evil to happen, and complementing them with that of the suffering God,[28] Volf rejected the position that the lack of health (or any other aspect of well-being) mirrored one's deficiency in spiritual life.[29]

Volf also sought to secure a dignified place for the faith and practice of Evangelical churches in Tito's Yugoslavia in a wider context of the Reformation doctrine of justification. His understanding of sin and the reasons for Christ's death was fully compatible with the common stance of the Evangelical churches in Tito's Yugoslavia. He thus presented sin in the Anselmian sense as an "offense" to God. Accordingly, Christ's incarnation and death were interpreted—without excluding the revelatory dimension or that of self-sacrifice—in the spirit of Anselm's satisfaction theory.[30] In this regard, he considered Moltmann's position, namely that Christ himself had left Christology open, as problematic.[31]

Volf also did service to Evangelical Christianity in his articles "When Should One Be Baptized?" and "Why Should One Be Baptized?" where he endorsed the opinion that only believers should be baptized.[32] Volf thereby extended his endorsement of the practice of Yugoslav Evangelical churches to the ecumenically problematic practice of re-baptizing those who had been baptized as children, which was a logical consequence of the correct view that the ritual performed over small children could not count as baptism, owing to their lack of personal faith. Only a very mild correction of the Evangelical understanding of baptism can be found in Volf's article "Why Should One Be Baptized?", where he—albeit only implicitly—questioned the significance of baptism as a sign of personal faith alone and of its public recognition, and emphasized the significance of salvation as related to it, although not entirely unambiguously.[33]

In his article "What's the Use of Theology?" Volf encouraged the community of Evangelical Christians to be a community interested in theology.

28. Volf, "Božja volja, bolest i izlječenje," I and V.

29. Ibid., V.

30. Volf, "Gorki grijeh i slatko otkupljenje" [Bitter Sin and Sweet Redemption]; "Ljubav: da li je san ili java?" [Love: Dream or Reality?]. Cf. Volf, "Zašto je Bog postao čovjek?" [Why Did God Become Man?]. Cf. Volf, "Krist: Spasitelj, Stvoritelj i Pomiritelj" [Christ: Saviour, Creator, Conciliator].

31. Volf, "Tko je čovjek" [Who Is a Man]; also in Volf and Gundry-Volf, "Teološka razmišljanja o filmu 'Posljednja Kristova kušnja'" [Theological Reflection upon the Film "The Last Temptation of Christ"], 153ff.

32. Volf, "Kada biti kršten?"; Volf, "Zašto se krstiti?" Cf. Volf, "Razgovor s profesorom Moltmannom," 4.

33. Volf, "Zašto se krstiti," 7.

Here he again showed tact and understanding for its anti-intellectualism, manifested in the fear that involvement with theology could only "spoil" genuine, living faith. Volf also showed profound understanding for the fear of "unspiritual theology," admitting that the fear was to some extent justified as theology could indeed become "unspiritual" and then nobody could have any use of it. Nevertheless, he tried to mitigate anti-intellectualism and surpass the fear of "unspiritual" theology by indicating the cognitive dimension of faith and the religious experience, the assistance that theology can offer in understanding one's own faith and one's own religious experience, as well as the apologetic "use" of theology in communicating with the "unfaithful." The critical task of theology as questioning certain beliefs and practices in his small community was nevertheless tacitly bypassed.[34] Regarding the fact that Volf was teaching at the time at the Biblical-Theological Institute and that he influenced his students in the way that they indeed often modified their narrow beliefs may certainly mean that this bypassing had pedagogical motivation. It may have resulted from Volf's intuitive judgment, perhaps not entirely rationalized, that people who felt safe in their convictions and lived a truly rare level of communal existence in their small communities should not be abruptly shaken out of their mode of existence, as it would only enhance the already present suspiciousness of these communities towards the "rest of the world"[35]—including the world of scholarly theology.

Volf discussed the relationship between faith (including the religious experience) and theology at the very end of his theological involvement in Tito's Yugoslavia, in his scholarly article "On the Cognitive Dimension of Religious Speech,"[36] in which he analyzed the relationship between religious experience and the cognitive dimension as presented in the book *Knowing and Believing* by Đuro Šušnjić, a renowned Yugoslav philosopher of science and religion.[37] Here Volf criticized Šušnjić's hypothesis that the cognitive dimension was not an essential part of religious experience and that, accordingly, one should neglect all cognitive approach to religious articulations. Volf, on the other hand, emphasized that the cognitive layer was an essential part both of religion and of religious experience,[38] as it was precisely the doctrinal aspect of religion, especially in Christianity, that mediated its very religious experience. That, of course, did not mean that

---

34. Volf, "Kakve vajde od teologije?" [What's the Use of Theology?], 1. Cf. Volf, "Bog kao model" [God as a Model], 6.

35. On this issue, see Volf, *Flourishing*, 10–11.

36. Volf, "O kognitivnoj dimenziji religijskog govora," 304–20.

37. Šušnjić, *Znati i vjerovati*.

38. Volf, "O kognitivnoj dimenziji religijskog govora," 306–7.

the cognitive segment of religion was the very realization of its goal. The doctrinal system had to pave the way into the reality it indicated and which eventually surpassed it. However, that did not diminish the fact that one could not reach religious experience without the help of cognitive or doctrinal elements of Christianity.[39] Moreover, Volf argued that "the specifically religious can be preserved in Christian religious experience (at least) only if it remains present (subjectively speaking) in Christian religious speech and implicitly asserted as a genuine cognitive component."[40] Thus, any kind of neglect or suppression of the cognitive dimension would eventually destroy the authentic Christian experience as such.[41] Even though Volf argued here against Šušnjić as a philosopher and philosopher of religion, his article offers a dignified articulation of the relationship between the religious experience of Evangelical communities and its cognitive dimensions, as well as a plausible articulation of the foundations on which those communities could build their self-image in the future.

Mild Criticism of the Community of the "Faithful"

The texts that Volf wrote during the time he was active in Tito's Yugoslavia reveal also certain elements of criticism of Evangelical Christianity.

He mentions as truly problematic the fact that these small communities were often detached from the realities of human life—a sort of visionariness that harbored an actual potential to turn faith into the "opium of the people."[42] In this respect, Volf criticized the models and the criteria of these small communities when it came to judging the authenticity of Christian life, as they were partly a result of vanity and arbitrariness.[43] In this way, the Evangelical communities could easily turn from proclaimers of the Gospel to Pharisee-like structures that preached themselves and their own spirituality, or rather some personal ideology of spiritual prosperity,[44] instead of God and his grace.

It is for this reason that Volf's articles written for *Izvori* shown signs of suffering in these small communities of the "faithful." It was the suffering of

39. Ibid., 308.

40. Ibid., 309.

41. Ibid., 309–10.

42. Volf, "Bog kao model."

43. Ibidem. Cf. Volf, "Duh u životu kršćanina"; Volf, "Kako ti je ime, Bože?" [What's Your Name, God?].

44. Volf, "Narod ne-narod" [People, Non-People]. Cf. Volf, "Razgovor s profesorom Moltmannom."

those who had difficulties with fitting into the patterns of prospering spiritual life—and preferred to sit quietly in a corner as observers in order not to disturb those who were spiritually successful.[45] Volf's article "Against Boring Christianity" implies that their numbers were far from negligent. Moreover, the reverse of the ideology of spiritual prosperity seems to have been the fact that a significant number of believers in the real world were feeling aimless and that their alternative was to turn on the TV and watch, for example, the popular American TV-series *Dynasty*, which was broadcasted by the Yugoslav television in those years. Sometimes they dedicated themselves to accumulating material wealth, which likewise tended to obscure the view of the reality, especially the suffering of others.[46] And this escapism—be it in the form of visionariness, resignation, or preoccupation with material gain—contradicted Christian hope as such, which is hope in God's new creation, which will not happen *ex nihilo*, after this reality had been extinguished in eternal death, but rather *ex vetere*, by God transforming this old reality into a new heaven and a new earth.[47] In that regard, the conviction that was common in Evangelical churches, namely that this sinful world would end in a general cataclysm, was malevolent and eventually godless.[48] Accordingly he also faced the Evangelical Christians with the problem of preserving God's creation and the issues of technological advance, including that of Christian responsibility for the ecological crisis.[49] He made it clear that Christians should not live in an activist illusion that their efforts could create a new heaven and a new earth, as only God can do that, which is why the essential segment of Christian engaged action for the good of God's creation was to be hope and expectation of God's intervention, with the aim of renewing the creation.[50] However, this hope should not be inebriating; instead, it should be a "sober" hope of Christians with their feet firmly on the ground.[51]

45. Volf, "Svatko treba svakoga."

46. Volf, "Protiv dosadnog kršćanstva."

47. Volf, "Krist: Spasitelj, Stvoritelj i Pomiritelj"; Cf. Volf, "Biblija i 'ekološka bomba," [The Bible and the "Ecological Bomb"]. Cf. Volf, *Flourishing*, 11.

48. Volf, "Biblija i 'ekološka bomba," 9; Volf, "Da li se Isus smijao?" [Did Jesus Laugh?].

49. Volf, "Biblija i 'ekološka bomba'"; Volf, "Tehnološki napredak" [Technological Advance].

50. Ibidem. Cf. Volf, *Flourishing*, 10f.

51. Cf. Volf, "Bog kao model."

In his articles "Why We Work"[52] and "No Pain, No Gain?"[53] Volf expressed his conviction that the Evangelical Christians should be "sobered up" regarding their attitude towards work, since many, as he said, "have started to behave as if their attitude towards work does not belong to the sphere of their Christian duties."[54] He reminded them that work was neither a consequence of sin nor a sign of damnation nor a necessary evil. Work belonged to the very essence of humanity as created by God, who was—as a working God—also the first worker.[55] This was the foundation of both the dignity of the working people and the dignity of work as an inalienable part of Christian life and the true divine service.[56] Its purpose was not to accumulate wealth, but to satisfy one's living needs, secure the protection of nature, and render service to others, especially the needy.[57] In this context, Volf invited the Evangelical Christians to truly live in their country and stop avoiding the meetings of their "Basic Organization of Associated Labor";[58] instead, they should participate both in the working process and in the process of workers' decision-making.[59]

Volf also considered it important to raise the awareness of his "visionary" community for the issues of social justice.[60] The community of believers that is so obsessed with its devotion to God that it has no mercy for the needy and fails to work on the liberation of the oppressed is on Satan's path, Volf concluded in his article "Sharing is Caring."[61]

Apparently foreseeing the dissolution of Tito's Yugoslavia, including its treatment of religious communities, which had partly favored the ghettoization of Evangelical Christians in its territories, Volf became somehow "sharper" with Evangelical Christianity towards the end of his activity in Tito's Yugoslavia. In his lecture on the Christian contribution to the

52. Volf, "Zašto radimo?"

53. Volf, "Umro pos'o, crko trud?"

54. Ibid., 10. Cf. Volf, "Brigo moja preÐi na—Boga" [None of My Business—but God's].

55. Volf, "Zašto radimo?"; "Umro pos'o, crko trud?"

56. Volf, "Zašto radimo?,"7. Cf. Volf, "Umro pos'o, crko trud?".

57. Cf. Volf, "Brigo moja preÐi na—Boga."

58. The Basic Organization of Associated Labor (OOUR) was the basic economic unit in Yugoslav self-management socialism.

59. Volf, "Umro pos'o, crko trud?"

60. Volf, "Bog osloboditelj"; cf. Volf, "Bog i bližnji." [God and the Fellow Man]

61. Volf, "Naše kese jesu sestre," 9. Cf. Volf, "Isus je radikalan" [Jesus Is Radical]; "Bog i bližnji"; Volf, "Siromasi i prepuna kuća." [The Poor and the House of Plenty]; cf. Volf, "Razgovor s profesorom Moltmannom."

democratization of socialist societies,[62] he seems to have wanted to shake
the members of his community, to force them to mature almost overnight.
He criticized the Evangelical Christians as the least awakened Christians
in terms of democracy in all socialist countries, as well as those with the
least awareness of their Christian political responsibility.[63] Even though he
showed some understanding for this deficiency,[64] he nevertheless pointed
out its absurdity, for it was precisely the Evangelical Christians that considered themselves heirs of the separatist tradition of free churches, which offered an important contribution to the development of Western democratic
thought with their endorsement of the separation of religion and the state.[65]
In order to accelerate them in their progress and help them shine forth
with their true light as sects, he offered them a crash-course in the basics
of Christian/Evangelical understanding of democracy. In his writings, he
advises the following: what the Evangelical Christians should be well aware
of when they come out of their small ghetto and begin searching for their
place in the construction of a democratic society, which will undoubtedly
happen soon, is that democracy is not recognized by the goals it seeks to
reach, but by the way in which it treats the individual. Therefore, if one can
say at all that democratic societies have a goal, that goal is to ensure that
no individual should become an instrument for the realization of a higher
goal and thus be deprived of his rights. For this reason, a democratic society
is open for the participation of all, as well as for the "individual and communal formulation of alternative visions of a collective future."[66] And since
some democratic societies consist in part of Christians, these should have
an equal right (neither more nor less) to "persuade the social community
to share their social ideals."[67] However, it should never happen in democracy that a particular vision of the society (be it Communist or Christian)
should be imposed upon either the majority or a minority against their will,
as that would mean violating human freedom. In order to prevent that, the
Evangelical Christians should watch over democracy together with other
citizens in order to ensure truly democratic structures.[68] They must therefore—keeping in mind the importance of personal change—deal with the

62. Volf, *Socijalizam, totalitarizam i demokracija* [Socialism, Totalitarianism, and
Democracy].

63. Ibid., 183.

64. Cf. Volf, *Flourishing*, 8–12.

65. Volf, *Socijalizam, totalitarizam i demokracija*, 184.

66. Ibid.

67. Ibid., 185.

68. Ibid., 186.

change in structures as well, since personal moral demands cannot be effective without structural change.[69]

Biblical Hope in the "Unfaithful" World—the Possibilities and Limitations of Dialogue with Marxism

In the same way as some of Volf's articles written for *Izvori* imply that the world of the "faithful" could not be unambiguously described as a community of sober Christian hope, other articles seem to claim that the "unfaithful" environment of self-management socialism was not entirely and by all means a world without hope. Moreover, that world, or rather its ideological substrate—Marxism—contained many things that made it worthy for Christians to take it seriously, as Volf wrote in his article "Opium of the People?"[70] Among the things that should be taken seriously was Marx's criticism of the Christian justification of the existence of oppressors and the oppressed, as well as the interpretation of welfare for the common man only as an otherworldly category. Another aspect of criticism that deserved attention concerned the Christian position that interpreted human suffering caused by injustice and violence as a just punishment for the sufferers' sins. What was, however, problematic in Marx's critique of Christianity was that it did not address its true principles, but rather their deviations. It also overlooked the fact that Christianity had not always betrayed the biblical principles throughout its history, but also nurtured them, so that it, for example, achieved the abolition of slavery. Nevertheless, it was Christianity itself that partly offered the reasons for these flaws in Marx's critique, as it often tended to confuse its principles easily and uncritically with its problematic manifestations. For this reason, Volf considered it justified to argue in his article "Convincing Mute Speech" that Marxist atheism was largely the fault of Christians.[71] Marxism posed a challenge to the Christian church to return to the social principles of its prophets, Jesus, and the early Church, who were truly revolutionary without calling for a revolution.[72] This did not mean that a line should be drawn between the believers and the non-believing world, but rather, as Volf stated in his article "Exodus without an Exit,"

69. Ibid., 187–88.

70. Volf, "Opijum naroda?"

71. Volf, "Uvjerljivi nijemi govor." Cf. Volf, "Svijet nasilja i crkva raspetoga" [The World of Violence and the Church of the Crucified].

72. Volf, "Opijum naroda?" Cf. Volf, "Krotki će naslediti zemlju" [The Meek Will Inherit the Earth].

a dialogue should be initiated with those who did not believe,[73] particularly a dialogue with Marxism, which could itself find its older and far healthier roots in Jesus and the prophets, that is, in biblical Messianism.[74]

Volf's own contribution to the dialogue between Christians and Marxists, or rather Christians and atheists in general, was his article "God, Freedom, and Grace," in which he entered into a dialogue with the Yugoslav Marxists, debating on the significance of atheism for Marx and Marxism.[75] Even though not explicitly questioning the hypothesis that Marx's critique of Christianity had its good reasons in the reality of Christian manifestations and in Marx's uncritical identification of the true principles of Christianity with its problematic historical forms, Volf was of the opinion that the reasons for Marx's atheism were too hastily identified in his disapproval of the life of Christian churches or his lack of knowledge about the tenets of Biblical faith, since Marx's atheism was not merely methodological, but also theoretical and as such based on his anthropology. And the basis of that anthropology was his understanding that human emancipation could never happen in any relation to God,[76] since God—whether understood as an advocate of the subjected position of human being or as the liberator—nevertheless diminished the humanity of the human being.[77] That is, Volf continues, only partly explainable from the fact that Marx, starting from Feuerbach, saw any relationship between human being and God as one of competition,[78] neglecting the fact that the relationship presented in the Bible was one of cooperation.[79] What made Marx's atheism so serious and fundamental was his radical rejection of any sort of human's dependence on God. In other words, this meant that the "stumbling stone that cannot be removed" in Marx's attitude towards Christian religion was nothing else but God's mercy.[80] The point in Marx's atheism was that humanity was generically the basis and the highest being for the human being, who therefore had to be emancipated not only from God as the advocate of the status quo of this world, but also from the idea of merciful God—as anyone who lived off the mercy of another had to be considered dependent and therefore unfree. This conviction remained unshaken, even though Marx believed

73. Volf, "Izlazak bez izlaska."

74. Volf, "Razgovor s profesorom Moltmannom."

75. Volf, "Bog, sloboda i milost," I and II.

76. Ibid., 314.

77. Ibid., 318.

78. Ibid., 319–20.

79. Ibid., 320.

80. Ibid. (II), 21.

at the same time that an individual did not owe his existence to himself, but remained dependent of his parents, other people, and nature, and was therefore primarily "given" to himself.[81] In this respect, Marx's atheism was also more than a mere "postulate of the practical mind" whose aim was to encourage people to rely on their own forces—which would be compatible with Christianity to some extent. Marx's rejection of God's mercy equaled a rejection of biblical faith in its most authentic expression, namely in the belief that the keys of human existence and salvation were in God's hands. In that respect, Marx's atheism was eventually a negation of God the Creator, since the existence of God the Creator meant that human life depended on another in the fullest sense of the word. And that was for Marx, as Volf emphasized when referring to Marx's *Economic and Philosophic Manuscripts*, incompatible with his postulate on human independence of God[82] and the real reason why Marx negated God's existence from the beginning to the very end of his evolution as a philosopher.[83] It was therefore possible to say, according to Volf, that both in Marx and in Christianity, "despite certain important discrepancies, God as criticized by Marx and God in biblical and authentic Christian tradition are nevertheless partly one and the same God."[84] With opposite philosophical outcomes, of course. In other words, even if Marx had better understood the truly liberating nature of the biblical message, he would have (probably) remained an atheist—as atheism was an essential part of his humanism.[85] Accordingly, Volf questioned at the very beginning of his article the concordance that was slowly emerging in the Christian-Marxist dialogue at the time, which consisted in the claim that atheism was not essential to Marx or to Marxism.[86] In his opinion, it would be truly useful to come back to the issue of the importance of atheism as posited in the dialogue between Christians and Marxists during the late 1950s and 1960s.[87]

By saying all this, Volf did not want to diminish the importance of self-criticism within Christianity as an important precondition for the Christian-Marxist dialogue and a cooperation between them on the task of humanizing the world. He merely indicated that Marx's atheism, and atheism generally speaking, if indeed theoretical, was a phenomenon whose

81. Ibid. (I), 318f (cf. II, 21).
82. Ibid. (II), 23.
83. Ibid. 27.
84. Ibid. 22.
85. Ibid. 24.
86. Ibid. (I), 311.
87. Ibid. 314.

sources were far deeper than a misunderstanding about the real principles of religion or its emancipatory nature. For even though some Marxists indeed claimed that, had they ever encountered the true Christianity, they would have never become atheists,[88] in theoretical Marxism atheism was eventually a fundamental position with regard to the ultimate reality. And that fundamental position could not be explained simply by the present state of the world or the current authenticity of a particular religion and its members. Instead, it was a fundamental and eventually not entirely comprehensible human "no" to the human's response to God's reality in faith, a "no" which Godself eventually respected. Therefore, the Christian-atheist dialogue could not really evolve in any form if it tended to downgrade this issue: be it by downgrading the seriousness of theoretical atheism or by perhaps giving up the belief in a personal and transcendental God, which was constitutive for Christianity.[89] This dialogue had to face its basic question, which was eventually the question of compatibility between God's mercy, or rather human dependence on God, and human freedom.[90]

The Voices of Prayer Outside
the Small Community of the "Faithful"

Volf did not allow the Evangelical Christians to live peacefully in the illusion that they were the only genuine segment of Christianity. This is clearly evident from a remark in his article "Saints: What about Them?" on the Evangelical Christians having forgotten that they were part of God's universal and transhistorical people,[91] and also indirectly from his interview with Moltmann, in which he critically addressed the ecumenical isolation of the Pentecostals on the global level.[92] For this purpose, his articles are equipped not only with biblical quotations and recommendation of books of a denominational nature, but also with a number of quotations from Christian antiquity, classics of the Reformation, and contemporary Protestant theology, and even one from the Eastern Orthodox theologian Berdyaev. His scholarly articles also contain references to the work of Thomas Aquinas, Walter Kasper, and other Roman Catholic and Eastern Orthodox theologians. However, it is interesting to note that Volf's writings from this period present the world of Tito's Yugoslavia as consisting almost exclu-

88. Cf. Volf, "Razgovor s profesorom Moltmannom."

89. Volf, "Bog, sloboda i milost," 23.

90. Ibid. (II), 29.

91. Volf, "Sveci što s njima?" 7.

92. Volf, "Razgovor s profesorom Moltmannom."

sively of Marxists and atheists on the one side, and the small communities of the "faithful" on the other, but barely give notice of other Christians or believers, even though a considerable segment of the population belonged either to Roman Catholicism or to Eastern Orthodoxy, and even though there were several important Roman Catholic theologians at the time of his activity in Yugoslavia who promoted the spirit of Vatican II. The presence of other Christians in Yugoslavia—as living people made of flesh and blood— is barely hinted at in Volf's review of the exquisite Croatian translation of the New Testament, the work of renowned Catholic Bible scholars Bonaventura Duda and Jerko Fućak—a translation that was just in the process of finding its way into the Evangelical churches—as well as in his mention of the Roman Catholic and Eastern Orthodox sacral spaces,[93] and in the article on the adequate form of baptism according to the New Testament.[94]

However, there is a notable exception to this silence, namely Volf's booklet of theological meditations on the religious poetry of Aleksa Šantić (1868–1924), a poet from Herzegovina, titled *I znam da sunce ne boji se tame* [And I Know that the Sun Fears not Darkness].[95] The idea of writing this book came to Volf quite spontaneously. During the 1980s the Pentecostal Church in Mostar purchased the birth house of Aleksa Šantić in order to use it for its own purposes, which triggered an avalanche of commentaries in the press about how inappropriate it was that the house where the poet Šantić had been born should become property of a Pentecostal religious community.[96] Such articles listed arguments that were typical of Yugoslav theoreticians of literature active after World War II, namely that Šantić had been primarily a socialist struggling for the rights of the oppressed and a critic of religion, and that his religious poetry was simply a consequence of his origins, as he had been born into a patriarchal Eastern Orthodox setting, and as such a negligible part of his poetic opus.[97] Since Volf was serving in the Yugoslav army in Mostar at the time, and he occasionally enjoyed the hospitality of the local believers, he decided to help the community of Mostar in that unpleasant situation. He started to read Šantić's poetry and came to the conclusion that it was an expression of a profound faith in the living God, as well as hope in the coming salvation. He also concluded that Šantić's poetry was in no contradiction with his great human and poetic sensibility for the issues of social justice and

93. Volf, "Sveci što s njima?," 6.
94. Volf, "Kada biti kršten?"
95. Volf, *I znam da sunce ne boji se tame.*
96. Ibid., 9.
97. Ibid., 16, and 23.

the suffering of his people. Quite the contrary, his religious poetry was permeated with the theme of liberation of the oppressed individual and the oppressed (Serbian) people.[98] It was for this reason that Volf decided to write a booklet of theological meditations on Šantić's religious poetry as an essential part of his artistic and human identity.[99]

Volf incorporated his previous reflections on the relationship between Christianity and Marx's critique of religion in his analysis of Šantić's religious poetry, positing the question on the extent to which Marx's criticism of religion and Šantić's attitude towards religion overlapped. He concluded that an aspect shared by both Marx and Šantić was the critique of all forms of oppression, even religion when it endorsed any relations of injustice. It was for this reason, and in a similar way as Marx did when speaking of the Christianity of his times, that Šantić described the Christianity of his own time as a form of human alienation. However, contrary to Marx, Šantić also acknowledged the liberating potential of authentic Christianity. Unlike Marx, he thus took over from the Bible not only the critique of religion, but also the biblical understanding of God as the liberator suffering with the world and for the world. Thus, for Šantić, God and humans do not compete with each other, but rather cooperate. In this respect, Volf argued—somewhat anachronistically—that Šantić could be considered as "the first Yugoslav 'theologian' of liberation."[100] The Pentecostal community of Mostar indeed could not have obtained a better defense. Volf plausibly showed that a poet who had been appropriated before World War II by the Serbian nationalists, and after the war by the Marxists or socialists, was in fact a follower of that same authentic biblical faith in God the liberator that was proclaimed by the Evangelical Christians—and that he thus stood indeed close to Evangelical Christianity.

However, the reason why I consider Volf's booklet on Šantić as crucial for his theological thought during his activity in Tito's Yugoslavia is not only that he defended the Evangelical Christians from the accusations voiced in the press, but far more—although it may not have been the primary purpose of his writing—because by indicating Šantić's closeness to them he defended them, or rather tried to save them from themselves: both from their isolation and from their fatal conceit, which was to a considerable extent nurtured by missionaries from the West. That conceit was manifested in their attitude that in Tito's Yugoslavia only the Evangelical Christians counted as the true Church and lived according to the Gospel.

98. Ibid., 9, and 13.
99. Ibid., 9.
100. Ibid., 16f.

Šantić, as Volf saw him, was not a lonely authentic Christian who found himself on the margins of Eastern Orthodox Christianity, almost like an outsider—someone who may have converted to an Evangelical church had he been born in different times. Volf's Šantić was a genuine Eastern Orthodox Christian.[101] To be sure, he was an Eastern Orthodox Christian who could criticize certain alienated forms of religiosity in his confession, among others the divine service that was very formal, hypocritical, and exclusively temple-bound, neglecting the everyday suffering and calamities of the common person.[102] However, that does not diminish the fact that Šantić was truly Eastern Orthodox in his heart and that he wanted to purify rather than abolish his religion.[103] Therefore, the Christian authenticity of his religious poetry, based on the prophets and Jesus Christ, was an authenticity inherited through Eastern Orthodoxy. And the buzzing of the true Christian prayer, of which he speaks in his beautiful poem "The Herzegovinian at Prayer," was indeed the voice of Eastern Orthodox Christians. It was the prayer to which the church bells called the believers from the actual Orthodox churches in Šantić's homeland of Herzegovina.[104] Thus I believe that I may say, albeit somewhat anachronistically, that Volf encountered in Šantić not only the first Yugoslav theologian of liberation, but also the biblical authenticity of actual Eastern Orthodox Christians in Tito's Yugoslavia. And Volf's booklet represents an encounter with that Christian authenticity for the Evangelical Christians as well. In this way, Volf mildly, yet convincingly reminded them that the number of those who venerated the true God in their surrounding was far greater than they might think. For it was a surrounding where, notwithstanding the Communist government, the church bells of Roman Catholic and Eastern Orthodox churches rang every single day, a surrounding in which the prayer to which those bells called had never gone silent. In this way, Volf reminded the Evangelical Christians of the demanding task of acculturation in the exceptionally specific religious and cultural area in which they lived.

CONCLUSION

Both in his early and in his later work, Volf often countered Adorno's claim that "there is no true life in the wrong one,"[105] since Christian joy and

101. Ibid., 15.
102. Ibid., 49f.
103. Ibid., 56.
104. Volf, *I znam da sunce ne boji se tame*, 77.
105. Ibid., 50. Cf. Volf, *Flourishing*, 17.

hope do not depend on the circumstances in which we live, but on God. Thus, people can be joyful even in a world that is more or less wrong.[106] In other words, those who are joyful always live joyfully in a world that is also "wrong" in one way or another—as another world does not yet exist.

This article on Volf is actually just another story of joy and hope in a world that is always "wrong" in one way or another; of joy and hope that— despite the atheist climate in that world—survived in the problematic world of self-management socialism; of joy and hope that survived in the majority religions in Tito's Yugoslavia—despite the unfavorable situation in which they existed and despite their sometimes questionable manifestations; of joy and hope that lived in the small world of Evangelical Christianity—likewise despite the "unfavorable" political situation and its sometimes questionable manifestations.

As a text on joy and hope in a world that is always "wrong" in one way or another, this article also speaks of the fundamental attitude of Christians towards the world they live in, both in terms of nature and the cultural or religious achievements of human beings who have been called and authorized to partake in God's creation. Thus, the joy and hope that one encounters in Volf's writings do not lull the reader into joyful endurance of that which is "wrong" in the world or into passive awaiting of the global cataclysm. It is also not the sort of joy and hope that would encourage or authorize someone to simply "crush down," "destroy," "demolish," or in any way "devalue" that world or any part of it because of its "wrongness," trying to—playing some sort of earthly god—create a better world or some part of it *ex nihilo*. And that is because even God will not destroy this "wrong world" in order to create a new one *ex nihilo*, but will create a new and better world from the existing reality—*ex vetere*.[107] Thus, the joy and hope that come from God's Spirit of creation gives us the strength to partake in God's new creation and to reshape existing reality—instead of blindly destroying, ignoring, or devaluing it—so as to be able to rejoice in the end because of that very reality.[108]

These reflections on Volf's early thought also speak of the basic attitude Christians should adopt towards all those who build this world in one way of another, making it a better place and thus partaking in God's new creation. That attitude basically consists of the following: not destroying, not devaluing, not trying to eradicate from memory any part of human history, any cultural or religious achievement of others. Instead, one

---

106. Ibidem.

107. Volf, "Biblija i 'ekološka bomba,'" Cf. Volf, *Flourishing*, 11.

108. Volf, *I znam da sunce ne boji se tame*, 51. Cf. Volf, *Flourishing*, 11.

should cooperate with other, different people—regardless of the differences in worldviews—to shape the existing reality so that we may all rejoice in the end. This position, which significantly determined Volf's later theological opus, was partly in its formative phase during the period in which he was active in Tito's Yugoslavia. However, this is not to say that it was less clear or less impressive for that reason. Moreover, the meekness with which Volf would never ever "break a bruised reed" or "quench the smoking flax" (Isa 42:3 KJV), but rather search, pick, and pluck like Cinderella, finding something exceptionally valuable first in his own small community and then in the religious and cultural environment of Tito's Yugoslavia, is a true exemplum of Christian joy and hope in a "wrong" world. This meekness is still adequate as a critique of all "earthly gods" who—regardless of whether they come directly from the world of religion or they have adopted some problematic models of religious behavior on the level of politics and economy—act as if they were able to create a new world *ex nihilo*. Thus they brag around, destroy nature, and annihilate everything before them, be it in open violence or by using some sophisticated methods to impose their domination, striving to erase, even from memory, entire parts of the world which others have created by their own efforts and with God's help.[109] And in their "heathenness" they cannot even dream that the earth, which God himself will eventually renew, will indeed be inherited by the meek.[110]

[Translated by Marina Miladinov]

---

109. Cf. Volf, *Flourishing*, 17.

110. Volf, "Krotki će naslediti zemlju," 16–17.

BIBLIOGRAPHY

Banac, Ivo. *Raspad Jugoslavije: Eseji o nacionalizmu i nacionalnim sukobima.* Zagreb: Durieux, 2001.

———. *With Stalin against Tito: Cominformist Splits in Yugoslav Communism.* Ithaca, NY: Cornell University Press, 1988.

Halik, Tomas. *Patience with God: The Story of Zacchaeus Continuing in Us.* Translated by Gerald Turner. New York: Doubleday, 2009.

Jakovina, Tvrtko. "Tito's Yugoslavia as the Pivotal State of the Non-Aligned," *Tito— viÐenja i tumačenja,* edited by Olga Manojlović Pintar, Mile Bjelajac, and Radmila Radić, 389–404. Belgrade: Institute for Recent Serbian History and Archive of Yugoslavia, 2011.

Orčić, Stjepan, *Ludost propovedanja: predavanja o propovedništvu,* Novi Sad: MBM– Plas, 2007.

Troeltsch, Ernst. *The Social Teaching of the Christian Churches.* Vol. 1. Translated by Olive Wyon. 1911. Reprint. Chicago: University of Chicago Press, 1981.

Šušnjić, Ðuro. *Znati i vjerovati, Teorijske orijentacije u proučavanju religije i ateizma,* Zagreb: Kršćanska sadašnjost–Stvarnost, 1988.

Volf, Miroslav. "Biblija i 'ekološka bomba.'" *Izvori* 6 (1986) 8–9.

———. "Bog i bližnji." *Izvori* 2 (1983) 4–5.

———. "Bog kao model." *Izvori* 3 (1987) 6–7.

———. "Bog osloboditelj." *Izvori* 10 (1986) 18–19.

———. "Božje praštanje i naše praštanje." *Izvori* 5 (1981) 4–5.

———. "Bog, sloboda i milost. Razmišljanja o bitnosti ateizma za Marxa i marksizam." *Crkva u svijetu* 4 (1988) 311–320.

———. "Bog, sloboda i milost. Razmišljanja o bitnosti ateizma za Marxa i marksizam (II)." *Crkva u svijetu* 1 (1989) 21–33.

———. "Božja volja, bolest i izlječenje I." *Izvori* 4 (1989) 8–9.

———. "Božja volja, bolest i izlječenje II." *Izvori* 5 (1989) 10–11.

———. "Božja volja, bolest i izlječenje III." *Izvori* 6 (1989) 10–11.

———. "Božja volja, bolest i izlječenje IV." *Izvori* 7-8 (1989) 10–11.

———. "Božja volja, bolest i izlječenje V." *Izvori* 9 (1989) 10–11.

———. "Brigo moja preÐi na—Boga." *Izvori* 1 (1985) 4–5.

———. "Crkva zajednica prijatelja." *Izvori* 1 (1982) 6–7.

———. "Da li se Isus smijao?" *Izvori* 2 (1987) 9.

———. "Duh u životu kršćanina I." *Izvori* 6 (1981) 8–9.

———. "Duh u životu kršćanina II." *Izvori* 7-8 (1981) 8–9.

———. "Duh u životu kršćanina III." *Izvori* 9 (1981) 8–9.

———. "Duh u životu kršćanina IV." *Izvori* 10 (1981) 8–9.

———. "Duhovni šund." *Izvori* 6 (1980) 19.

———. *Flourishing: Why We Need Religion in a Globalized World.* New Haven: Yale University Press, 2016.

———. "Gorki grijeh i slatko otkupljenje." *Izvori* 4 (1987) 4–5.

———. *I znam da sunce ne boji se tame. Teološke meditacije o Šantićevu vjerskom pjesnišvu.* Zagreb-Osijek: Izvori, 1986.

———. "Isus je radikalan." *Izvori* 11 (1985) 4–5.

———. "Izlazak bez izlaska." *Izvori* 2 (1985) 4–5.

———. "Kada biti kršten." *Izvori* 1 (1988) 4–5.

————. "Kako do Boga?" *Izvori* 2 (1988) 6–7.

————. "Kako ti je ime, Bože?" *Izvori* 5 (1986) 10–11.

————. "Kakve vajde od teologije?" *Izvori* 11 (1984) 4–5.

————. "Krist: Spasitelj, Stvoritelj i Pomiritelj." *Izvori* 4 (1988) 6–7.

————. "Krotki će naslediti zemlju." *Izvori* 9 (1982) 16–17.

————. "Ljubav: da li je san ili java?" *Izvori* 6 (1987) 10–11.

————. "Naše kese jesu sestre." *Izvori* 7-8 (1985) 8–9.

————. "Narod ne-narod." *Izvori* 12 (1986) 10–11.

————. "O kognitivnoj dimenziji religijskog govora. Teološke opaske uz Šušnjićevu knjigu 'Znati i verovati." *Crkva u svijetu* 4 (1989) 304–320.

————. "Obrazloženje nade." *Izvori* 5 (1983) 6–7.

————. "Opijum naroda?" *Izvori* 6 (1983) 20–21.

————. *A Public Faith: How Followers of Christ Should Serve the Common Good*. Grand Rapids: Baker, 2011.

————. "Protiv dosadnog kršćanstva." *Izvori* 10 (1984) 4–5.

————. "Razgovor s profesorom Moltmannom." *Izvori* 2 (1982) 16–17.

————. "Razgovor s profesorom Moltmannom." *Izvori* 3 (1982) 4–5, 23.

————. "Ričući lav." *Izvori* 1 (1986) 8.

————. "Socijalizam, totalitarizam i demokracija. O kršćanskom doprinosu demokratizaciji socijalističkih društava." *Crkva u svijetu* 2 (1990) 188.

————. "Siromasi i prepuna kuća." *Izvori* 7-8 (1981) 11.

————. "Starješine i vjernici." *Izvori* 4 (1983) 16–17.

————. "Svatko treba svakoga." *Izvori* 5 (1985) 4–5.

————. "Sveci što s njima?" *Izvori* 6 (1985) 6–7.

————. "Svi su nadareni." *Izvori* 4 (1985) 6–7.

————. "Svijet nasilja i crkva Raspetog." *Izvori* 4 (1981) 6–7.

————. "Što s vikendom." *Izvori* 10 (1983) 4–5.

————. "Tehnološki napredak." *Izvori* 9 (1983) 6–7.

————. "Teološka razmišljanja o filmu 'Posljednja Kristova kušnja." *Crkva u svijetu* 2 (1989) 149–156.

————. "Tko je pravi čovjek?" *Izvori* 1 (1983) 19.

————. "Umro pos'o, crko trud?" *Izvori* 5 (1987) 10–11.

————. "Uvjerljivi nijemi govor." *Izvori* 3 (1985) 4–5.

————. "Vrijedan si zato što jesi." *Izvori* 7-8 (1983) 4–5.

————. "Zašto je Bog postao čovjek?" *Izvori* 12 (1985) 8–10.

————. "Zašto radimo." *Izvori* 1 (1984) 6–7.

————. "Zašto se krstiti." *Izvori* 10 (1985) 6–7.

12

Reconciled in the Embrace of the Crucified

*The Notion of Enemy
in the Theology of Miroslav Volf*

Ivan Šarčević

CONFESSING RATHER THAN DENYING our own wrongs, remembering rightly, avoiding future violence, repentance and forgiveness, the establishment of new relations between enemies, in a word, reconciliation before the graceful God is an indispensable theme for Miroslav Volf. Volf discusses this process of reconciliation at three interconnected levels. The first level of reconciliation is interethnic reconciliation. At the foot of this process there are layers of long historical ill—memories of collective suffering; ethnic, religious, and ideological conflicts; stereotypes and demonization of neighbors; and the recent wars for "Greater Serbia" in his former homeland, Yugoslavia. This is what Volf draws on in his valuable theological discourse on remembering and forgetting, truth and justice, the relation between the victim and the wrongdoers, as a faithful and theologically reasoned offer for overcoming conflicts in post-conflict societies and countries.

At another level, Volf deals with reconciliation in the global world. On the one hand, our world is defined by social and economic inequalities, and increasing secularization and atheism and agnosticism, seeking not simply to separate politics and religion, church and state, but to remove religion from the public sphere. Despite this postmodern ideological secularism, in the same world, religion(s) are increasingly present in the public arena as integrating social factors and as the most powerful national and cultural identifiers. In some parts of the world, religion even assumes the role of bearer of social transformation, and even revolution. The global world thus becomes not only technologically unified but also increasingly pluralized, causing internal friction of confrontational (and religious) values. We are witnessing the clashes of political religions giving rise to horrendous and disastrous "holy terror" fought in the name of God, which calls for a proper response through reconciliation rather than through violence.

The observation above leads us to the conclusion that Volf, thirdly, deals with relationship, dialogue, and reconciliation between the two most powerful world religions: Christianity and Islam. Despite their long history of conflict, ignorance, and mutual contempt, these two religions, or their members, are searching for a new mode of coexistence for our times that, as Volf points out, must stem from their belief in a common God rather than from secular ideologies and political interests. With their shared Jewish origin and heritage, these two monotheistic religions, inherently and according to revelation, are understood as prophetic religions, meaning that they are obligated by God to get involved in society and change the *saeculum*.

In changing the world it is necessary to note that in the economically and militarily powerful West, rather than being a personal faith, Christianity is more a cultural given, a cultural identifier and signifier, in particular in its encounter with foreigners, notably with the growing number of Muslim immigrants. While the majority in Muslim societies considers Islam as the "total faith," the only one which can justly and legally preserve their societies and their world from the threats of a new Western (global and Christian) colonialism, the increasingly islamophobic West perceives Islam as and inherently violent religion and Allah as the God of exclusion and violence. The unavoidable responsibility for peace in the world, argues Volf, lies with Christians and Muslims. Unless they walk the path of reconciliation, unless they accept the imperative of "embracing the enemy," which is derived from an indicative of faith in the God of unconditional grace and forgiveness, our world will sink deeper into the growing darkness of xenophobia and persecution, wars and violence.

PEOPLE, RATHER THAN IDEOLOGIES, ARE RECONCILED

Volf's book *Exclusion and Embrace* addresses the first level of reconciliation. Besides bringing him fame and recognition in the theological world,
this comprehensive and polyphonic book is Volf's programmatic work. It
serves as a source providing varied and widening directions that this theologian can take in his further theological development. And that is exactly
what Volf does. We could argue that almost all of Volf's writings have their
theological origin in *Exclusion and Embrace*. Thus, for instance, his rather
autobiographical work, *The End of Memory*, follows out questions about
the role of memory in reconciliation that are found already in *Exclusion
and Embrace*. In *A Public Faith*, Volf discusses a level of reconciliation, that
between the secular world and religions, between Christianity and secular
society, that did not take center stage in *Exclusion and Embrace*. And the
third area of Volf's interest in reconciliation, that of the relationship between Christianity and Islam in the modern world is discussed in his rather
systematic work *Allah*, in which Volf, aside from providing a concise history
of Christian–Muslim relations, grapples with a difficult theological question—Christian and Muslim understanding of God/Allah; but this project
can be seen to grow out of the questions of truth, justice, and violence that
arise in Volf's seminal text.

Volf, however, does not address the issue of reconciliation in everyday
and, so to say, ordinary life, or reconciliation in smaller living environments
such as family, institutions, academic or religious communities, where people spend most of their effective time, and which can also be marred by less
than harmonious relations and everyday conflicts, and divisions that spring
from mandatory requirements of religion, and are in constant need of reconciliation, too. Even when he expresses his own personal experience, his
personal struggle and pain of reconciliation, and when he tries to provide
a theological argument—which is a thread running through all his works,
evident particularly in *The End of Memory*—Volf's predominant interest
remains with the possibility of reconciliation between adherents of conflicting worldviews, more precisely, the reconciliation of the individual believer/
Christian with the adherents of totalitarian ideologies or with a religious
fanatic, including the possibility of sharing true and just memories.[1] With

---

1. In *The End of Memory* Volf makes personal confessions from many sides regarding forgiveness and reconciliation with Captain G. who interrogated him as "the
enemy" of the regime and the state in the Yugoslav army. The work is a kind of personal theological purification of memory in a dialogue with Christian tradition and
contemporary literature, whereby the author frees himself of bitterness, anger, and the

this in mind, the discussion of the personal character of reconciliation is set more within the first mentioned area, rather than at the level of everyday personal relationships.

Although he never pinpoints or makes direct references to it, Volf rightly assumes, and thus formulates his theological reasoning, that there is no reconciliation between ideologies or between political religions. Only the people, the concrete individuals may want to reconcile. Subjects of reconciliation are neither institutions nor ethnic and religious collectives, nor religions, but conscious and free individuals, or if they are office holders, then particular people who act on behalf of their respective communities and institutions as well. Whether they are purely political or economic in nature, whether they, as political religions, assume the form of secular ideologies shrouded in God's name, ideologies are mutually irreconcilable.

Volf's theological engagement bears a strong autobiographical mark. He "theologizes" his personal experience and, first and foremost, addresses an individual, a believer. Above all, he addresses a Christian, a follower of Jesus Christ. Volf constantly insists—and assumes himself to be among those addressed by this insistence—that the individual, bound by God's revelation and God's merciful relationship toward human beings and humanity, is responsible for himself, others, and the world.

GOD LOVES GOD'S ENEMIES

Responsibility for other human beings, for peace and reconciliation in ethnically, religiously, and ideologically plural societies and in the world, from the perspective of God's love for all people, including the "ungodly," also subsumes an unavoidable responsibility for the wrongdoers,[2] for the enemy. This is the subject matter of the present article. The choice of this theme—to present a brief account of the understanding of the enemy[3] in Volf's works—is grounded in the fact that Volf, either directly or indirectly,

---

possibility of revenge, in a continuous conversation with the "Captain" which should bring forgiveness and mercy. It is about "embracing" our enemies, entering into the new reconciled relationship in the way God did it for all people at the Jesus's cross: to reconcile human beings not only with God but also with one another.

2. "It is the wrongdoer whom God calls me to love." Volf, *End of Memory*, 13.

3. Under the term "enemy" as the broadest concept, Volf subsumes other concepts, from the most politically correct in our times (wrongdoer) to the most specified ones such as adversary, perpetrator, oppressor, torturer, and enemy in the broadest sense. Our author never makes a semantic differentiation of these concepts but uses them according to their context.

grapples with that most difficult human and religious challenge—our relationship with our enemy—practically in all of his writings.

The love of the enemy, as Volf constantly reminds us, is the most specific Christian distinction in relation to other religions and world-views. And this love, writes Volf, is derived from the basic axiom of the Christian faith: God is merciful not only towards the righteous but also towards the unjust, not only towards believers but also towards unbelievers. The love of enemies is the pinnacle of Jesus's commandment of love of neighbor,[4] and it is the culmination of Jesus' practices and the fullness of the revelation of God that is unsurpassably manifested in the crucified Jesus. At the heart of the Christian faith is, therefore, "God's reconciling self-giving for the ungodly,"[5] and it bears consequences for Christian practice, i.e. the practical decision of Christians to show this unconditional mercy towards wrongdoers. Bound by God's practice of love, Christians, in order to remain Christian, ought to practice forgiveness and love for their enemies.

Along with other authors addressing our relationship with the enemies, Volf is following a theological path that is particularly dear to Reformation theology, from Luther to Moltmann.[6] The reconciliation between human beings, between all people, and therefore between enemies, takes place only through God's unconditional love in the Crucified. Reconciliation between people is a pure outcome of God's grace. "Without wanting to disregard (let alone discard) the theme of divine solidarity with victims," Volf writes at the beginning of his *Exclusion and Embrace*, "I will pick up and develop here the theme of divine self-donation for the

---

4. In *Allah*, in the context of the commandment to love, when comparing the sacred texts of Muslims and Christians, Volf says: "An explicit command to do so is not found in Muslim sacred texts. Though Christians have not always obeyed this command, to say the least, the command to love enemies is nonetheless central to the Christian faith—as central to the way Christians should live in the world as is the message of God's unconditional grace to their standing before God. It is a clear consequence of the Christian conviction that God is love." (108). Cf. The difference with Muslims in terms of relationship with the enemies, 179–84.

5. The full sentence goes: "But if God's reconciling self-giving for the ungodly stands at the center of our faith, then nothing stands in the way of opting for grace, with its pain and delight, of forgiving and ultimately releasing the memory of suffered wrongs." Volf, *End of Memory*, 209. Volf uses very similar vocabulary in Allah: "God's love for the ungodly and human love for enemies are inextricably tied together" (177).

6. On solidarity and self-giving for the enemies in Moltmann, based on Paul's words that "Christ died for the ungodly" (Rom 5:6), in self-giving of the one for many, see Volf, *Exclusion and Embrace*, 24, 47. Cf. also the section entitled "Enmity and Reconciliation." Ibid., 115–17.

enemies and their reception into the eternal communion of God."[7] And this thread is evident in his subsequent work.

On the path of Christian discipleship and following of Jesus's love for enemies—where Volf echoes Luther or, perhaps, both of them echo the Apostle Paul—there is that particularly unattainable goal of "covering the sins of our neighbor," because Christ loved and gave his life for his enemies too.[8] This thought will be developed even in his discussion with the Muslim understanding of Allah, especially in consideration of one of the Islamic names of God—*Al-Gafur*, which is found in the work of Al-Ghazali, where forgiveness is not simply "covering up" the sins, or closing one's eyes to the evils and failure to call the perpetrators to account. Forgiveness means much more, since it emphasizes the positive aspects of the other, drawing our attention to the positive aspects of people who, by virtue of human merit and understanding, deserve only condemnation and punishment.[9]

Even when inspired by their most ethical aspirations, human beings, Volf argues, cannot be reconciled with each other without God. In Christ's cross God reconciles human beings. Reconciliation is the work of God with free and informed consent of human beings, with a total act of faith. In Jesus's cross, God shows solidarity with those who suffer, but he also saves the sinners, the ungodly, and his enemies with the cross. God is not revealed in this world,[10] nor in Jesus Christ, to punish his enemies, but to love and redeem them, and to enable new relationships between human beings. Therefore, the believer's ultimate reason and obligation to reconcile with his enemy is found only in Christ's cross. "Hostility can be 'put do death' only through self-giving. Peace is achieved 'through the cross' and 'by the blood,'"[11] continues Volf, echoing Paul in the Epistle to the Ephesians (2:13–17). This shows that Volf's theology is entirely grounded in theonomy, in God's revelation in Jesus Christ to all people, as reported in the Gospels and especially in Paul's writings. In this respect, human liberty

---

7. Ibid., 23.

8. See Volf, *End of Memory*, 64. Volf makes it very clear that Christ's death was undoubtly meaningful. He continues: "Not all wrongs suffered are meaningless. Above all, suffering that we take upon ourselves for the sake of others is not meaningless; by definition, it is laden with positive meaning (see John 15:13: 'No one has greater love than this, to lay down one's life for one's friends'). But its meaning often consists precisely in relieving others of pain and guilt that cannot be rendered meaningful." (190).

9. See Volf, *Allah*, 161–62.

10. "God came down to earth not to punish or kill enemies (which we all are); instead, God gave God's own self as a sacrifice on their behalf, Jews and Gentiles alike." Volf, *End of Memory*, 95.

11. Volf, *Exclusion and Embrace*, 48.

is always acknowledged and respected as the source of human dignity and the possibility to radically reject this offer.

EXERCISING "DOUBLE VISION"

According to Volf, then, the process of reconciliation is initiated by God's love for sinful humanity, out of his love for enemies that was ultimately made evident at Christ's cross. This process has several stages: contrition (not only of perpetrators, but also of victims), forgiveness instead of revenge, forgetting (for the sake of the other),[12] and embracing. In other words, love of the enemy has its foundation in the universality of human sinfulness, including the sinfulness of the victims, and in the primacy of God's grace. We do not love others because they are innocent, but—like God in Christ's cross—precisely because they are sinful. Therefore, we should embrace the other even when we consider them wrongdoers.[13] Integral discipleship to Jesus means to "love those who do me harm," and that is, Volf continues, "a hard path on which Jesus called me to follow him—a path that reflects more than any other the nature of his God and mine."[14] In doing so, it is not up to human beings to determine our or God's enemies, sinners and wrongdoers, as priests often determine, but to start with the fact that all human beings are sinners, including those who are the real victims, and that all are reconciled by Christ's cross—both victims and perpetrators.

Volf often varies his main theological thesis that "God's reception of hostile humanity into divine communion is a model for how human beings should relate to each other."[15] Hence the call to repentance, prior to forgiveness, is addressed not only to the perpetrators but also to victims, who can envy and hate their enemies, mimic or dehumanize their oppressors. "Devotion to wealth and hatred of the enemy," Volf emphasizes, "are sins of which the followers of Jesus must repent."[16] In an act of repentance,

---

12. In *The End of Memory* Volf speaks on forgetting not as a denial or intentional repression or as the wiping out of the memory but as a non-remembrance of the suffered wrongdoings, as non-recollection or not bringing to mind, with the goal of giving the wrongdoer the new gift of innocence (109–10). We are not dealing here with forgetfulness for the sake of ourselves but for the good of the other.

13. See Volf, *Exclusion and Embrace*, 85.

14. Volf, *End of Memory*, 17.

15. Volf, *Exclusion and Embrace*, 100.

16. Ibid., 115. "The dominant values and practices can be transformed only if their hold on the hearts of those who suffer under them is broken. This is where the repentance comes in. To repent means to resist the seductiveness of the sinful values and practices and to let the new order of God's reign be established in one's heart. For

the victim protects herself or himself from becoming a future offender,[17] and allows the creation of a new social order in accordance with the norms and values of God's Kingdom.[18] In forgiveness, which marks a transition from exclusion to embrace, we are bringing before God not only our unjust enemies, but also our own vindictiveness and *anger*. Moreover, we "make our own God's miracle of forgiveness."[19]

Forgiveness, whose apex is "non-remembrance of the suffered wrong-doings" and a new relationship with the enemy, points in two directions: on the one hand, it brings down the wall of hostility and divorces the act of wrongdoing from a wrongdoer, exposing the original humanity of the torturer and returning the excluded enemy to the community of human beings, and, on the other hand, it admits oneself (the victim) into the community of sinners.[20] This is what God has done in the Crucified on the cross, for everyone, and therefore everyone ought to "make space for others in ourselves and invite them in—even our enemies. That is what we enact as we celebrate the Eucharist. In receiving Christ's broken body and spilled blood," Volf concludes, "we, in a sense, receive all those whom Christ received by suffering."[21]

And even if all of that is done, reconciliation and forgiveness are by no means guaranteed in advance. Even if we emulate Jesus's crucified arms on the cross embracing his enemies, the believer's embrace of enemies does not warrant reconciliation as a final outcome.[22] Embrace is, so to say, an asymmetrical practice of mercy in which there are no guaranteed outcomes. It is dicey, it is risky. In a world of hostilities, giving ourselves, while emulating persons in the Trinity, "is the risky and hard work of love," Volf soberly

a victim to repent means not to allow the oppressors to determine the terms under which social conflict is carried out, the values around which the conflict is raging, and the means by which it is fought. Repentance thus empowers victims and disempowers the oppressors. It 'humanizes' the victims precisely by protecting them from either mimicking or dehumanizing the oppressors. Far from being a sign of acquiescence to the dominant order, repentance creates a haven for God's new world in the midst of the old and so makes the transformation of the old possible." Volf, *End of Memory*, 116.

17. On many occasions Volf correctly warns that "histories of individuals and peoples are intertwined and the longer they engage in conflict, the more the lines between victim and victimizer blur. Yesterday's victims became today's victimizers and today's victimizers tomorrow's victims." (Ibid., 90).

18. See Volf, *Exclusion and Embrace*, 117–19.

19. Volf, *End of Memory*, 266.

20. Cf. Volf, *Exclusion and Embrace*, 124–27. On the basic axiom of Christianity that God rejects the ungodliness and loves the ungodly, see Volf, *Allah*, 170–73.

21. Volf, *Exclusion and Embrace*, 129.

22. Cf. Ibid, 147.

emphasizes. "There are no guarantees that self-giving will overcome enmity and that the wrongdoers will not try to invade the space that the self has made and crush those willing to give themselves for the good of others."[23]

Along with the Trinitarian self-giving, in addition to Jesus's out-stretched arms on the cross, Volf states that it was Jesus's parable of the prodigal son—especially the stretching out of the father's arms to embrace the repentant—that gave rise to the idea of a "theology of embrace." The father's "extravagance" in preservation of relationships,[24] his attempts at restoration of filiation, and his refusal to follow the logic of the elder son, to consent to the order of exclusion on the grounds of moral precepts, is what constitutes the meaning of faith in God and theology of embrace. Embrace is an offer at reconciliation, not coercion; gift, not compulsion.

In the context of talk about God's and human justice, without which there is no reconciliation, when the two poles clash, and especially the perspectives of victims and their perpetrators, Volf uses the concept of "enlarged mentality" or "enlarged thinking" by the philosopher Hannah Arendt. "Enlarged thinking" means "letting the voices and perspectives of others, especially those with whom we may be in conflict, resonate within ourselves, by allowing them to help us see them, as well as ourselves, from *their* perspective, and if needed, readjust our perspectives as we take into account their perspectives."[25] More than an "enlarged mentality," Volf argues for the necessity of a "double vision."[26] In "double vision" we open ourselves to the "unbearable" other, we allow the enemy to speak to us, we acknowledge the "opposing justice," and we learn from other traditions. In doing so, says Volf, "the most important theological reason for practicing 'double vision' lies not in the example of Jesus, but in the inner logic of the theology of cross." It is because, and now Volf returns to his theological counterpoint, "on the cross God made space in God's very self for others, godless others, and opened arms to invite them in."[27]

---

23. Ibid., 193.

24. Cf. Ibid., 164–65.

25. Ibid., 213.

26. Volf discusses double vision with reference Thomas Nagel and his concept of the view from nowhere. However, Nagel advocates a total distance from oneself, i.e. a view "from no point of view," as opposed to the view "from here" (i.e., one's own perspective). Quoting Charles Taylor, Volf suggests replacing the view "from nowhere" with the view "from there," from the perspective of the other. However, God is the only one that sees "from everywhere" (see Volf, *Exclusion and Embrace*, 250–53). On "double vision" see also *Allah*, 204–5.

27. Volf, *Exclusion and Embrace*, 214.

What is important in "double vision" is not merely taking the position of the other, or indifferently and shamelessly denying the facticity of the victim's or the perpetrator's status, but to acknowledge in faith that God on the cross, "receives the godless," "and exposes their godlessness in the very act of providing for its forgiveness." This movement, which we could term a "perspective altruism," for Volf, is derived from the basic datum of faith, i.e. "that *we* are the perpetrators who crucified Christ, *we* are the godless whose godlessness God exposed."[28] The consequence is clear: if Christians want to be consistent with the Crucified, then they ought to provide in themselves room for others and their perspective.

According to Volf, we can say that in order to achieve justice it is necessary to suspend the righteousness of our own perspective and have willingness to see justice through the eyes of the other. It is necessary to transcend oneself and be repositioned from riveted "embeddedness" in our own correctness, to step out of oneself towards the other,[29] to make a step towards the embrace. This "will to embrace the unjust precedes agreement on justice,"[30] and precedes even "doing justice," which is an integral part of faith. One cannot know God without doing what is just, Volf concisely claims. But justice cannot be realized by creating new injustices. And as there is no justice without a will to "embrace," as there is no "embrace" without justice; neutrality[31] is not an option, and one cannot consider differing points of view as equivalent. Drawing from the Scriptures, and God's understanding of justice, Volf emphasizes God's "bias" in favor of those who are in need, because he acknowledges that in "double vision" one should preserve both the "initial suspicion against the perspective of the powerful," and the "epistemological privilege of the oppressed."[32]

28. Ibid., 214–15.

29. Double vision presumes the view from here, from oneself, and from there, from the perspective of the other. It means stepping out of oneself and distancing from oneself and from one's own "situated self" as much as possible. It means crossing the social boundary, moving into the world of the other, inhabiting it, accepting the other in one's own world and repeating that process. (See ibid., 251–53).
In *The End of Memory* Volf emphasizes that "the highest aim of lovingly truthful memory seeks to bring about the repentance, forgiveness, and transformation of wrongdoers, and reconciliation between wrongdoers and their victims." (65)

30. Volf, *Exclusion and Embrace*, 215.

31. "Even more than just encouraging inaction, neutrality is positively harmful. For one, it gives tacit support to the stronger party, independently of whether that party is right or wrong. Second, neutrality shields the perpetrators and frees their hands precisely by the failure to name them as perpetrators. Third, neutrality encourages the worst behavior of perpetrator and victim alike." (Volf, *End of Memory*, 219).

32. Volf, *Exclusion and Embrace*, 219.

Volf's special contribution to theological practice of reconciliation lies in the attitude that God's "bias" concerns not only the poor and the oppressed, those who are deprived of the possibility to participate in debates, publicity, and power, but God is "biased" and even "unjust" in the eyes of the people, because he is incomprehensibly merciful to the rich and powerful, sinful and ungodly. God relates to each human being individually in his forgiving way, because his justice is neither equalizing nor abstracted, but approaches everyone in an unconditional love and understanding for his or her personal needs, and in accordance with the movement of justice which is concerned with the wellbeing of each person, and his or her own "measure" of mercy, following the definition of justice to give each his own: to each his accompanying grace. Ultimately, if one strives only for justice, the result will be injustice. "If you want justice without injustice," Volf concedes, "you must want love. A world of perfect justice is a world of love."[33] With Carol Gilligan, Volf argues that "the ethics of justice" ought to be replaced by the "ethics of care."[34] This is based on the belief in one God, on the interdependence of all people, on the fact that we all belong to each other, on the concern of all for all, and for enemies. The whole of *The End of Memory* is advanced from the viewpoint that one should hear—before the Judgment Day, and before the eschatological wrath of God—the other who has done one wrong, and reconcile with them.[35]

Double vision does not deny justice; neither does it deny the truth. The truth is not possessed; rather one searches for the truth and aspires to it. And as justice is reached through love, so is truth. Volf cites the Apostle Paul: "speaking the truth in love" (Eph 4:15).[36] Willingness to embrace the other for the truth is to create a community of righteous and truthful people. As with justice, it is not enough to tell the truth, but the truth needs to be done. We need to make sure that the truth does not become, as was the case with Pilate, a despised truth, the truth of power, the truth of social status and position, which is ultimately nothing more than the power of violence.[37] The person of the other should not be sacrificed to my under-

33. Ibid., 223.

34. Ibid, 225.

35. "The last word was to be spoken on the Last Day by the Judge who knows each of us better than we know ourselves. Before then, the Captain would be allowed to speak and I would listen—with ears attuned to detect any attempts to white-wash his crimes. Still, I would listen to his protests, corrections, and emendations about the way I remembered him and his wrongdoings as I continued to hold firmly the reins of my remembering." Cf. Volf, *End of Memory*, 14.

36. Volf, *Exclusion and Embrace*, 256.

37. Cf. Ibid., 264–71.

standing of truth, as was the case with the chief priests and elders of people in relation to Jesus. The truth, rather, is liberating because it is non-violent. The cross of Christ breaks the cycle of violence constituted by the truths of the powerful. It is not easy to practice non-violence in a world of violence, but our refusal to take revenge, and our endeavor to act as Jesus is the only form of discipleship worthy of Christian name and identity. For what is redeemed in Christ's cross is not only a victim's truth, but also the truth of his or her enemies.

BELOVED HUMANITY AND RESURRECTION IN THE CROSS

This brief outline of Volf's notion of "enemy" within the process of reconciliation is offered as a possible way of true reconciliation, a possible way of new relationships between the opposing persons, and as a way of coming together in our big and small worlds, ridden with conflicts and hostilities. Volf makes this pledge of personal faith: God has already achieved it, and continues to do so with people in history, but most excellently and fully in the cross of Jesus Christ. Without equating the victim and the wrongdoer, without denying justice and truth, all people find their reconciliation in the cross of Christ, because all are sinners and all need to be justified.

Now, following in the footsteps of Volf's stimulating thinking, a set of issues arises as a modest offering for theological dialogue and discussion. These issues are not novel, having been the subjects of multiple discussions by religious geniuses and saints and many theological giants in the long history of Christianity. They appear to be gaining importance in our own times, calling us to revisit them with our own experiences and theological apparatuses, and in dialogue with Volf's well-founded opinion, even if not to answer them, then at least to let them resonate between us and our contemporaries.

One such issue is certainly a question of understanding human beings. Volf, in fact, consistently follows Reformation thought regarding the simultaneously righteous and sinful man (*simul iustus et peccator*). The anthropological precept established in Christianity, starting from Paul and Augustine (especially his understanding of original sin), insists that the first human experience in the presence of God is the experience of sinfulness. God saves the sinful man, without any human merit, and redeems him, particularly through the cross of Jesus. Our question is: Is not the first and fundamental human experience that of being loved?

The answer to this question changes the starting point in the issue of memory and reconciliation. What is it that we remember more, love or evil? On the other hand, in our world torn by hostilities—as Volf often emphasizes—how are we even to talk about sin and sinfulness? Is not the concept and awareness of sin something that has vanished from the enlightened consciousness of modern people? Does not it seem that sinfulness is acknowledged only in relation to love, an undeserved love of God, as it is so often implicitly highlighted by Volf?

Volf's opinion confirms that for people of all times, including us today, the question of faith or unbelief in God, is not just a casual question, but the question that underlies the meaning of human existence. At the same time, the question of all questions is the human himself or herself, the human as a neighbor, a beloved neighbor or complete foreigner, opponent and enemy. Out of this issue, wrapped in an unconquerable mystery, arises unquenchable and insatiable human longing for love as well as the "dark" issue of human propensity towards lying and sin, violence and evil. Volf is convinced that Christians are offered God's love in Jesus Christ as a compelling and meaningful answer to the mystery of God and the mystery of human being. Discipleship of Jesus is given as a meaningful way in which God's salvific grace encounters humans and the world, the sinful and godless human and tells him or her: I love you always and unconditionally.

Among the issues that we would like to share with Volf is the issue of the resurrection, or soteriology. Consistent with his Christian tradition, from Luther to Moltmann, with his sound knowledge of and in openness to other Christian theologies, particularly Roman Catholic, Volf unreservedly witnesses that our world, and we in it, can be saved only by God's graceful forgiveness and love manifested in the cross of the Crucified. This inevitably brings about our commitment as believers to carry on the discipleship and following of God's practical love and forgiveness towards all people, including our enemies; the gift of renewed innocence, a new beginning to all, and new relationships while building new togetherness before the graceful God.

Jesus's cross is undoubtedly the most material, the most physical manifestation of God's love for people. Without the cross of Jesus, without his suffering and death for his friends and his enemies, for the victims and wrongdoers, God's revelation would remain only a word—without doubt powerful and strong a word—but it would have missed the final confirmation, another intervention of God, one that abounds with grace, one that borders with the impossible (i.e., with the religious illusion and atheism). Does it not seem now that with the resurrection as the foundational event of the Christian faith, with that last act of Jesus' Passover (leaving), the incarnated and crucified Word reaches the pinnacle of God's revelation and revelatory joy? With resurrection, Jesus's cross becomes final justice and truth, it becomes truly good news in the darkness of violence and in the grimness of death. And this in particular in the world of boundless suffering and myriads of crosses, excruciating experiences of loneliness and forsakenness by fellow humans and by God.

Without resurrection, without this gratuitous act of God's grace and unconditional love, without a newness of life, the cross would have slipped out as one of the "ethical," probably valuable but still insufficient offer that provide intrinsic value and meaning to human suffering. Of course, without the cross—without the radicalness of God's embrace, the embrace of love not of death—the resurrection could be easily turned into a false comfort, into an immunizing eschatological myth and spiritualists' illusion of escape from reality.

Finally, isn't it the unforeseen and decisive Easter embrace of God's newness that we can spot in God's love on the cross, in that universal embrace of all people in the Crucified, of those who suffer, and of those who are sinners, of those who are just, and of those who are godless, of those who are victims, and of those who are wrongdoers, on which Volf rightly insists and which he believes in? Embracing a new life, which is not merely a life beyond an empty or a full tomb, but already here on Earth, in our own environment, whether big or small, in our world eroded by the forces of tormenting conflicts and hostilities, being a Christian, being a follower of the Lord and Master Jesus Christ, means to live from the viewpoint of God's love manifested in the cross and confirmed by the radical grace of resurrection.

I am convinced that engaging with Volf's theological writings will not turn readers into mere passive recipients, but rather meet Volf's intentions, (i.e., initiate a "hermeneutical enrichment," or "double vision") and Christian readers will—obliged by the immense grace and love of God—become actively involved in order to turn their enemies into God's and their own friends in their own, whether large or small, but always plural worlds.

[Translated by Entoni Šeperić]

BIBLIOGRAPHY

Volf, Miroslav. *Allah: A Christian Reponse.* New York: HarperOne, 2011.
———. *The End of Memory: Remembering Rightly in a Violent World.* Grand Rapids: Eerdmans, 2006.
———. *Exclusion and Embrace: A Theological Exploration of Identity, Otherness, and Reconciliation.* Nashville, Abingdon, 1996.
———. *A Public Faith: How Followers of Christ Should Serve the Common Good.* Grand Rapids: Baker, 2011.

13

The Weight of the Past in the World of Love

Linn Marie Tonstad

MIROSLAV VOLF DIDN'T SHOW up for class on the first day of my first class with him. It was the end of my first week as a student at Yale Divinity School. During orientation the previous week, I had sought permission to take his advanced seminar on the Trinity in a conversation in which—in memory, at least—he loomed terrifyingly over me interrogating me about my background in theology as I stammered awkwardly. (The answer was, as soon became painfully clear, not very much!) As I sat in the basement room in the Religious Studies department on College Street that Tuesday afternoon, a PhD student explained that Miroslav was trapped in Manhattan, where he had been participating in a UN prayer breakfast. It was September 11, 2001.

I had entered divinity school firmly convinced that theology had little if anything to say about real problems. I had a head full of prejudices about Constantinianism and substance metaphysics, and was then as now deeply concerned about Christianity's maltreatment of women and queer persons. I had decided to spend a couple years figuring out my own Christian beliefs before going on to work in another academic field, likely philosophy or intellectual history. Yet here, less than a week in, I was encountering a theologian who seemed to be in the right place on that particular day.

The sense Miroslav gave of theology as an engaged discipline was deepened for me after that first non-encounter. In another memorable scene that fall, he participated in a panel discussion about how Christians are to respond to terrorists, insisting without compromise that dehumanization of terrorists is incompatible with Christian faith despite their horrendous acts. In strong agreement with his position, I thought: perhaps theology does have something to say. Perhaps *theologians* have something to say. By the end of the semester it was clear that I would be applying to PhD programs in theology.

That essential sense of Miroslav's vision of theology as a conversation in which the most abstruse discussions have real implications for how people are to live together was deepened over the following years. In courses, reading groups, over a beer or a glass of wine, during comprehensive exams, and beyond, Miroslav and I argued text after text, issue after issue. Throughout, he gave me the one thing I—a woman, queer person, and feminist plagued by self-doubt about my capacities and about the hostility of systematic theology to people like me—needed more than anything: his absolute faith that I could do this. Over and over, his reassurance allowed me to continue despite my own fear and sense of inadequacy. At the same time, he pushed me to try harder and dare more. In one memorable case, his comment on a final paper of mine was: This is not as good as it could be, not even as good as it should be. Yet knowing that he would tell me when my work was not good enough allowed me to trust him when he told me what I had much more difficulty believing, that there was a place in systematic theology for someone like me.

During those years, Miroslav was working on *The End of Memory: Remembering Rightly in a Violent World* (2006). The book undertakes an experiment in eschatology, developing an imaginative proposal for what might happen to memories of sins and offenses suffered in the life to come, and drawing out the consequences as well as discontinuities between that vision and how we ought to remember now. It is in honor of that work, and in gratitude to a onetime mentor transformed into friend and colleague, that I offer the following reflection.

Volf's theological interest in how people who have suffered and perpetrated evil acts can become reconciled with one another runs through much of his work. As a student of Jürgen Moltmann, it is no surprise that this interest has often been accompanied by a view to eschatology: while humans may become reconciled to one another already in this life, in some cases and to some degree, full reconciliation awaits the establishment of a kingdom of perfect love in which humans will live with one another and God in indefeasible communion and mutual joy. That kingdom of perfect love will be populated by former enemies, now reconciled. Eschatology is a particularly Christian mode of thinking about human flourishing: it treats questions of ultimate flourishing, of what is good for humans absolutely, and of the definitive ends for which we are made. Eschatological visions of flourishing have consequences for how we envision our lives together in the here and now, although Volf has always been careful to avoid any simplistic or exaggerated continuities between this life and the life to come.

In the world of perfect love, when redemption is completed and reconciliation has taken place among human beings as well as between God and human beings, insistence on the eternal memory of wrongs destroys heaven. When wrong has been *made right* in the judgment of the cross—not merely consigned to the past—it need not and will no longer come to mind, Volf argues.[1] Volf's account invites a number of interesting questions and has received both approbation and pushback. Without quite agreeing or disagreeing with his proposals, I want to draw attention instead to some less-discussed aspects of his vision: the status of Christ's body in the life to come, and the more general question of whether an irreversible past can, in a meaningful sense, be redeemed at all. Both relate to the issue of what John Thiel—whose alternative proposal will accompany my discussion of Volf's through part of the essay—terms the "eschatological imagination."[2] At the heart of Volf's proposals stands a real worry about the heavy weight of evil and suffering in human lives, and the Christian proclamation of a world of perfect love to come.

Illuminating these questions requires a brief rehearsal of Volf's general understanding of the "eschatological transition,"[3] developed in some detail in a series of essays around the turn of the millennium, as well as his rather more controversial proposal regarding the status of memories of "suffered wrongs."[4] The eschatological transition refers to multiple transformative events that take place as this world comes to an end and the world of perfect love is established: the resurrection of the dead and transformation of the material conditions of existence, the last judgment, justification, and social reconciliation. For Volf, the condition of the establishment of an irreversible world of love—a world no longer threatened by even the possibility of sin—is that "somewhere between this world and the coming world of perfect love, a transformation of persons and their complex relationships

1. See Volf, *End of Memory*, 192–214. An earlier and somewhat different version of nonremembrance appears briefly in Volf, *Exclusion and Embrace*, 131–40.

2. Thiel, *Icons of Hope*, 13.

3. Volf, "Enter Into Joy," 257.

4. Volf, *End of Memory*, 177.

needs to take place."[5] That encounter takes place after judgment, as part of justification,[6] and involves two further steps: humans must reciprocally give and receive grace,[7] and must subsequently "want to be in communion with one another."[8]

Volf notably refuses either the notion of a "lived life" as the object of eschatological preservation, or a turn to God's memory of individuals as the content of any hope of eternal life. Instead, he insists that humans will be raised *as human*. The totality of the person is the object of justification, and the totality of the person is the subject of reconciliation.[9] In the life to come—in the world of eternal joy and perfect love—time and space will not disappear, but will marked by plenitude and fullness rather than fragmentation.[10] Volf holds on to something like time and something like space—plenitudinously transformed. It is because of this crucial move that some sort of sequence can characterize the eschatological transition without threatening its absoluteness. The transition from this life to that life is neither instantaneous nor temporally extended over a vast period of time. Rather, the eschatological transition is a temporally delimited process involving multiple events: social reconciliation is its "cultural" aspect.[11] Social reconciliation represents the need for appropriation of forgiveness by sinners and our concomitant reconciliation with each other.

Divine forgiveness of sin is unilateral. As sinners knowing ourselves "at the foot of the cross," however, we learn that as we are sinners already forgiven, we must also forgive.[12] And such forgiveness is not merely abstract, distanced from our offenses against particular human beings. For Volf, the eschatological transition involves a social dimension in which we—more or less literally—confront each other and learn to embrace each other as forgiven sinners. We enact the dimension of reconciliation in an active, postresurrection/pre-eschaton period of encounter with each other, as part of our entry into heaven. Volf has not to my knowledge stated the latter aspect of this account quite as crudely as this, but it seems entailed by his account.

5. Volf, "The Final Reconciliation," 91–92.

6. Volf, "Enter Into Joy," 262–63.

7. Ibid. 264.

8. Volf, "Final Reconciliation," 93.

9. Volf, "Enter Into Joy," 263.

10. Ibid., 265–78.

11. Volf, "Final Reconciliation"; see also Volf, "Social Meaning of Reconciliation."

12. Volf, *End of Memory*, 122.

This dimension of appropriated reconciliation precedes the transformation in which forgiven sins are allowed no longer to come to mind. The imperatives of justice and mercy have both been fulfilled: sin has been acknowledged, admitted, and appropriated—from the perspective of sin's forgiveness. Offenses between people have been acknowledged between those same people, and forgiveness has been offered and received. Since sin has received its "due" and sinners are being transformed, it is now safe for the memories of wrongs committed and suffered no longer to come to mind as the human being is drawn out of themself toward the intrinsic attractiveness of perfect love and beautiful goodness.

Postmortem reconciliation involves every single "social" sin[13] "whether miniscule or grand, whether committed intentionally or not," thus abrogating any radical distinction between perpetrator and victim as such while respecting the differentiated seriousness of violations.[14] Volf seeks to remove the possibility for anyone to hold themself truly innocent—not only, I think, because he doesn't think anyone is innocent in such a way but more significantly because of the relationship between being forgiven and justified, and offering forgiveness to others. But given Volf's consistent emphasis on love and grace as affirming rather than transcending justice, as well as on the relationship between truth and justice, *all* sins must be uncovered, made visible, "narrated."[15] The transformations he envisions, including the not-coming-to-mind of wrongs suffered, follow the intolerability of sociality were the regime of visibility a permanent state rather than a transitional moment in which *justice is done*, made absolute.

The subsequent encounter between victim and perpetrator is mediated by "a judge who suffered the victim's fate and was judged in the perpetrator's place."[16] In contrast to Roman Catholic understandings of purgatory, in which pain is generally concomitant with the "amount" of sin to be purged, Volf wants the perpetrator to suffer only "the pain of remorse" at this stage. Finally, the transformation is not only one that victims offer to perpetrators; victims too are liberated from "(possible?) bitterness and vindictiveness"[17] and from the "perverse bond" of injustice suffered that ties them to those who have done wrong to them.[18] As all admit themselves sinners, "giving

13. I think "social" here is contrasted with non-social sins, i.e. sins not committed against another person as suggested in Volf, "Final Reconciliation," 110 n.41. See also the distinction between personal and social sin in "Final Reconciliation," 100.

14. Ibid., 98.

15. Ibid., 102.

16. Ibid., 98.

17. Ibid., 99.

18. Volf, *End of Memory*, 119.

up on self-justification," the appropriation of justification generates inter-human forgiveness and reconciliation.[19] Reconciliation requires embrace; forgiveness alone is not enough.[20]

A significant part of Volf's argument for nonremembrance or "not-coming-to-mind"[21] hinges on the assumption that some suffering, some evil, is irredeemable in memory even after the wounds such evil leaves have been healed.[22] That is, the evil could not be remembered without its memory destroying the world of perfect love that achieved redemption establishes: "Put starkly, the alternative is: either heaven *or* the memory of horror. Either heaven will have no monuments to keep the memory of the horrors alive, or it will be closer to hell than we would like to think."[23] Anything else requires the belief that, in the world to come, God will render horrendous evils meaningful.[24] That belief, if extended to all experiences of horrendous evil, implies a theodicy in which suffering is eventually justified—a position Volf finds intolerable.

Nonremembrance hinges on the body's transformation. Without going into detail, Volf says: "to the extent that memories of wrongs are inscribed in the bodies of those who suffered them, the re-creation of a new body from the ruins of the old one is clearly relevant to my topic in that it makes non-remembrance possible."[25] Does that mean that the condition of nonremembrance is the creation of a new body without the inscription of memories of wrongs suffered; or that the condition of nonremembrance is that the body's memory remains intact or recreated (and so reinscribed?). It seems likely that the former ought to be the case.[26] If the body retained its inscriptions, those inscriptions would be noticeable, and so lead the mind to the memory of the cause of such inscription, as a consequence of the unity of mind and body. Indeed, the body's history would itself continue to

---

19. Ibid., 103.

20. Ibid., 104.

21. Volf, *End of Memory*, 145–47. In *Exclusion and Embrace*, Volf describes what happens to memory as loss (138) and says that "the Lamb has . . . erased their memory," referring to the redeemed in Revelation 22 and John 1:29 (140). In *End of Memory*, he says that such memories will not be erased (145) although he leaves the possibility open (145n37).

22. Volf, *Exclusion and Embrace*, 134.

23. Ibid., 135–36.

24. Volf, *End of Memory*, 183–86.

25. Ibid., 179.

26. Volf suggests the opposite, using the analogy of a computer file that is never opened, in Volf, *Free of Charge*, 177, although he is primarily discussing this-worldly forgetting in that passage.

mark the body. Alternatively, memory becomes a purely cognitive reality rather than a bodily-borne history, an arguably undesirable consequence of nonremembrance. In *Exclusion and Embrace*, Volf's argument for nonremembrance reads the cross as "a paradoxical monument to forgetting" that stands "at the center of God's all-embracing memory": the cross is a monument to God's forgetting of forgiven sins.[27] In *End of Memory*, the possibility of nonremembrance hinges on the redemption of the *person* rather than the totality of the lived life; redemption gathers together fragments but does not require the redemption of every single event.[28]

Since Volf reads suffering freely undertaken for the sake of another as meaningful, it may seem that he leaves room for the memory of the cross in the life to come. Not so, however: not only will Christ's body no longer be wounded, the cross itself will no longer come to mind (even though it is itself a monument to nonremembrance):[29] "True, our being new creatures in eternity will have been achieved in part through Christ's death. But it does not necessarily follow that life as a new creature is predicated on the eternal display of the means by which such life was achieved."[30] Achievement of an irreversible world of perfect love requires the creation of true innocence,[31] an innocence that knows nothing of good and evil, following Friedrich Nietzsche. There is an ontological aspect to this series of events. A world of perfect love, once achieved, cannot be undone because of its character: it is a world in which active mutual embrace between people continues even as all are rapt in contemplation of the good. There is no "room" where sin or fracture could once more enter in.[32] Note that Volf does not for this reason rule out a kind of temporality—to the contrary, he affirms it. So change is possible (presumably something like an ongoing enjoyment of actually existing human beings in something like sequence), as well as ongoing enjoyment of God, which involves growth in knowledge and so also love of God.[33]

While I too have argued—with different concerns in mind—that resurrection in a sense overcomes the cross in the world to come,[34] I wonder whether Christ's wounds could be retained even if the memory of the cross

27. Volf, *Exclusion and Embrace*, 140.

28. Volf, *End of Memory*, 187, 189.

29. Ibid., 190–91.

30. Ibid., 191.

31. Volf, "Enter Into Joy," 274.

32. In Volf, "Enter Into Joy," 275, time means "*continuation* in the unthematized good."

33. Ibid., 276. See also 270, where he firmly holds on to both temporality and change.

34. Tonstad, *God and Difference*.

did not come to mind, on Volf's account. The question has to do with the relationship between Christ's scars and their significance—and by implication, the relationship between our scars and their significance. Human bodies are vulnerable to scarring. The course of life marks us on a most "visceral," and visible, level—reforming us over time, leaving us with marks, tracing our histories in skin. These marks may seem constitutive of our identities, or they may seem distortive. Some scars may encode fondly remembered accidents, as with the scar on my palm that commemorates an afternoon of roughhousing with a cousin as well as the pride with which my pre-teenage self removed the resultant stitches. Many scars encode far less cherished, and more identity-forming, memories, yet selfhood always involves forgetting as much as remembering.[35]

The eschatological criterion for self-identity is whether "we could experience ourselves without a sense of loss."[36] Volf reads the self as "dispersed in all centeredness, discontinuous in all continuities, fractured notwithstanding all attempts to render ourselves coherent, and ever changing while manifestly always being self-same."[37] Thus the possibility, at least, of self-identity without the full presence of one's history to memory remains. The central question about Christ's wounds, and by implication ours, becomes whether the body might retain a mark that no longer has its meaning, whether the cause of the mark might not come to mind even if the mark remained. In theory, it seems possible that scars might become no more meaningful than, say, differences in the shape of an earlobe.[38] Yet because Christ's wounds encode a history of violence, the other side of the question asks why his body should retain its wounds at all if the cross no longer comes to mind. Isn't the "thing" itself the point, rather than its traces?

At the heart of all these discussions is the question of what it might mean to redeem the past. Given the irreversibility of time and the cumulative and multiplying injustices, histories of violence, and experiences of horrendous evil that human history involves, can the past be redeemed at all? And if the answer is yes, what does such redemption involve? For Volf, horror and injustice in that past is in a sense irredeemable. The persons—victims and perpetrators—involved in such events can be redeemed, but the

35. Volf, *End of Memory*, 197.

36. Ibid., 196.

37. Ibid., 198.

38. Note that since my concern here is whether Christ's wounds could be retained on Volf's own account, I am not concerned in this discussion with the question of whether nonremembrance is justified on a more general level, nor with the important issues raised by theologians of disability regarding the relationship between how we envision our bodies in the life to come and contemporary approaches to disability.

events themselves cannot. To say otherwise would be, for him, a betrayal of the injustice of those events, their evil. While critiques of Volf's view of non-remembrance typically hold that he discounts the significance of experiences of evil, the truth is just the reverse. It is precisely because experiences of evil are so significant that the events themselves cannot, in a sense, be redeemed—that is, they cannot remain what they were and be woven into the fabric of a blessed life to come. It may be that the demand that memories of evil become integrable in the life to come reflects their significance now, and one wants to make sure that it is the person now (the historical person) that is reconciled. Yet with some memories, we could imagine becoming more ourselves were those memories not to come to mind. I was bullied rather brutally as an adolescent, and those memories infect me so deeply that I do not know myself without those memories and their concomitant effects on my responses to other people: defensiveness, a kind of reserve, and distrust. While my adult life has been lived entirely as a person marked by such memories, I would be thrilled to be released from them since overcoming their effects in my life is an ongoing project. The self unmarked by those memories is a self I would love to be—a freer, more joyous, more trusting self. Not all memories of evil suffered are so easily detachable from one's sense of self, however. Sometimes, the gift of forgiveness given to another is already central to one's selfhood in a situation of wrong suffered. Given that such forgiveness reflects a life and character shaped in very particular ways, doesn't the prospect of nonremembrance invalidate the way in which the one who forgives a wrong suffered is shaped and shapes herself in the image of a forgiving God?

Here Volf's sense that the relevant kind of personal continuity lies in "*being* and *feeling* ourselves if we did not remember such experiences"[39] becomes significant, as does his view that personal transformation continues eschatologically. The one who forgives in the image of God now remains the person she becomes through that forgiveness, even if the event precipitating forgiveness is no longer present to her consciousness. But this kind of personal continuity, as well as the types of postmortem change that Volf allows for, also suggest that our typical visions of eschatological transformation—in the moment, in the twinkling of an eye—elide just how much change we might have to undergo in order to enter a world of perfect love.

One approach to the need for such change is found in the idea of purgatory. In an intriguing footnote, Volf discusses an alternative notion of purgatory as a place where reconciliation could happen. According to Father Hubert, forgiveness happens at the moment of entry to purgatory, whereas

39. Volf, *End of Memory*, 196.

"immediate and perfect" friendship develops between former enemies while both are in purgatory.[40] Both the possible relationship to something like purgatory and the notion of heaven that eventuates emerge if Volf's proposal is compared in more detail to John Thiel's recent eschatological speculations in *Icons of Hope*. He too believes that happy heavenly sociality hinges on the accomplishment of interhuman or social reconciliation in an interim state that looks a lot like purgatory.

Thiel argues that the activity of the "blessed dead" is the accomplishment of forgiveness and actualization of reconciliation.[41] Like Volf,[42] Thiel assumes a relatively high degree of continuity between this life and the life to come,[43] although Thiel surpasses Volf regarding just how high a degree of continuity is assumed. Both see forgiveness as central to any actual redemption—not just divine forgiveness of human sin, but interhuman forgiveness. A crucial difference lies in the direction from which eschatological speculation takes place. Thiel derives his "hermenutical rule for eschatological imagination" from "our existential experiences of redemption, which is to say, in our present experience of already standing in a resurrected life gracefully secured by the life, death, and resurrection of Jesus Christ."[44] The work of saints in their historical existence determines what we should imagine the "blessed dead" doing. Since we already live in a (partial, fragmentary) experience of redemption, and since a high degree of personal continuity is assumed, a high degree of continuity of activity follows. Thiel justifies that degree of personal continuity precisely in the wounded resurrected body of Christ.[45] The continuity of activity lies in Jesus' refusal to blame his tormentors both before and after his resurrection, as well as in his pre- and post-resurrection acts of forgiveness.[46] Thiel thus assumes a high degree of continuity also between activity in purgatory and heaven: "The negotiation of sin is certainly the business of the dead in purgatory. But it is important to imagine heavenly life continuing that task in its own way."[47] Since the forgiveness of sin provides the continuity between Jesus' pre- and

40. Volf, "Final Reconciliation," 113 n.72, quoting Hubert, *Mystery of Purgatory*, 32.

41. Thiel, *Icons of Hope*, 49–50.

42. Volf, "Enter Into Joy," 275, where he holds to the importance of "the continuity of creatures' being on a time line."

43. Thiel, *Icons of Hope*, 21.

44. Ibid., 27.

45. Ibid., 42.

46. Ibid., 52.

47. Ibid., 54.

post-resurrection activities, and the eschatological imagination depends on that continuity, heavenly life must include it too.

Again the sequence is reversed: where Volf sees grace as preceding judgment, so judgment is also justification through the affirmation of justice in its overcoming, Thiel sees judgment as preceding grace.[48] After death, divine judgment of sin presses on resistant sinners who continue to deny the truth of God's judgment until "God's own presence and perhaps the irresistibility of the Beatific Vision . . . breaks through sinful resistance and gracefully causes an acceptance of judgment."[49] The gift of grace—equivalent to the acceptance of divine judgment?—encourages the blessed dead to seek and offer forgiveness from and to each other. Only so do the blessed dead remain themselves: "the effects of sin truly must endure eschatologically, since those effects . . . have shaped our identity in ways that continue to make us the persons we are."[50] These effects allow the entry of the "redeemed, and yet unreconciled" into heaven.[51] To my mind, the perverse consequence is that sin becomes *defining* of personal identity and continuity between this life and the life to come. This account of heaven does not just expand the function that purgatory allowed in a time of greater anxiety about the Last Judgment, as Thiel argues.[52] It transforms heaven *into* purgatory, or maybe into something closer to hell.

Since Thiel intentionally allows license to the imagination, let us try to imagine what this life of the blessed dead looks like on his account. A victim and a perpetrator encounter each other and rehearse the true history of the violation of one by the other, recognizing the act in all its true horror. As long as history continues, though, the act may not be reconciled in any individual such encounter, because the consequences of acts reverberate through the entirety of history in unexpected ways—reconciliation between the victim and perpetrator might thus need to be followed by reconciliation between the perpetrator and every other person throughout history who was further damaged by the perpetrator's act, even to the end of time. With the horror of the act between them, the victim offers the perpetrator forgiveness, or the perpetrator requests forgiveness from the victim. Such forgiveness is given, and the victim and perpetrator then move on to the next encounter with another victim or perpetrator. The presence of the Beatific Vision with its grace extended to each individual perpetrator and

48. Ibid., 145.
49. Ibid., 146.
50. Ibid., 147.
51. Ibid., 168.
52. Ibid., 98–105.

victim allows the interhuman extension of the grace given to each. Each such extension of grace entails the rehearsal of the deed at stake, in all its horror and horrendous consequences. Forgiven by one victim, the perpetrator of a horrendous act then goes on to the next victim victimized by that act, begging for forgiveness, once more rehearsing the deed, then again gratefully accepting forgiveness. During this period, the bliss of heaven, if any, must be rather restricted, given that the entire business of heaven is the rehearsal of every injustice, no matter how small or large, perpetrated or suffered in one's life.

Let us assume that the temporality of the life to come is such that, eventually, this process reaches its end: every single evil act throughout human history has been rehearsed and forgiven.[53] What then will happen to the past, with all its weight of evil? And what happens to the cross? The contrast between Thiel and Volf may reach its apotheosis at the point where Thiel opts for "a small strain in Christian imagery that portrays the abiding presence of the cross in heaven."[54] The heavy "price" of redemption—a price paid in suffering—needs to be commemorated in heaven.[55] Eternally, he finds "a kind of sadness . . . prompted by the guilty burden of the effects of sin."[56] Even though "grace itself . . . costs nothing,"[57] its cost must never be forgotten, nor must heavenly delight ever be untinged by the sadness that attends human evil acts.

Thiel illustrates well an alternative view of the role of forgiveness in the establishment of the kingdom of love. In his imaginative vision, the weight of sin and evil lies very heavy within and among human beings, as it does for Volf. But Thiel also demonstrates that Volf may have good reason for positing the incompatibility of any vision of heavenly bliss and redeemed

---

53. Presumably this takes place at some point "after" the Last Judgment. As long as history is ongoing, the process can never be completed, since the effects of past sins continue to reverberate in the lives of ever new human beings who then become subjects of reconciliation when they enter the community of the blessed dead. Alternatively, there must be a gap between the death of the last human being to enter heaven and the resurrection of all at the Last Judgment, in which case that gap would be the heavenly "time" that the process of reconciliation requires. "The resurrection adds nothing to the redeemed encounter with God in the Beatific Vision," according to Thiel (*Icons of Hope*, 48). Yet if "the blessed dead anticipate the last judgment as the fullest revelation of the effects of sin . . . that their eschatological virtue must continue to engage" (Ibid., 151), then it seems that heavenly "life" both before and after the Last Judgment is taken up with the kind of reconciliation described here.

54. Ibid., 184.

55. Ibid., 185.

56. Ibid., 186.

57. Ibid., 169.

sociality with the ongoing presence to memory of evil. While Volf insists that the cross is, in the end, only a small interlude in the history of God with God's beloved creation, Thiel sees rather the cross as entailing a permanent distortion, a non-transcendable sadness that marks the life to come. There is a sense, then, in which Volf and Thiel agree about a central presumption: the past cannot, as such, be redeemed. It must be transformed or overcome. Its sedimented weight of evil and sinful human acts cannot be lightened without distortion of the truth of that evil—without in some sense denying the evil of that evil. But Thiel's alternative solution cannot provide a vision of a joyful, desirable, *redeemed* sociality. To consider, as he does, that those in heaven work to "defeat the burden of sin that they both made and suffered" since "less a conception risks the loss of ourselves in all their integrity"[58] is to place personal integrity in the wrong place in a vision of judgment and reconciliation. Our sins become the site of our integrity, but sin is integrity-destroying, not integrity-forming. In Thiel's vision, something like human guilt persists eternally, offering an attenuated vision of salvation.

Volf's controversial thesis of eschatological nonremembrance, and his yet more controversial suggestion that Christ's wounds do not persist following eschatological consummation, may then turn out to be less costly than an alternative vision, illustrated here by Thiel, in which what is given up is not the conscious presence of human history to its subjects but a vision of eschatological bliss itself. While both share an appropriate emphasis on the need for human social reconciliation to be a part of any vision of eschatological transformation—an emphasis that reflects the essentially social constitution of human beings—their disparate visions allow us to think in some (speculative) detail about what eschatological transformations *can* reconcile people to one another.

Could these visions be joined by positing that, in slightly different ways, each gives something like a positive vision of purgatory a role in the eschatological transformation? Rather than purgatory as the site of sin's punishment, a positive purgatory would be the anteroom of heaven in which we become reconciled to each other *before* the establishment of the world of perfect love in its final form. Would Thiel's vision still require eternal sadness and a cross-centered heaven? Given his stipulations about the justification of the eschatological imagination, it seems that it must, at least as a site of speculation in this life. Volf might, however, be able to allow for Christ's wounds to be retained without their significance marring the joy of heaven. Eschatologically reconciled selves would be ourselves because we would continue to be the "subjects" of our experiences of transformation.

58. Ibid., 54.

Such transformations, when achieved, would allow something like the positive effects of our experiences to remain, without their horrendous aspects coming with us into a world of perfect love. In a world in which God and human beings love each other face to face, however, it does not seem necessary to assume that the cross has a place. We will be in the presence of the one who loves us as much as we were loved "then." But we will know that one much better when we see face to face and are changed in that beholding.

BIBLIOGRAPHY

Father Hubert. *The Mystery of Purgatory*. Chicago: Franciscan Herald, 1975.

Thiel, John. *Icons of Hope: The "Last Things" in Catholic Imagination*. Notre Dame: University of Notre Dame Press, 2013.

Tonstad, Linn Marie. *God and Difference: The Trinity, Sexuality, and the Transformation of Finitude*. New York: Routledge, 2016.

Volf, Miroslav. *The End of Memory: Remembering Rightly in a Violent World*. Grand Rapids: Eerdmans, 2006.

———. "'Enter Into Joy!' Sin, Death, and the Life of the World to Come." In *The End of the World and the Ends of God: Science and Theology on Eschatology*, edited by John Polkinghorne and Michael Welker, 256–78. Harrisburg, PA: Trinity Press International, 2000.

———. *Exclusion and Embrace: A Theological Exploration of Identity, Otherness and Reconciliation*. Nashville: Abingdon, 1996.

———. "The Final Reconciliation: Reflections on a Social Dimension of the Eschatological Transition." *Modern Theology* 16 (January 2000) 91–113.

———. *Free of Charge: Giving and Forgiving in a Culture Stripped of Grace*. Grand Rapids: Zondervan, 2005.

———. "The Social Meaning of Reconciliation." *Interpretation* 54 (2000) 158–72.

Made in the USA
Columbia, SC
19 May 2020